Advance Praise for *Grateful, Not Dead*

"Many of us really do not want to retire but rather continue working in ways that take advantage of our years of experience and skill. People who have been forced to make mid-career changes, retire, or else choose to work past 'retirement age' need help. Art Mitchell's ten-step program can help you repurpose your lifetime of experience and become a 'modern elder,' sharing wisdom and experience while at the same time remaining curious and open to learning."

– *Chip Conley*, founder of Joie de Vivre Hospitality, strategic advisor for hospitality and leadership at Airbnb, founder of Modern Elder Academy, and author of *Wisdom @ Work*

"Art Mitchell is a passionate champion of aging consciously and is helping to broaden the conversation about both the challenges as well as the opportunities of the third stage of life. We need more such voices in the world!"

– *Kerstin Sjoquist*, Director of Experience and the IONS Conscious Aging Program, Institute of Noetic Sciences

"Eric Berne, author of *Games People Play*, creator of transactional analysis, emphasized that we set the cause and age of death at an early age and then live our life script to fulfill that plan. Whether you remember that script setting later is not important, but rewriting the script to a more rational, happier one is the wisest thing you can do. *Grateful, Not Dead* is the best I have read to assist you in resetting your life script for the happiest, youthful aging!"

– *C. Norman Shealy, M.D., Ph.D.,* President of Shealy-Sorin Wellness Institute, founding President of the American Holistic Medical Association, and author of *Living Bliss* and *Medical Intuition: Your Awakening to Wholeness*

"Art Mitchell has written an indispensable guidebook for people entering the territory of old age. He knows the territory and he's got all the landmarks down. More importantly, he also realizes that each of us must make the actual journey on our own."

– *Harry R. Moody*, retired Vice President, AARP

"Art Mitchell is a good storyteller and has taken the difficult topic of 'the third act' and made it accessible. As a Certified Sage-ing Leader with Sage-ing International, I would recommend this book as a resource across the entire landscape of conscious eldering and the process of connecting with purpose and passion as an elder."

– *Jerome Kerner*, CSL, Co-Chair of Sage-ing® International and author of *Be It Ever So Humble*

"The information in this book is relevant to all boomers on a quest for ongoing relevance – and vitality! After decades in careers that have defined us, what's the next step? Guided by the author's life wisdom and skills as a coach, readers find their own answers through inspiration and exercises that tap into personal power and purpose."

– *Lois Guarino*, What's Possible Life Mentor and author of *Writing Your Authentic Self*

"Art Mitchell's book presents a remarkably comprehensive contrast between the current mainstream disempowering paradigm for aging and an understanding which recognizes and supports the potential of older adults to truly thrive, grow, and serve as vital and important members of their human communities and the larger planetary community. Within his organizing structure of REWIREMENT, he provides a compelling conceptual framework and a rich variety of practices to help elder adults tap into their beliefs about their aging, their core values, their innate sense of purpose, their signature strengths and gifts, and many other dimensions of life's elder chapters well lived. It is clear that Art is deeply committed to living what he teaches, and his heartfelt and often-entertaining stories of his personal journey of conscious aging make *Grateful, Not Dead* an engaging work that speaks to both head and heart."

– *Ron Pevny*, founder and director of the Center for Conscious Eldering, certified Sage-ing® leader, and author of *Conscious Living, Conscious Aging: Embrace and Savor Your Next Chapter*

"This book represents an invitation to coaching that will help anyone overcome the money shame and scarcity mind-set that keeps so many of us from achieving financial security in retirement. As such, the topic fills a gap in 'self-help' books that focus on conscious aging."

– *Pam Prior*, host of "Cash Flow" podcast, money coach, and author of *Your First CFO: The Accounting Cure for Small Business Owners*

"With his book, Art Mitchell has gracefully acknowledged the massive yet underserved demographic of the Aging. Presenting a conscious and well-integrated framework of spiritual embodiment and proactive life skillsets, this manuscript will benefit anyone who is in transition to mature stages of the human experience – all of us."

– *Sherree Malcolm Godasi*, founder of PsychedeLiA: Psychedelic Integration, Los Angeles

"This is a veritable encyclopedia of elder wisdom – a rich, wide-ranging and inspiring survey of the new paradigms of aging. There is so much to process here, so many wise teachers sharing their wisdom, that you will find yourself transformed before you're even finished. A banquet of transformational advice, Art's book is a call to re-invent yourself, transcend your ageism, and come alive again. Let it work on you and get back in the saddle."

– *John Robinson*, Ph.D., D.Min., author of nine books and numerous articles on the psychology, spirituality, and mysticism of the New Aging and frequent speaker at Conscious Aging Conferences

"Art Mitchell has put together a rich sharing of his thoughts, wisdom, inputs from others, and exercises to help the reader chart their course through retirement in a positive and growth-promoting manner. He brings light to how this time of life, the elder years, can be full of vitality, meaning, and fulfilment."

– *Dr. Tom Pinkson*, author of *Fruitful Aging: Finding the Gold in the Golden Years*

"A guidebook to navigating opportunities for intentional living with passion and purpose in tune with a person's gifts, talents, values, and vision. Art has compiled a wealth of information that nurtures heart, soul, and a legacy of service leadership."

– *Sandra Strauss*, author of *Dancing through Life with Guts, Grace & Gusto!*

"A delightful read full of wisdom, straight-up facts, and a sprinkle of Boomer cultural references. At the heart, this sunshine daydream book is a love song to any sentient being seeking guidance on 'what's next' in the second half of life."

– *Ingrid Hart*, facilitator, Midlife Renewal, and author of *My Year in California: A Journey Toward Midlife Renewal*

"Art Mitchell is a natural storyteller who masterfully infused real-life stories, experiences, science, and wisdom of great leaders in the field of Aging. With a combination of humor and depth of knowledge, he takes us on a journey where we can experience the possibilities of living life consciously."

– *Dr. Katia Petersen*, President of Petersen Argo, Inc., former Executive Director of Education at Institute of Noetic Sciences (IONS), and author of *Safe & Caring Schools*

Grateful, Not Dead

GRATEFUL, NOT DEAD

REWIRE, Not Retire.
RE-FIRE Your Purpose

By Art Mitchell, CPC, Ph.D.

Foreword by C. Norman Shealy, M.D., Ph.D.

NEW YORK

LONDON • NASHVILLE • MELBOURNE • VANCOUVER

Grateful, Not Dead

Rewire, Not Retire. Re-fire Your Purpose

Published in New York, New York, by Morgan James Publishing in partnership with Difference Press. Morgan James is a trademark of Morgan James, LLC.
www.MorganJamesPublishing.com

ISBN 9781642796629 paperback
ISBN 9781642796636 eBook
ISBN 9781642796643 audio
Library of Congress Control Number: 2019943025

Cover Design Concept: Jennifer Stimson

Cover Design: Christopher Kirk www.GFSstudio.com

Interior Design: Chris Treccani www.3dogcreative.net

Editor: Moriah Howell

Book Coaching: The Author Incubator

Morgan James is a proud partner of Habitat for Humanity Peninsula and Greater Williamsburg. Partners in building since 2006.

Get involved today! Visit
MorganJamesPublishing.com/giving-back

Dedicated to

St. Hildegard of Bingen,
who called to us then and warns us now to "Wake Up,"
"to bring light to the dark places in our lives,"[1] and thus
rise above our self-destruction and denial of a Sacred Earth
and
Sr. Maureen of Chardon, who, with a servant's heart,
shows me how to listen.

"Humanity, take a good look at yourself.
Inside, you've got heaven and earth, and all of creation.
You're a world – everything is hidden in you."

"The earth which sustains humanity must not be injured.
It must not be destroyed!"

– Hildegard of Bingen (1098 – 1179)[1]

1 Image: "*The Man in Sapphire Blue*" mandala by St. Hildegard of Bingen. Manuscript Illustrations of the Scivias by Hildegard Von Bingen, Scivias-Codex Plate Eleven. Collection by Elles Lohuis ("The 35 images contained in the manuscript illustrate 26 of Hildegard's most vivid visions."). Pinterest.

Table of Contents

Foreword		xiii
Introduction		xv
PART 1	**RELEASE the Myths and Rethink Your Retirement**	**1**
Chapter 1:	I Know You Rider	3
	Wake Up! Cheer Up! Push Back!	*3*
Chapter 2:	Attics of My Life	13
	Odysseus's Long Journey Home	*13*
Chapter 3:	Mississippi Half-Step Uptown Toodleoo	27
	Walking the Wizard's Labyrinth of Conscious Aging	*27*
PART 2	**RECEIVE Guidance and Rewire, not Retire**	**37**
Chapter 4:	Death Don't Have No Mercy	39
	Step 1: Recognize Your Ageism	*39*
Chapter 5:	Touch of Grey	53
	Step 2: Embrace Conscious Aging	*53*
Chapter 6:	Beat It on Down the Line	73
	Step 3: Wake Up to Your Values and Strengths	*73*
Chapter 7:	Sugar Magnolia	85
	Step 4: Identify Your Vision and Goals	*85*
Chapter 8:	Ripple	101
	Step 5: Re-Fire Your Purpose	*101*
Chapter 9:	Uncle John's Band	109
	Step 6: Envision Your Work	*109*
Chapter 10:	Ship of Fools	123
	Step 7: Manifest Your Prosperity	*123*

Chapter 11:	Turn on Your Love Light	135
	Step 8: Expand Your Consciousness	*136*
Chapter 12:	China Cat Sunflower	155
	Step 9: kNow the Numinous	*156*
Chapter 13:	Not Fade Away	171
	Step 10: Take Back Your Power	*171*
PART 3	**RETURN to the Game Rewired**	**185**
Chapter 14:	Friend of the Devil	187
	Pitfalls and Logjams	*187*
Chapter 15:	Eyes of the World	197
	You Can Make the Difference You Want to See	*197*
Endnotes		209
Appendix 1	Additional Resources	231
	Books: Discover and Learn!	*232*
	Organizations: Get Involved!	*240*
Appendix 2	Conscious Aging Articles by Ron Pevny	251
	Claiming Your Elderhood	*252*
	The Inner Work of Eldering	*257*
Acknowledgments		263
Thank You!		267
About the Author		269

Foreword

Eric Berne, author of *Games People Play*, creator of transactional analysis, emphasized that we set the cause and age of death at an early age and then live our life script to fulfill that plan. Whether you remember that script setting later is not important, but rewriting the script to a more rational, happier one is the wisest thing you can do. Interestingly, Eric Berne told his inner circle of friends that his script called for him to die at age 60 of a heart attack, and he did. A few years later I gave a talk at the Transactional analysis meeting and I said "He was such a brilliant man. Why didn't he change his life script?" One person replied, "But, Norm, what better way to prove his point?"

In 1974, I saw one of the few true miracles I have witnessed. A 50-year old woman was flown to my clinic by air ambulance, dying of widespread metastatic breast cancer. She kept saying "I came here to get rid of my pain, not to be brainwashed." I replied, "Listen, I am teaching you how to get rid of your pain." I did a life script exercise with her, and it became clear that she had set herself at age 16 to die of cancer at age 50 when a very dear aunt of her's died at age 50 of cancer. On the 17th day of our one-month pain treatment program, I did a guided imagery exercise to the whole group of patients. At the end, she got up and walked for the first time since her arrival. She then flew home on a commercial plane. Three months later, her cancer was totally gone. Eighteen months later, she picked me up at the airport in Los Angeles where I was to talk at the hospital where she had once been unsuccessfully treated with chemotherapy and radiation. She told me that during the exercise 18 months earlier, she had realized how much she hated her family, who were only preparing her for death. When she got well, her husband committed suicide. She then lived another eight years and died of kidney failure from the earlier damage caused by chemotherapy. There was no cancer found at autopsy!

Over the decades, I have seen many miracles when individuals have reprogrammed their life plan. Unfortunately, over 94% of people have one to five unhealthy habits: obesity, smoking, no exercise, eating only two daily servings of fruits and vegetables, or sleeping less than seven hours a night. The average life expectancy would be 100 instead of 79 if everyone just adopted these habits. When you have these unhealthy habits AND a negative life script, you are unlikely to make it even to the seventy-nine average.

The greatest problem is not recognizing that your life purpose is to help other people, and every job that helps other people is just as valuable as any other! The persons publishing this book are just as important as the author or me, and so on. Once you recognize that your job is helping others, and you enjoy the daily gift you provide to others, you may not desire to or even need to "retire." Indeed, for most people true retirement is unwanted, boring, and unfulfilling. Here is where you need to follow Art's advice: re-fire your purpose, envision your work, expand your consciousness, know the numinous, and reset your life script to live happily and healthily to 100 or longer. *Grateful, Not Dead* is the best I have read to assist you in resetting your life script for the happiest, youthful aging! This is true CONSCIOUS AGING!

C. Norman Shealy, M.D., Ph.D., President of Shealy-Sorin Wellness Institute, founding President of the American Holistic Medical Association, and author of *Living Bliss* and *Medical Intuition: Your Awakening to Wholeness*

Introduction

"Thoroughly unprepared, we take the step into the afternoon of life. Worse still, we take this step with the false presupposition that our truths and our ideals will serve us as hitherto. But we cannot live the afternoon of life according to the program of life's morning, for what was great in the morning will be little at evening and what in the morning was true, at evening will have become a lie."

– Carl Jung, *Stages of Life*

Let's begin with a question: "So, what's next?"

Facing aging and retirement, you are experiencing the world you knew changing in unsettling ways. Yet, the dust is not even close to settling; a new world has yet to emerge. Now that you have retired or are soon approaching the thought or prospect of this stage in life, willingly or unwillingly, you are having some reservations because changing jobs, being in a transition, can be tough! Or quite possibly, you do not want to retire at all. But what happens when you do retire, when you finally go out the door with – does anyone really get one? – a gold watch and a handshake?

What happens then – when your identity has been so wrapped up in a thing, a job, and now it's over? But internally nothing has really changed; you still have a lot to give. Do you now feel the need for a reboot, a redefinition, a course change, seeing possibility and opportunity with new eyes? Have you tried repeatedly to make changes only to fall back into old patterns? Have you made goals? Are your goals and objectives what you think you should be striving for, what you really want, or is the push coming from somewhere else? So are these goals really yours or someone else's? Are you telling yourself, day after day, "I'll start that tomorrow?" Is it the discomfort of uncertainty, the need to somehow have a guarantee of a positive outcome – that all will turn out just fine – that keeps you from taking action? Do you need that guarantee before you will start anything? Are you just not following through on what you say you want? It is, after all, quite comfortable on the couch, having the sincere intention to get off it, making a real change for the better, but never following through – as though this defines your life, this inaction, your depression.

And you worry about money – obsessively. You may expect to live another twenty or thirty years. That should be a good thing, right? You want to figure out how to keep funding your retirement and stop worrying so much about the money. You want that so much – so you can get back to enjoying life and being of service to others – isn't that right? And you do want to keep working, to have a reason to get up in the morning – a purpose that is in line with your values, strengths, and experience. You still do have a lot to offer. And you may say you have tried. Oh, yes, you did try, but …

Understand that the challenges, problems, and dreams of our generation directly relate to you – and that you are not alone. You don't really have a problem. You are facing a type of discrimination called ageism, and you are suffering from its cumulative effects. You have bought into it – unconscious acceptance, a co-conspiracy – as though it were a real thing and not the trickster illusion it really is. With all the "-isms" calling for our attention and correction, our materialistic, youth- and media-oriented consumer society continually tries to minimize the real impact of ageism, even making it laughable – think of those Hallmark greeting cards that make fun of age, as if that's normal and acceptable, or the phrase "senior moment." Ha. Ha. Not funny. But the scourge of ageism is deep; it is insidious, a killer of dreams, opportunities, and of life itself – we are giving up and dying way too soon.

Scourge is a funny word, but I cannot think of a better way to describe ageism. It is defined as "a whip used as an instrument of punishment" or "a person or thing that causes great trouble or suffering." *Grateful, Not*

Dead will focus on how you can combat this scourge – what society is continually telling us and what we have told ourselves our entire lives as willing scourge co-conspirators – to slow down, be quiet, diminish, dissolve, become invisible. "Move along, nothing to see here."

We, the baby boomers are, by definition, those of us born between 1946 and 1964. We have brought many new challenges and opportunities to the economy, politics, and social institutions while passing through each life stage. We are the generation that came of age in the 1960s and '70s idealistically protesting and resisting an unjust war, working for civil rights and women's rights, fighting for environmental protection, exploring alternative lifestyles, and expanding our consciousness. At least I did, maybe you did too, maybe not. But the outcomes of those progressive social and environmental changes are with us today. And we made compromises; we fully bought into an American dream of working hard and receiving, hopefully, prosperity, a family, and a house – with a mortgage. After all, we bought into it: "Cash rules everything around me. Cream! Get the money. Dollar dollar bill, y'all."[2] And now many of us don't want to retire. What does that even mean? We still have so much to offer – if only …

The issue here is not about how to retire well but about becoming revamped, upgraded, or rewired in your so-called Third Act. I completely dislike the word retirement. Matthew Fox, the theologian, agrees with me and has said we should "retire the word retirement. It's an obscene word." We should "replace retirement with the words re-firement and rewirement."[3] To be honest, my use of the word retirement in this book's original title was a boldfaced marketing ploy. Unashamed. But would you have picked up this book if the title said something like "Learn All about Conscious Aging or Spiritual Eldering or Sage-ing into your Golden Years?" Maybe. I would have. But I don't know you. Now, retirement – everyone seems to know what that's all about. Having free time for travel, grandchildren on your knee, reduced responsibilities, playing cards, golf, knitting, woodworking, or engaging in some other innocuous hobby. Right? Good times at last. Flipping the bird to all those still in the game.

But also, it can imply to me, and many others, a beginning to an end – a lack of purpose, becoming invisible, a life of diminishment, a Bataan Death March toward nothingness.

Retirement, as it pertains to career, is a new word, derived from and generated by our modern society with its unrelenting passion for consumerism, continual consumption, and productivity. David Orr reminded us that the word "consumption" long ago also commonly referred to a fatal disease, a wasting away of the body. [4] Once we are seen to no longer serve that justification and role in society, we are told most emphatically it is time to "retire," let the youngers do your job, and we are now even more under attack as "niche consumers." Chapter 9 will address more on this.

How about renewment instead of retirement? I like that. In her book, *My Year in California: A Journey Toward Midlife Renewal*, Ingrid Hart described how she courageously moved past her comfort zone on a quest for self-discovery and purpose to arrive at her renewal and reengagement at midlife.[5] For example, Project Renewment is a grassroots movement of women nearing or already in retirement and who are seeking mutual support. They are a group founded on the belief that retiring is all about change and increasing self-awareness. In their 2008 book by the same name, Bernice Bratter and Helen Dennis have given us this alternative to the word "retirement," which they associate with negative stereotypes and clichés that emerged from sexism and ageism. The authors provided a clear and comprehensive retirement model for career women that promotes emotional health and physical well-being. The authors wrote, "The combination of retirement and renewal, Renewment suggests optimism and opportunity, growth and self-discovery." As women "redirect the commitment and passion previously dedicated to their careers, they transform and reshape their lives. Project Renewment provides these women with an enriched and safe environment in which to explore and confront the challenges that lie ahead as they leave behind a lifetime at the office, hospital, studio, or courtroom."[6]

Now that you're still with me, and my "retirement in the title" ploy seems to have worked, let's recognize that while retirement may still be seen as a key aspect of a certain well-established life stage, my focus in this book is to move you toward an alternative perspective – conscious aging – and why I deeply believe it is so important for you to understand this. But more on that in Chapter 5.

I wrote this book specifically for you – and for myself – because we need to retrain, rewire, and change and our minds in ways that will shatter a lifetime of conditioning, limiting beliefs, and deep inner critics that scream, "I'm too old. Why bother? The best has come and gone." In this way, we begin to dramatically increase our well-being in ways that are aligned more with our values. Our challenge is to translate that alignment into daily activities and healthy relationships that continually reinforce our attitude shift. We do this through consistent actions that reinforce our wholeness and in support of a valuable goal of greater connection to others and the planet – and with sustained self-actualization that emphasizes service to others. But this book could be relevant to anyone at any age interested in living and aging creatively and with dignity no matter how they are occupied.

After decades of working as an environmental consultant on technical assistance and leadership projects in seventeen countries, I have changed gears and am now trained and certified as a transformation coach. Coaching for consciousness transformation requires a supportive, integrative, and sincere partnership that empowers people to more fully live the life they want, one that is rewarding and in line with their fullest potential – who they really are. More specifically, I work with people focusing on career or life transition and confronting so-called "retirement age," addressing conscious leadership, and engaging with rapid global change through social and environmental activism. Based on my own transformations and work as both consultant and coach, I have empowered myself and others to believe in themselves, take action, and move into greater emotional and financial security. Entering "retirement age," I have struggled to redefine myself and career path, with its financial ups and downs, been through debilitating bouts of depression as well as one bankruptcy and survived.

Grateful, Not Dead is a guidebook of sorts, a compass to help you begin navigating your later years and maximizing your overall happiness and well-being. You will metaphorically follow the three phases of a labyrinth walk – release, receive, and return – to learn how understanding the myths and truths about aging can change everything for you. A labyrinth in not the same as a maze, but rather a unidirectional spiral into the core and back out again, transformed. This book is also intended to serve as a framework for individual and group coaching and as a guide to workshops I hold on conscious aging, rediscovering purpose, and reinforcing an empowered mindset that confronts ageism. The intention of this book is to help fill a conspicuous gap in the self-help field regarding positive aspects of growing older and in support of conscious aging. Most books focus on so-called "successful aging" of the super geezer or wonder crone, staying young, fighting aging, or else ensuring economic security in retirement. Some Botox, "wise" investing, and more exercise – that's all you need, right? Hmm.

Dr. Norm Shealy, in his Foreword to this book, has stressed the importance of resetting your life script to live happily and healthily to 100 or longer. To do so, to increase your longevity by adding quality rather than quantity of years, will require health and lifestyle changes, including a healthy diet and regular exercise. What you eat, how you eat, how you move your body and how frequently are all important. Dr. Shealy has presented his formula for health in several books, journal articles, and videos from conference presentations.[7] And of course there are many other programs, some reputable, appropriate, and feasible, some not.

In this book, I do not focus on these physical improvements or lifestyle changes or make recommendations on improving your health. But Dr. Shealy recommends that the essentials include having 80% of your diet as fruits and vegetables, exercising a minimum of 30 minutes 5 days a week, and not smoking. This added focus on good health and longevity would fill my own conspicuous gap in the conscious aging process presented in this book. However, my primary focus is on mindset or mental attitude, which is logically viewed as equally important to reinforce your mental clarity, positive outlook, and quality of life as you continue to age.

By following the ten R-E-W-I-R-E-M-E-N-T steps in this book – outlined at the end of Chapter 3 – and then – most importantly – taking action, you will open to your creativity and potential as well as allow and maintain spiritual and physical abundance in your later years. What you'll learn here are some steps and lessons toward gaining or refining some skills that most of us need for a life of greater mindfulness and enjoyment but were never told.

So, it is time to ask yourself a few questions: What do I really want? Where am I now with getting that? Where do I want to be? What am I willing to do to get there? And how can this writer help me?

PART 1

RELEASE the Myths and Rethink Your Retirement

Chapter 1:
I Know You Rider

*"No, no, no, no. I'm too young to be a grandmother. Grandmothers are old. They bake, and they sew, and they tell you stories about the Depression. I was at Woodstock, for Chr**t's sake! I peed in a field! I hung on to The Who's helicopter as it flew away!"*
– Dianne Wiest as Helen Buckman in *Parenthood* (1989)

Wake Up! Cheer Up! Push Back!

Feeling down? Really low? Guilty even? Having made a permanent dent in the couch, you know something is wrong. Really wrong. Seriously. Just puttering around? There's something you're not doing, something you're avoiding, something big, but then you could, if only, but …

No one needs to tell you this is worse than just some annoying but mildly amusing bout of procrastination, a temporary avoidance of getting a thing done – after all, there is always tomorrow. No, this is deeper – a sort of denial. Something is holding you back, and you're beginning to get scared. Maybe you're OK now, physically and financially comfortable even, but the fear of running out of money, losing control and independence, has been nagging away at you - something's just not right, an existential crisis "like a splinter in your mind."[8] You know all this.

Seriously, though – congratulations! You're in retirement or plan to be soon. But financial insecurity is the number-one reason we put off retirement – why we put off our dreams. Our money keeps dwindling, paying down the loans, the mortgage. Retirement plans, investments, and home equity are not what we imagined. Cost of living keeps going up while the income does not. How can you enjoy these years when you worry so much about "retirement" and the money? How can you focus on self-improvement, personal development, being of service to your community, when this cloud hangs over you – daily? How will you survive? Bankruptcy? Fearing "the home" instead of staying in your home? Fearing the scary "A Place for Mom" TV people? Think you are worth more dead than alive to your loved ones? Ask yourself, "How would 'the best years of my life' be different if I could overcome these aching fears about money, these worries that keep me up at night?"

So, what are we talking about here? Clearly money is not the only issue, but a sort of depression has set in. Therapists and coaches might say you are out of alignment – but what's that and how? How did this happen? I remember only really connecting to the words of Pink Floyd's "Comfortably Numb" when I began to "feel old" and regretful and that something maybe was even wrong with me: "When I was a child, I caught a fleeting glimpse … The child is grown …The dream is gone."[9]

No, that's not right; not it at all. You see, I didn't really feel "old" as I entered my sixties. Apart from having lost partial sight in my right eye, everything was working just fine, and nothing hurt. But I felt like I was supposed to be old and maybe even act like it. Society had been telling me and now I was telling myself it was "that time of life." And I was looking for the signs – those so-called senior moments, which are all BS by the way, but more on that later. Whether intentional or not, Pink Floyd's lyrics spoke to me about the pain of giving up on our dreams as we get older – time's up on that – and trying to dull the pain, the regret, keeping myself numb, even though I know this can and should all be better somehow. I came to understand, in part, the avoidance and origins of our current alcohol and opioid epidemic – and that maybe I would not remain immune, and came close – and I got scared, then angry.

But why are you now stuck? You know this is such BS, a deceit, and a conceit. A dangerous game that keeps you where you are even though you say you want change. You know how wonderful the world can be, how it really is. You have experienced that. So why this? Why now? What has changed? Maybe because you are trying to do something – to make a change – the way you have always done it. And it's not working. Or you are not allowing yourself to think outside the box, to be flexible and adaptable, just believing what you have been told. Einstein or somebody said, "Insanity is doing the same thing and expecting a different result"[10].

A client of mine (or maybe it was me – yep, it was partly me; no, it was me) once said something to the effect, "I thought my life would be better at this age. I planned, but then there was the 2008 recession and so many debts have piled up. Some of these debts cannot be paid off until about 20 years after I'm dead. I think all I need is a better job to pay my bills and live without worry. But time keeps moving, and I'm no closer to getting out of this financial hole. I feel like I'm stuck, stuck in this story. I fear dying with so many regrets. But my more immediate concern is being able to stay in my own home with financial control of things."

I know how that held me back. But what is it costing you to stay this way? "Comfortably numb" may not be so bad, but how long can that last? How long before there is the next crisis? What is this depression, this nagging – *j'ne sais quoi*? – this ennui? Webster, or somebody like him, defined this as "a feeling of listlessness and dissatisfaction arising from a lack of occupation or excitement,"[11] as in "Oh, ain't it a shame. Poor old Ralph. He succumbed to ennui and despair." Now, your depression may most likely be situational, typically triggered by maladaptive coping mechanisms, not surprising in our current complex soup of political, social, and environmental chaos; social media nonsense; and the continual onslaughts from the TV and elsewhere that you should be afraid, very afraid, and clearly are not good enough on just about every parameter and level – but here, try this. Good old days? Make America great again? Uh, no, that's not it, so no point in pining about mythologies.

Where to start? Maybe you have just left your job of thirty or forty years; you are confused. Maybe, in your quest to find meaningful and lucrative new work, something to pay the outstanding debts and bills, you have just been rejected by some HR person half your age even though you are hugely qualified. This was my trigger for what was clearly an elusive dream job, something that respected and maximized my years of experience – a job that was clearly tailored just for me. But then, poof! – gone! I was too old, apparently – the convenient excuse was typically "overqualified," ageism otherwise never stated – "Why? Oh, no, we would never do that," says the HR woman as she dreams up a lame alternative reason to disguise the truth. Yawn.

My personal scourge of choice that drove my own despair? Hmm. That would be money, or the instability thereof – or, more accurately, the worry about an impending scarcity and loss of control and freedom. There just wasn't enough to consider a long-term retirement – forget about a vacation home in Belize, two happy, gray-haired people walking some tropical beach hand in hand with their sweaters slung over their shoulders like in the Prevagen or Geritol or reverse mortgage commercials. Nope, that's not going to happen – not while I have these debts and lowered prospects of earning what I had before. And if prospects are so bleak, if I believe they are unlikely to change anytime soon, then I'll never be able to retire. Such a failure. Such feelings of shame. I've done the bankruptcy thing years ago – turned out to be not so bad, a sort of miserable reprieve, a stay of execution – but I never, ever want to go back there. And although I still have my "moments," money shame is now largely under control as I moved away from a dysfunctional, disempowering, and destructive mind-set of scarcity. But more on our money myths and mind-sets in Chapter 10.

As alluded to in the Introduction, the challenges, problems, and dreams of our generation directly relate to us – and you are not alone. I am of a generation defined in part by the counter-culture and its music of the '60s and '70s. I was informally initiated into this culture at the tail end of the'60s – August 1969, somewhere in the middle of a big, sweaty, psychedelic throng at the Atlantic City Pop Festival to be exact, two weeks before Woodstock. But that's another story again (Chapter 11). And then we grew up, became reasonable facsimiles of adults with adult responsibilities and challenges, careers, marriages, mortgages, and kids – most, if not all, of the "warning signs of adulthood" fulfilled.

And then there's the Grateful Dead; love them, hate them, few are on the fence, but each of us was impacted by them in some way. They never had a number-one song, not even close; that was never their objective. The Dead led a decades-long utopian or spiritual practice, if you will, of "the transformation of the everyday," supporting an urge to transcend and a dedication to community. Historical revisionism, fueled by our commercial media culture that for some reason requires a cartoon version of the Dead, typically depicts the band as "grizzled hippie throwbacks with a cult following of burned-out stoners." Nudge. Nudge. Wink. Wink. But the Dead were on "no simple highway." Jerry Garcia in 1972 said, "The Grateful Dead is not for cranking out rock and roll; it's not for going out and doing concerts or any of that stuff. I think it's to get high. I'm not talking about unconscious or zonked-out; I'm talking about being fully conscious."[12]

Unlike our parents, the so-called Greatest Generation,[13] we were pampered, yes; but we were also in search of meaning, not just prosperity. And now we are conscious of not going gently or willingly into this "retirement." The word itself conjures up all sorts of negative, oddly humorous, stereotypes. Most of us are happy with our work, having overcome our challenges and obstacles – with contributing and being an important member of society and all that – with a role, a function, having something to offer. So now what? Do we now just "retire" under a tree? Take a long nap? I see a coconut palm on a tropical shore (paradise always has a coconut palm), maybe somewhere south of Miami Beach where life is easy, unlimited piña coladas and no one making any demands on us or our time. Hmm. Really? OK, and then do what? Play cards? And then we die? Free at last like Russell Crowe falling nobly, heroically, to the dirt in that *Gladiator* movie? Really? What's that all about? Well "it ain't me, babe," it ain't me going down that road, babe. Beach or no beach, coconut palms or not.

We are the baby boomers, part of a significant throng of aging achievers, some moving into retirement, others holding on and maintaining their current work positions, some still climbing their own "ladders of success." In 2018, as I write this, baby boomers are, by definition, between ages fifty-four and seventy-two – give or take. Author Terry Pratchett has written, "We have been so successful in the past century at the art of living longer and staying alive that we have forgotten how to die. Too often we learn the hard way. As soon as the baby boomers pass pensionable age, their lesson will be harsher still."

A 2015 report from the Population Reference Bureau (PRB), *Aging in the United States*, examined current trends among American adults aged sixty-five and older and how we are reshaping or redefining the older population. The report noted we are living longer than previous generations, with higher education levels and greater work experience. PRB predicted the number of Americans ages sixty-five and older will more than double from today's forty-six million to over ninety-eight million by 2060; the proportion of the total population age sixty-five and older will thus rise to about 24 percent from 15 percent today. Average US life expectancy was sixty-eight in 1950; in 2013 it was about seventy-nine years, likely increasing due to "the reduction in mortality at older ages."

According to Mark Mather, principal author of the PRB report, "The growth in the older population is fundamentally a success story from a public health perspective – new advances in medicine and living standards have led to longer life expectancies." Also, the life expectancy gender gap appears to be closing. According to PRB, "In 1990, there was a seven-year gap in life expectancy between men and women. By 2013, this gap had narrowed to less than five years (76.4 years versus 81.2 years)." The report also presented several key challenges to an aging population, including (i) "Obesity rates among older adults have been increasing, standing at about 40% of 65-to-74-year-olds in 2009-2012;" (ii) "More older adults are divorced compared with previous generations. The share of divorced women ages 65 and older increased from 3% in 1980 to 13% in 2015, and for men from 4% to 11% during the same period;" (iii) "More than one-fourth (27%) of women ages 65 to 74 lived alone in 2014, and this share jumps to 42% among women ages 75 to 84, and to 56% among women ages 85 and older;" and (iv) "The aging of the baby boom generation could fuel a 75% increase in the number of Americans ages 65 and older requiring nursing home care, to about 2.3 million in 2030 from 1.3 million in 2010. This also means that Social Security and Medicare expenditures will increase from a combined 8% of GDP today to 12% by 2050." [14]

Oh, and there's more. According to William F. Benson of the CDC Healthy Aging Program, "An estimated 7 million of the nation's 39 million adults aged 65 years and older are affected by" (clinical) "depression, which is a persistent sad, anxious, or empty feeling, or a feeling of hopelessness and pessimism. Depression in older adults is often not recognized or treated."[15] Anxiety is even more common, with one in five, or sixty million, people in the United States diagnosed with an anxiety disorder.[16] Benson has provided some additional statistics, including (i) "20% of adults age 55 and older have a mental health disorder (such as anxiety, cognitive impairment, or mood disorder) that is not part of normal aging (American Association for Geriatric Psychiatry, 2008);" (ii) "15–20% of adults older than age 65 in the United States have experienced depression (Geriatric Mental Health Foundation, 2008);" and (iii) "people aged 65 years and older accounted for 16% of suicide deaths in 2004 (Centers for Disease Control and Prevention, 2007)."

Boomers have shown some of the steepest increases in suicide rates and highest rates overall. We know of the tragic, well-publicized suicides of Robin Williams, Kate Spade, and Anthony Bourdain, for example. Gladys Bourdain said of her son, "He is absolutely the last person in the world I would have ever dreamed would do something like this."[17]

Quentin Fottrell has written, "Among men, the greatest increases in suicides were among those aged 50 to 54 (up 49% from 1999 to 2010, to 30.7 per 100,000) and for those aged 55 to 59 (up 48% to 30 per 100,000 people). Among women, suicide rates also increased with age, and the largest percentage increase in suicide rate was observed among women aged 60 to 64 years (up 60% to 7 per 100,000 from 1999 to 2010)."[18] It is recognized that men in general, for reasons known and not so well known, have a greater resistance to emotional honesty, expressing feelings, and being open to emotional support, leading to isolation, depression, and an earlier death. The life insurance companies all know this.

A "midlife crisis" is one thing, but privileged white men, such as me, have never faced overt discrimination in a significant way. If we are sufficiently aware, we come to understand this new insult, this rage, this discriminating unfairness, is a significant factor in the everyday lives of women and people of color in the United States regardless of age. Thus, when we come to retirement age and lose our previous status, our identity – what we tell people we are and do – we are faced with our first (or additional) disempowering "whammy-ism": ageism. But more on that in Chapter 4.

According to the US surgeon general, "Depression is not a normal part of aging. While older adults may face widowhood, loss of function, or loss of independence, persistent bereavement or serious depression is not normal and should be treated."[19] Clinical depression, or major depressive disorder, has no known cause but is believed to result from several genetic, biochemical, environmental, or psychological factors[20].

I am not going to pretend or presume to understand your or anyone else's depression or the reasons, the triggers, for your "dark night of the soul;"[21] I know mine. But a trigger is a trigger and comes from resistance to change or more specifically from an inappropriate behavioral response to a particularly difficult situation, criticism, or disappointment. How you react to any negative trigger may include your response becoming multiplied; that is, becoming manifested in other unrelated areas of your life, like a snowball effect. But regardless of who we are going to blame this time, when depressed, no one can convincingly tell you this state is (1) imaginary, "just in your head, get over it;" (2) temporary, "you'll be right as rain again very soon;" or maybe even (3) a profound and fortuitous spiritual lesson that arises from reaching an impasse that you chose to learn or overcome before you can enter a greater and sustained state of consciousness that resonates with greater creativity and happiness. That is to say, "you are lucky to be experiencing this; this is critical to your soul's evolution." Uh, excuse me? Seriously? You tell me this when all is dark, empty, and hopeless? Go clear your own crystals; get out of my face.[22] Stay with me here.

I know you want to be happy, to retire comfortably – not numbly – and with enough money to do what is important to you. It all boils down to freedom. I know you sincerely do want to be living the best years of your life in the next twenty, thirty, or more years, with a positive outlook and openness to possibilities, opportunities, challenges, new work that keeps you active and financially secure – to just be happy and fulfilled. I suspect all that is a no-brainer. And I think this is all critically important – starting with confronting ageism in its frustrating face. But how?

It's October 2018 at the Bioneers Conference in San Rafael, California. Sitting next to my daughter, I am listening to an inspiring talk by Ashton Applewhite, not unlike her TED talk,[23] based on her book *This Chair Rocks: A Manifesto against Ageism.* I managed to speak with Ashton afterward, and she gave me some sage advice, possibly not all well-taken, for writing this book and for all of us boomers struggling with aging. We struggle with our negative thoughts about a future as an "older" (as she prefers to call us) and confront the angst produced by society's and our own disempowering myths about ageism. When she signed my book she wrote, "Wake Up! Cheer Up! Push Back!" Thank you, Ashton. I like that! I try.

Chapter 2:
Attics of My Life

"A man who has been through bitter experiences and traveled far enjoys even his sufferings after a time."
– Homer, *The Odyssey*

"But how could you live and have no story to tell?"
– Fyodor Dostoyevsky, *White Nights*

Odysseus's Long Journey Home

Getting older. What does that mean, this acute self-realization you are beginning to "get old?" Does it first happen when AARP finds you on your fiftieth birthday and sends you an annoying mailer and invitation to join? Or is it, perhaps, when you start looking up old friends – trying to connect with the past – on Facebook? Could it be that remarkably memorable moment of angst when you first find a lump in your armpit? Or when your friends start dying? When your older relatives go one by one, and you realize you are now part of the family's oldest generation? When you purchase and then locate your burial plot in the family cemetery? Apparently, "my people" go to Richmond, Virginia, to get buried. I don't know. Or does it happen when you reach sixty and for some strange reason you care much less about some earlier pressing concerns? After all, you've had a good life, not too many regrets.

But when you hit sixty-four, you cannot escape the Beatle's "When I'm Sixty-Four" mocking and taunting you with Vera, Chuck, and Dave bouncing on your knee – indeed! And you wonder how you ever even remotely liked that little ditty and got to this place. "And why is my mind still like a twenty-year-old's?" you say. So, maybe there is an afterlife, a continuation, another chance, after all? Maybe there isn't. But if I'm wrong – or right – then it won't matter, or I'll deal with it then. But, with a grateful acknowledgement to Monty Python, the Grim Reaper comes to us all – one way or another – if not from the salmon mousse.[24]

James Hollis, Jungian analyst and author of *Under Saturn's Shadow*,[25] said, "Every man has an appointment with himself." Once we admit our mistakes and the lies we tell ourselves we begin to heal and realize we can more deeply connect with one another. That connection becomes like looking into an old mirror wiped clean. I am no better, no worse. Just me. Many times during my life I wanted to be someone else – anyone other than this inadequate numbskull, the "loser" I perceived myself to be. But I came to understand the root causes of that insecurity. Today I am comfortable with myself, pleased with who I have become, the family I have and, more importantly – because it's what matters most – who I am becoming.

I did not like who I was because I could never measure up to the unattainable high standards I held for myself. I am a recovering perfectionist. These notions were absorbed during childhood. At age thirty-nine, my father died suddenly when I was seven. Unknown to me at the time because he seemed outwardly healthy and not bed-ridden, for two years he was slowly dying from cancer. He appeared to me to be very difficult and judgmental. It seemed I could never do anything right, and what I did do was frivolous. I remember being happy, adventurous, curious, and free. But during that time, I subliminally absorbed or bought into the lie, perceived or imagined, that I was stupid, clumsy, not good enough. After all, at a young age, it appears our parents hold up a mirror to us about how we are doing, who we are, good or bad. Over the years, this negative self-image took root in a variety of forms. There were lessons I needed, or chose, to learn. But I am not a victim; I did buy into it.

My story, change the names, places, and circumstances, is the story of most men who grew up in this society – the primary message was "you will never *ever* measure up. You will always be less than, and you better do your best to cover it all up, hide your feelings and disguise any genuine emotion."[26] If we take all this at a soul contract level, and I do, the apparent parental abuse, while never physical, was in reality a great self-sacrificing act of loving kindness – and although it has been hard, great lessons have been learned – and for that discovery, I am very grateful.

John Robinson, clinical psychologist, ordained interfaith minister, and prolific author, has written an engaging book on the *Odyssey* as a parable of male aging[27]. While the parallels between Odysseus, hero and warrior, and modern men may be easily recognized, the transformational challenges of these stories presented in his book, *What Aging Men Want*, unquestionably have great universal relevance and significance for all ages and genders. If you would like to experience some of these captivating stories, interpreted from a modern perspective and through the lens of transformational challenges, pick up his book.

More than 2,500 years ago, a blind philosopher poet possibly from Anatolia in present-day Turkey penned the *Iliad* and the *Odyssey*, two epic poems that archetypally and metaphorically describe our life's journey of consciousness and transformation. While the *Iliad* is the story of our Greek hero Odysseus (Ulysses) fighting in the Trojan War, through battles and power struggles, the *Odyssey* describes his many misadventures and challenges after the war had ended, lost at sea, and traveling for ten years to get back home to Ithaca and his beloved wife, Penelope. Themes in the *Odyssey* include homecoming, wandering, friendship, challenges, transformations, and omens – even a magical elixir or two. Each of these many misadventures – from encountering the uncivilized one-eyed giant Cyclops to spending a year with the beautiful witch-goddess Circe, who turned his men into pigs, to descending to the underworld and encountering

Hades and Persephone – represents yet another transformational challenge on Odysseus's quest to get back home.

What Homer conveyed in these epic poems was an archetypal collective truth, the Hero's Journey. The *Iliad* may be seen metaphorically as our journey through adulthood, our own personal war of struggles and attainment, losses and wins, finding our place, having a career and family, and making our mark in this world. The *Odyssey*, on the other hand, is that long journey traversing the challenges we encounter symbolically as we struggle with age, coming to a point in life when we begin to realize, internalize as a reality, the shortness of this life. We shift from a life of war and ambition to peace and meaning. We aim to come home after our war of adulthood, our *Iliad*, and some seek to be guided on this path. The *Odyssey* consists of twenty-four books, each its own story, adventures on the way home to deeper transformation and meaning. These epic poems depict the subconscious realm of the psyche or soul, a developmental stage, a collective growth in consciousness toward self-realization or self-actualization, potentially leading to our greatest life stage of psychological and spiritual growth – our so-called Third Act. And here we are!

What follows are just a few of my stories, transformational challenges encountered on my own *Odyssey*. They represent a few stops on my journey to get home, figuratively and, in my case, literally. Wanting to get back home (my "Ithaca") after working in so many countries and return to my wife (my "Penelope") was a cry for wanting stability, security, peace, and community. This is a little of my story – often not so easily written – just a few of my personal struggles with transformation and themes presented in this book. My stories connect in one way or another with where I was, where I wanted to be, or where I am now – and to six stories in the *Odyssey*.

The Odyssey Begins: Understanding the Meaning of Coming Home

"The Odyssey begins with the goddess Calypso holding Odysseus captive on her island. He fell in love with this beautiful sea nymph on his journey home,

and she promised him immortality if he would be her husband. After several years of apparent happiness, however, Odysseus begins to ache painfully for his wife and homeland. He is tired, sad, and homesick. Homer tells us that the gods ordained his homecoming, but it was Athena, Zeus's daughter, concerned about Odysseus's growing depression, who finally begs her father to set him free."[28]

For over forty years, I worked in seventeen countries as a senior consultant on projects that sought to mediate environmental changes, protect biodiversity, and reduce poverty of those most impacted by these changes. It seemed that the bigger it was, the greater the financial investment, the less a project actually accomplished or made any difference at all. I became cynical; there was so much arrogance, corruption, and lack of political will despite obvious harm to the environment, natural resources, and the often-marginalized communities most dependent on them. Short-term gains always seemed to trump long-term sustainability. I felt a real sense of powerlessness, weariness, disappointment – that my work, for the most part, had been an exercise in futility. It makes no difference whether that was true or not; that is how I felt. And all this travel left me without any sense of community. And I got really, really depressed.

Did you ever see the movie Trading Places? There's a wonderful scene where actors Don Ameche and Ralph Bellamy, the wealthy Duke brothers, are explaining to Eddie Murphy, "Billy Ray," what a commodities broker does.

Ralph Bellamy: "And the good part, William, is no matter whether our clients make money or lose money, [we] get our commissions."

Eddie Murphy: "Sounds to me like you guys are a couple of bookies."

Ralph Bellamy (laughing to Don Ameche): "I told you he'd understand."

This is how I was feeling, not unlike a commodities broker; in my case, self-serving, cynical, pessimistic, and jaded. I wanted something more, to be home, have a community, follow a different passion – or rather the same but in a new context. After this long career, mostly overseas, I decided I had enough of the traveling, changing gears from one assignment to the next, from one country to the next. The novelty of travel had worn off. I wanted to finally stay home, get involved in a community, be of service. This desire is common as we age and begin to think about "retirement."

Based in the Washington, DC, area with its plethora of government agencies and NGOs, I assumed it would be easy to find work in my field, international natural resource management and biodiversity conservation, given my forty years of work experience in seventeen countries and a good education and reputation and all that stuff. But a dose of humility and futility was presented to me on several occasions when interviewing – unsuccessfully – for positions that were very suited to my background and experience; just what I wanted.

Due to my apparent less than ideal coping skills, this ate at me bit by bit and caused me to slip into a severe depression (on several occasions each time I tried to "get back home") for which I sought counseling. Details not required. Being continually referred to in rejection e-mails as "overqualified" is not a compliment – news flash – it is code for ageism. Clear and simple.

But one interview, or rather its outcome, is still painful and vivid. It still makes me angry. As much as I would like to name names and the organization, I will resist that temptation. I had applied for an ideal senior position exactly in my field of expertise and was accepted for an interview at a company headquarters in northern Virginia where I lived. They were the gatekeepers, three young professionals sitting across from me, asking all the right questions, determining if I was the right fit. I thought it went well, I answered everything just fine and felt confident, but something troubled me – a gut feeling, my intuition. A few weeks later, I found out I was right. I didn't get the job. I was viewed through a different lens, one that was clouded by ageism; I know this. At age twenty-eight, I too may have felt threatened or maybe bemused by this older guy and might even have said to myself, "He's just not a good fit for our corporate culture" or some such thing.

Tsk. Tsk. I get it.

Now, I must acknowledge that as an educated, privileged, cisgender, white, WASP male in America, ageism was my first significant encounter with discrimination – and it made me both sad and mad. How very unfair, after all! But others have been facing this and more insidious and endemic forms of discrimination all their lives. I've had it relatively easy; I get that. We'll look more into the issue of ageism and in the context of other isms in Chapter 4.

The Island of Thrinakia: Stumbling on Divinity

"*Both Circe and Tiresias warned Odysseus about visiting Thrinakia, the beautiful island home of the sun god Hyperion. Here goddesses care for seven herds of sheep and seven of oxen and, miraculously, these animals neither give birth nor die. But if any are slaughtered, punishment from the gods is harsh – the offender shall lose his ship and all his companions.*"[29]

Everyone is on the Hero's Journey, a personal expedition – for many, it's a slow path taken up and out of an uncaring universe, from a depressing hopelessness, lack of direction, certainly more than a few poor choices. It is a path toward greater understanding of self, a spiritual awakening of sorts, and a path toward self-actualization – discovering a promise and tendency to become actually what we are potentially. "You must just learn to let it happen; you cannot force anything. You must stop persuading. For when you are ready, it comes."[30]

On June 24, 2015, when I was sixty-three, something happened to me. I was leading an environmental planning project in Bangladesh. That afternoon, I was in my apartment in Gulshan 2, Dhaka, washing a dish. Nothing extraordinary. Just what I like to call my "enlightenment at the kitchen sink,"[31] not really an enlightenment but astonishing and illuminating, nonetheless. "When the context of your life shifts from becoming satisfied to being satisfied," wrote Werner Erhard, "an essential shift has occurred. You no longer seek satisfaction – you are satisfied. You no longer seek completion – you are complete. You shift from chasing satisfaction and completeness to expressing or manifesting satisfaction and completeness."[32] It occurred to me that I was happy.

I had no idea life could be this good – an intellectual, creative, physical, and spiritual awakening of sorts. I recognized something extremely important and valuable had happened to me. This was no sudden epiphany, no flash of brilliance. In retrospect, elements of it had been building up over the last several years, especially the last few months. This did not involve any prescription drugs or mind-altering substances. At that time, the only substance I was using to alter my consciousness was an occasional beer. And while washing that dish, there was a realization. I recalled – from nowhere – something from Psych 101 so very long ago, and it was the psychologist Abraham Maslow and his hierarchy of needs and something about self-actualization. Not sure what that was all about, so I looked it up. Maslow described self-actualization: "It refers to the person's desire for self-fulfillment, namely, to the tendency for him to become actualized in what he is potentially."[33] On reading the self-actualization characteristics, it seemed I had come to meet each one! I will discuss that theory later in Chapter 6 on assessing your needs, values, and strengths.

What emerged was a sort of letting go, a spontaneity. There had been signs leading up to this. I felt more comfortable with myself and relaxed socially, nothing particularly dramatic. But what was happening came as a pouring out of ideas and energy. Not manic, not a temporary productive high interspersed within a series of depressive episodes. I had more energy, ideas, and optimism, as well as what appeared to me to be greater social skill. And I was told something like, "There is a power in you that has been calling you since day one."[34] Each morning, I awoke thinking it might be gone. But it stayed; it held, this amazing grace. Tedious rote activities could not hold my attention for very long, but if something needed to get done, I just did it – no more soul-sapping procrastination. I was more creative and started organizing and writing outlines and text for my first twenty books! I'm serious. And it lasted for almost a year.

And "Nagarjuna said, 'Lord, it has been taught exhaustively that focusing mindfulness on the body is the single path traversed by the *sugatas*. Adhere to this and guard it. When mindfulness degenerates, the entire Dharma will be destroyed.'"[35] And when mindfulness degenerates, all will be lost. Or put another way by the Dead, "'Cause when life looks like easy street, there is danger at the door."[36] It slowly crept up on me until I realized these feelings of confidence and creativity were dissipating, replaced with doubt and procrastination. Now, instead of happiness and optimism, I awoke on most mornings to a subtle sense of dread. I had fallen back into old, comfortably numb ways of dealing with people and my future. And the depression returned. No further explanation required. It was an avoidance of my potential, a blockage to creativity, not honoring my purpose.

In *Living Deeply: The Art and Science of Transformation in Everyday Life*, a book based on a ten-year research program at the Institute of Noetic Sciences (IONS), the authors wrote, "Even when a transformative experience is deeply profound, new realizations can be fragile. To take hold, transformations must be reinforced. As Reverend Lauren Artress told us, 'Transformation disappears if you don't honor it' (2003). Changes in your worldview can happen in an instant, but mastery of new kinds of thoughts or behavior often requires the cultivation of new ways of being. George Leonard, author of *Mastery* (1992), put it this way: 'if you want to catch the grace of the wind, you must put up your sales. Practice!' (2002)."[37] I learned this was key.

Between Skylla and Charybdis: Moving Through Fear and Depression

"*Circe now warns Odysseus about the narrow and extremely dangerous straits of Skylla and Charybdis through which he must pass next. On one side, concealed in a cave high on a cliff, is Skylla, an evil monster with twelve feet and six heads, each with three sets of teeth. Her heads shoot out of the cave like arrows taking six sailors from every ship that passes. On the other side of the strait dwells a ferocious Charybdis, a once beautiful water nymph that Zeus turned into a monster.*"[38]

Lachesism is "the desire to be struck by disaster – to survive a plane crash, to lose everything in a fire, to plunge over a waterfall," [39] a desire to be diagnosed with an illness even though you are perfectly healthy, a tangible calamity – anything but this agonizing mental condition that no one can see, that you can't seem to justify to yourself or anyone else. That condition is major depressive disorder. How odd that such a word exists; apparently, I'm not alone.

I had a history of depression even before a suicide attempt when I was nineteen followed by a week or so spent in a hospital recovering. I am not proud of that – no one should be – but I don't deny it either. Author William Styron, more articulate than I, wrote *Darkness Visible*, an autobiography of his experience with major depressive disorder. His depiction of this disorder reveals its physical and mental pain. Then, fortunately rarely, there would be a trigger that would send me into depression again albeit never so dramatic as the first episode. Over the years, well-meaning doctors have prescribed Prozac, Zoloft, other antidepressants I cannot remember, Xanax for anxiety, and Adderall for focus, finally settling on Effexor, for that was, after all, what really helped my mother. And with my questionable "depressed ancestral mitochondria" theory that seemed to make sense.

As discussed in Chapter 1, depression may very well be a symptom of a physical condition or some biochemical imbalance, complicated by possible genetic roots. There are no simple causal answers to depression. Some are easily explainable, some from life circumstances, but others such as birth and childhood trauma or even past life conflicts left unresolved are difficult to uncover. In the search for a biochemical explanation, there is some evidence, for example, that mitochondrial DNA dysfunction or its gene expression, epigenetics, may be associated with abnormal brain function and mood disorders, such as depression.[40]

In my own family (and I know more about mine than perhaps I should), relatives and ancestors back to the mid-1800s (and possibly further), who shared my maternally inherited mitochondrial DNA, showed a high propensity toward depression and suicide. Certainly not all, but some battled alcoholism, some were periodically institutionalized; at least three of which I am aware took their own lives. And this was, possibly still is, prevalent among those who shared this mitochondrial

DNA, people who I trace back from my mother, to her mother, and her mother's mother's mother (you get the idea), to a woman born in 1748 on a farm near what is now Shippensburg, Pennsylvania, and then further back into a Scottish fog. These behaviors are not so apparent, if at all, among my "non-mitochondrial" relatives and ancestors as far as I know. Relevant perhaps? I really do not know. But what I am painfully aware of is that I was not spared, be it from genetics, childhood issues, poor coping skills, or a combination of all more likely. It doesn't really matter; and I know now, I had placed these burdens on myself and accepted the challenge to overcome them. I do hope, for now, successfully.

Call of the Sirens: Resisting Illusions

"*The goddess Circe now addresses Odysseus and his men. … Then, after feeding them, she tells Odysseus how to survive their next challenge – the Sirens. Enchanters of men, these mermaid-like beings sing so beautifully that sailors completely forget home and family and are lured to their death. Circe instructs Odysseus to fill the ear canals of his crew members with soft beeswax to block their hearing.*"[41]

In 2008 I had what my wife might refer to as a "mid-life crisis." Although a bit bemused, she was fully supportive, and I will always be grateful for that – for allowing me to take a risk on achieving something better. At age fifty-six, I wanted something more, something new, something more in line with my values – and I wanted a community. I desired to live in a place of beauty, where people were more creative, progressive, and engaged, "like-minded" if you will. I had lived in Northern California in my twenties and was "California dreamin'" again. I found that community first in Fairfax, house sitting, which only required walking two happy dogs each day. Then I lived in a nearby hamlet, Forest Knolls, in the San Geronimo Valley of western Marin County. My goal was to find work and relocate from the other side of the continent, from another Fairfax, in Virginia.

I wound up spending a lot of time across the creek from my house at the Papermill Creek Saloon, a bar with quite a history. A tiny, rather obscure place, but Janis Joplin, Jimi Hendrix and his Experience, the Dead (Jerry Garcia spent his final days in Forest Knolls), and many others performed there and lived nearby in the '60s and '70s. Some would say the local bands that play there now are just as good, just not so famous. I felt comfortable; I felt at home in San Geronimo Valley. But this relocation attempt fell apart when the reality of not getting the work needed to support me caused me to return to consulting overseas. And unprepared for such a move, however noble and idealistic it may have been, resulted in bankruptcy about a year later.

Feast of the Phaeacians: Celebrating Home

"Odysseus sails for seventeen days on Calypso's raft when Poseidon spots him. Determined to avenge his son's blinding, Poseidon sends a vicious storm completely destroying the raft. With the aid of a sea nymph, who provides a magic veil of immortality for protection; Athena, who manipulates the winds and guides them through rocky outcroppings; and Zeus, who stills the water, Odysseus finally comes ashore on the island of Scheria, home of King Alkinoos and the Phaeacians."[42]

I'm sure I am not the only person in my house to think I should shower more. When I do, I get ideas, inspiration – sometimes. In 2017, I participated in a Hay House writers' workshop in Orlando and had a mild epiphany while taking a shower – OK, I know, stay with me here. It was Monday, October 23rd, in the shower, 6:30 a.m., to be precise – I took notes – the day after attending the final workshop. I already had two books published with Balboa Press, a division of Hay House, and was now resurrecting a novel called *Angels in Dhaka*, written and published while I was working in Bangladesh in 2015 – not very good, trust me. Don't go looking for it. And I thought I was going to go deeper with that novel, develop it further and be creative and all that. But while dripping wet, I recognized a need for personal revelation – to not write another novel that attempts to cathartically expunge some demons from a comfortable position of anonymity using invented, fanciful fictional characters. Something like that.

Then, for a variety of reasons, I decided on a sort of self-help book – right, another self-help book – meh. But this would be different, this would be about the pain and opportunity of aging baby boomers and the problems that arise from ageism; it would be about and for me, hopefully others. But I wasn't a coach or therapist, not a counselor with years of experience helping people. I had a PhD in monkeys and trees after all. It was Nancy Levin who did it for me. She had spoken the previous day in the workshop about her books *Worthy* and *Jump,* and the writing process and struggle. Nancy was all about writing as your authentic self and putting yourself, those embarrassing aspects of yourself, out there if you want to make a difference in the lives of others. I was so affected, touched, that when I went to speak to her after the talk, all I could do was stand there like an idiot and tear up; she understood.

But I had to quickly change gears because a few days later, I was on a plane to New Delhi to begin working again as a consultant, this time leading a performance evaluation of a forest conservation project in India. It turned out to be a happy evaluation (the project was successful) with great colleagues and exciting project sites to visit in four states. So, nothing hurt, and it was a job well done. But the understanding remained with me that I was OK with not being a trained or certified counselor or a therapist. What I did have was my own story to tell, and maybe that story and what I have learned along the way could help others. Here is that book, all cleaned up after my shower.

Stranded on the Isle of Aeaea, Home of the Beautiful Witch-Goddess Circe: Coming to Terms with the Feminine

"After fleeing the giant cannibals, and greatly relieved to still be alive, Odysseus and his crew arrived at the island home of the dreaded sorceress Circe. … The following morning Odysseus realizes that he is now completely lost and disoriented. He has no idea where he is or what to do, and his men still feel the grief of their recent failure. … Odysseus splits his crew into two divisions and sends one to the house of Circe. Lions and wolves, enchanted by the goddess's evil drugs, surround the house, wagging their tails like friendly

dogs. … Odysseus knows he must confront Circe and asks Eurylochos to show him the way to her house. … She then remembers … that the great Odysseus would one day visit on his way back from Troy and asks him to share her 'bed of love, that we may have faith and trust in each other.'"[43]

The idea for this book gave me other ideas. Retirement never made any sense to me – what was I retiring from? I decided to "reinvent" myself from consultant to coach. So, I embarked on a transformation, a transition or reinvention of my work and my life. I decided to become a transformation coach, something I could do from home, from anywhere really. I like to think it represented a shift from getting people to believe in me as a consultant to, as a coach, getting people to believe in themselves. I prefer to spend my time doing the latter. This was about transforming consciousness – so that sounded pretty good. And the process transformed my own consciousness through nine months of rather intensive training and practice coaching. The course was, for me, a very positive self-examination and transformation, a coming to terms with the "feminine" part of my psyche, a reawakening of a new kind of consciousness and capacity, including learning to trust my intuition. Despite many years of performance and life experience, many men have not explored their inner world, which includes the often-confusing symbols and experiences of a "feminine side." As a man comes to know and express his feminine side, he grows in maturity. This inner work required reconnecting with my intuition and a sense of the spiritual. I felt I became more sensitive, compassionate, and inclusive as a result.

In the next chapter, you will learn more about the purpose of this book, what you can expect to get from it, its structure, how to use it – and a few things about Wizards.

Chapter 3:
Mississippi Half-Step Uptown Toodleoo

"A wizard is never late, Frodo Baggins. Nor is he early. He arrives precisely when he means to."
– Gandalf in *The Fellowship of the Ring*

Walking the Wizard's Labyrinth of Conscious Aging

The world has changed much since we kicked around as kids oh so long ago; our parents often could not even fathom these changes, more dramatic in scope. Remember your childhood. Can you go home again? Is it gone, still there but altered beyond recognition? When I was around the age of five, I could begin wandering on my own – great adventures, often alone, in the fields and forests around my home in what was then rural western Alexandria, Virginia. Yes, I do realize if that happened today someone would frantically call Child Protective Services, but it was a different time and place. Today, I only live a few miles away, but it is too painful to go back. Those horse pastures and woods so fondly remembered, the wonder and awe of it all, are now for the most part covered in concrete, asphalt, condos, and bedroom community housing developments.

Aunt Bertha, my grandfather's aunt, my great-grandfather's sister, lived comfortably all her life in her father's house in Georgetown, until she died at 103 years of age. Over the years during my childhood visits to her Victorian museum-like home on 30th Street between N and Dumbarton, Aunt Bertha told me lots of stories from way back when. One was about riding horse-drawn streetcars with straw on the floor to keep her feet warm during the turn-of-the-century winters in Washington. Before she died, men had walked on the moon.

I listened to these stories; I respected and remembered them. Now paradigms have shifted, and mind-sets have adapted, not always for the better. As a species, *Homo sapiens* (Latin for wise or intelligent man), we have amazing opportunities and capacities today, but these have also created new crises with the power to destroy the biosphere that sustains all life. Arthur C. Clarke once said, "It is yet to be proven that intelligence has any survival value." And Einstein has supposedly and famously said we cannot fix such problems with the same mind-set that made them. We need to find a way to move past this, individually and collectively, to move into a new consciousness, a new mind-set, that both embraces new opportunities and addresses the crises we have created. We can live in denial, along the banks of a river in Egypt, or we can strive to go upward with an urge for higher, nobler things.

So everything changes; that's a given. Not very profound. But what do we do about it? Carl Jung said that when people refuse to open themselves and allow in new and unfamiliar experiences, which may be threatening to their ego or sense of self, they are preventing themselves from being independent, fulfilled, and happy. Our consciousness moved further and further away from the natural world as we passed from childhood to adolescence to adulthood. Jung likened this to saying "goodbye to childlike unconsciousness and trust in nature" and hello to the complexities of human culture, the world of Man. The question we must ask was, "What kind of person shall I then become in this strange new world? Each of us must confront it."[44]

Beginners, Journeymen, and Wizards

I want you to understand more about the purpose of this book, what you can expect to get from it, its structure and how to use it. But first, let me speak about a metaphor of human potential and our evolving consciousness – a little story about Beginners, Journeymen (or women), and Wizards.

Our personal and collective growth in consciousness may be reflected in three metaphorical stages: Beginner, Journeyman, and Wizard.[45] Beginners, the first stage, are provided with structures, stories, concepts, rules, and labels – all they need to know to function or "live" effectively in the world. Beginners learn the rules, understand, and respect the rules. They do not question the rules because these rules are necessary for them to be confident as they move through the world. These structures, stories, concepts, rules, and labels were passed down by those who came before them – often enabling us to survive in earlier more precarious times. In a very real sense, they subscribe to a sarcastic, yet profound comment made famous by a popular hotdog vendor in Berkeley, California, "Believe what you're told. There'd be chaos if everyone thought for themselves."[46]

Beginners continue to operate from that foundation until, through life experiences and newly gained knowledge, they begin to question the rules, the stories and then the structures. They are now Journeymen, metaphorically in a period of wandering and exploration, embarking on dangerous journeys and adventures beyond the bounds of generally accepted authority. Now they begin to question and ask, "What if"? "Why not?" They expand their horizons beyond their own community. They will continue to apply and use the "old" as they seek ways to expand meaning and redefine the words and labels to fit the "new" to which they find themselves exposed. And the key is that they have begun to question and refine their opinions and reactions with minimal or no sense of guilt.

Then, at some "ah-ha" point, or gradually over time, these transforming Journeymen come to realize it is, in fact, they who are maintaining those old labels, those old rules. So why not challenge and redefine the structures, stories, concepts, rules, and labels and create something new? They realize they are the ones also making these labels. And as emergent Wizards, they come to recognize that they are the ones who create their reality by how they label what happens. When the wizard stops labeling everything and every action, categorizing, pigeon-holing, obsessing over making sense of something by giving it a name, they see these things afresh, with new eyes. And they know that "reality comes into being through our interactions."[47] That is their – our – power. How do we learn to do that? Useful and timely resources are all over the place – teachers, books, recordings, the Internet, entheogens, yourself – Google whatever you want or need and take it from there – meditation, mindfulness, experience. And what is now available to us has broadened tremendously.

Deepak Chopra described a wizard as "not someone who can simply perform magic but someone who can cause transformation," an alchemist who metaphorically turns base metal into gold. Wizards do not accept that humans are limited by time and space. "The wizard is beyond opposites of light and dark, good and evil, pleasure and pain."[48] Finding your wizard within – the way of the wizard – involves reclaiming what is already yours, what already exists within you – the chrysalis that already holds the freedom of the butterfly. The wizard's essence is one of transformation. And while wizards in our mythology are most often associated with an older male – think Merlin or Gandalf – a seer or wizard is not tied to any gender.[49]

To the Wizard, the world is no longer an "either-or" world; it is a "both-and" world, no longer a duality (black or white, right or wrong, this or that) as seen by the Beginner and the emerging Journeyman but rather a polarity. In the Wizard's view, polarity implies a spectrum of choices and options. Reverend Toni Fish, from whose lecture this story is derived and used with permission, has identified three big polarities that are worthy of effort and how they show up; namely, success versus failure, fault versus responsibility, and positivity versus negativity.[50]

Success and Failure: Did you give up the first time you failed? We "knew" as a child trying to walk that just because we fell, we were not a failure; we just got up and tried again until we got it. But over time we were taught and then told ourselves, the origins of our inner critic, our negative self-talk, our perfectionist hall monitor, that if we did not do it right the first time, then we were clearly a failure. What is failure but perhaps just not completing the task as envisioned, not having all the information or abilities needed in the moment. Admitting I was wrong, made a mistake, does not mean I am bad. In every failure lies a success, provided we learn from our mistakes. A client of mine once reminded me of what Yoda told Luke Skywalker, "Do or do not. There is no try." Doing and completing something with an outcome unlike what I had perceived, does not make it – or me – a failure, just that I completed a task without the expected outcome. So, what is success? A house in the suburbs, fast car, two kids, a job to support all that, listening to the smart money boys about wise investing, your adoring fans? So finally, I have it and then what? We may have trouble when we retire because what we deemed success was defined on a very limited basis, thanks in large part to the onslaught of all the "not good enough, you need this" advertising annoyances everywhere.

We need to redefine success. "The plain fact is that the planet does not need more successful people," wrote David Orr. "But it does desperately need more peacemakers, healers, restorers, storytellers, and lovers of every kind. It needs people who live well in their places. It needs people of moral courage willing to join the fight to make the world habitable and humane. And these qualities have little to do with success as we have defined it."[51]

Fault and Responsibility: Your situation now, what you are experiencing, this angst, may not be your fault. But that said, it is still entirely your responsibility to choose how to deal with it. Eleanor Roosevelt wrote, "No one can make you feel inferior without your consent."[52] My responsibility is how I am going to respond to a thing, and this is based on my ability to respond. What is my responsibility now in response to what happened? What is my response to that? You do have a choice, a responsibility to yourself to never beat yourself up – there is nothing wrong with self-love! It's easy to place blame and fault on yourself and others, be a victim or a martyr, but the Wizard learns to ultimately take full responsibility.

Positivity and Negativity: We talk about affirmations and seeing the positive, and that is important. The other side of affirmation is denial. Denial is not about ignoring something, but rather saying, "Oh, that's happening. Now how do I move through that without giving it, as something external to myself, the power over me?" The power of positivity says you can do whatever you want if you envision it, just manifest it, but my experience tells me this does not often happen. I know that I will at least get through it – I can create from that situation a goodness and a peace even when it hurts and causes suffering. I grieve when my friend dies but then find the joy in remembrance. To stay positive does not mean all will turn out OK. It means that no matter what happens, you will be OK. Again, it is entirely your responsibility to choose how you will respond.

The Wizard works with these three polarities and is then able to go beyond the limiting "rules" to create something new, something better, more adaptive, the ability to adjust when we get something wrong. That ability is our strength. The Wizard recognizes the new challenges of aging, of retiring, of the new world we live in and the power we have to succeed through our apparent failures.

Steve Jobs spoke of these Wizards. There is a quote often attributed to him but actually written by advertising executive Rob Siltanen, who was hired by Apple to create the television commercial promoting Apple's slogan "Think Different." Jobs narrated this famous 1998 commercial, but it was Siltanen who wrote of the Wizards, "Here's to the crazy ones. The misfits. The rebels. The troublemakers. The round pegs in the square holes. The ones who see things differently. They're not fond of rules. And they have no respect for the status quo. You can quote them, disagree with them, glorify or vilify them. About the only thing you can't do is ignore them. Because they change things. They push the human race forward. And while some may see them as the crazy ones, we see genius. Because the people who are crazy enough to think they can change the world, are the ones who do."[53]

Wizards take responsibility for their actions and know that in every failure lies a success – that staying positive is to know you are OK. These are the self-actualizing souls, those who are in the meaning phase of their lives, creative and using their potential, detached from outcome and free of any overbearing need for approval and the good opinion of other people.

Structure of This Book

Each chapter title is a Grateful Dead song title. A title was selected as being somehow relevant to the chapter content, sometimes obvious, other times obscure and only known to me like a private joke.

This book is assembled in three parts based on the labyrinth, a mindful walking meditation, a metaphor of journey, and a powerful tool for personal transformation. Though they are often falsely equated, a labyrinth is not a maze; you follow the same way in as out, and the purpose is not to lose but rather to find yourself. This book is thus structured on the three main steps or phases of walking a labyrinth. This approach to visualizing the transformative power of walking the labyrinth is based on the threefold path of:

1. *Release* – walking in, likened to purgation, letting go of the details of your life
2. *Receive* – being at the center, likened to illumination, receiving what is there for you if you listen
3. *Return* – walking back out the same way you came in, likened to union, empowered to take back into your life and the world what you discovered at the center.

A labyrinth walking meditation is an archetype, a mystical ritual found in most religious and secular traditions back thousands of years. In Chapters 5, 11, and 12, I use this metaphor for describing the three stages of our journey into conscious aging, consciousness expansion, and as a spiritual practice, respectively, for personal transformation.

A Ten-Step Program for REWIREMENT

Part 2, to Receive, provides a ten-step process – an integrated program to rewire and re-fire your mind, purpose, and life through positive and empowering thoughts, emotions, behaviors, and – most importantly – actions. Our time is not about becoming retired; it is about being rewired, changing our minds. Navigate this ten-step walk and forget about the "rule" of retirement. You know it's not retirement you really want or need; it's **R-E-W-I-R-E-M-E-N-T**:

Step 1: **Recognize** Your Ageism
Step 2: **Embrace** Conscious Aging
Step 3: **Wake Up** to Your Values and Strengths
Step 4: **Identify** Your Vision and Goals
Step 5: **Re-fire** Your Purpose
Step 6: **Envision** Your Work
Step 7: **Manifest** Your Prosperity
Step 8: **Expand** Your Consciousness
Step 9: **kNow** the Numinous
Step 10: **Take Back** Your Power

Many of these steps include adapted and modified tools from a variety of time-tested sources, including the IONS Conscious Aging program,[54] for which I am trained and certified to facilitate intensive workshops. Also, as a certified professional coach, I am trained to use the Coaching for Transformation and Leadership That Works[55] "pathways to alignment," processes that support people to become more aligned with their authentic self or core, and other coaching methods. I am also trained through Veriditas[56] by Lauren Artress to facilitate labyrinth walks as a spiritual practice. All these methods and approaches are adapted to uncover and re-fire your purpose and rewire your mind-set, to reimagine new work, and reinvent yourself as the renewed person you want to be and know you can be, happily living the life you want for the next twenty or thirty years or more – this is your Third Act.

How to Use This Book

The ten steps of the REWIREMENT Program are designed to be done sequentially, in order. However, this is not necessary; you can choose those steps that most interest you. However, I recommend you just follow the ten steps as designed. Each chapter gives you a summary, an introduction into the step and what can be explored further on your own with selected resources – or with me.

Sprinkled throughout the text but mostly in the Endnotes, active Internet hyperlinks (in Kindle) will take you to videos, assessments, original sources, and other topics for more exploration. Appendix 1 provides some additional resources – a very limited list of organizations and books relevant to each step – that I have found to be excellent and of good benefit to me and others.

This book is action-oriented, off-the-couch, and most chapters or steps have several recommended actions you can take now. But I often find when reading a "self-help" book that those end-of-chapter exercises, albeit useful and clearly defined, can sometimes be irritating, bog me down, block the flow of the book, as though I cannot proceed to the next step, the next chapter, until I have done the exercises for that step. In fact, I have paused reading a book, book-marked it to return to do the exercise later and then never did. My bookshelves are full of half-read books like that. I debated whether to include exercise sections as most people are unlikely to do them anyhow, but then perhaps I am overly pessimistic – I just know myself! Yes, I am overly pessimistic.

However, that's not the same case here. You can easily read through the chapters and steps of the program without taking any of the actions if you so wish. The actions are designed to give further depth to what you will be learning during the program and in some cases build on the preceding steps. So, if you choose not to take the actions on the first read through, then I strongly encourage you to return to them and do those that most resonate with you. And despite myself, I sometimes do go deeper – to my benefit.

Welcome to your ten-step REWIREMENT program – to rewire your life, re-fire your purpose, change your mind, stop worrying about "retirement", and participate as a positive force for change in the world on our journey together into conscious aging. But what is conscious aging? The next two chapters will address that by focusing first on a recognition and release of our debilitating myths about ageism and second on embracing the more positive life plan of conscious aging.

PART 2

RECEIVE Guidance and Rewire, not Retire

Chapter 4:

Death Don't Have No Mercy

"Age is not a particularly interesting subject. Anyone can get old. All you have to do is live long enough."
- Groucho Marx

"Old age, especially an honored old age, has so great authority, that this is of more value than all the pleasures of youth."
- Marcus Tillius Cicero (106–43 BC)[57]

Step 1: Recognize Your Ageism

Getting old. Individually, these two words elicit no special feeling but put them together and – bam! – a whole slew of mixed, confusing emotions springs forth. Getting old. As in, "not young anymore." You've been sensing its advent ever since you were young. It's been creeping up on you all your life, "like a splinter in your mind." But, like death, it all seemed so remote. It seemed to be something that happened to other people; it was not a part of your world. You have been excessively obsessed and devoted to a youthful adulthood. You have spent a lifetime making comparisons, and those comparisons typically had to do with age – I am older than he is, therefore, or I am younger than she, therefore ... You may have had models of aging both good and bad. Nevertheless, there was this small sense of impending doom when thinking about your own aging. Or is that just me? I doubt it.

I remember just before I turned fifty, a youngster had I only known then, when like clockwork the AARP had found me. Now, AARP, as it turns out, is a respected and helpful organization. But I still resented the letter and the come-on to join. Me? Retired? Getting old? Uh, I don't think so! I found it humorous and made a joke of it. Becoming what my parents were? Hmm. Nope. Not now, not ever. Thanks, but no thanks – and consigned the letter happily to the trash.

Erica Jong, author of *Fear of Flying*, an influential book of our generation, wrote in *Fear of Fifty*, "We have extended the limits of life, yet we dare to rage at growing old. … It seems damned ungrateful. But then we baby boomers are a damned ungrateful bunch. Nobody gave us limits. So, we are good at squandering and complaining, bad at gratitude. And when we discover life has limits, we try to wreck ourselves in anger before we learn the importance of surrender. We are the AA kids, the qualification generation. We have to be hurled to the bottom again and again before we come to understand that life is about surrender: And if the bottom doesn't rise to meet us, we dive into it, carrying our loved ones with us. Only a lucky few swim back up to air and light."[58]

In this first step in our REWIREMENT partnership, we begin by understanding our myths about ageism, how to confront them and how they affect our ability – today, right now – to thrive as we age. After all, what we want is to "thrive not just survive." We will consider what can be done about this scourge and then act to avoid succumbing to its debilitating impacts, impacts that affect our ability to find purpose and new work and manage our finances – keeping us from being secure and happy as we age. I want nothing less – I expect you feel the same.

For the record, just so we are clear on this, ageism is "stereotyping of and discrimination against individuals or groups on the basis of their age. This may be casual or systematic. The term was coined in 1969 by Robert Neil Butler to describe discrimination against seniors and patterned on sexism and racism. Butler defined 'ageism' as a combination of three connected elements. Among them were (1) prejudicial attitudes toward older people, old age, and the aging process; (2) discriminatory practices against older people; and (3) institutional practices and policies that perpetuate stereotypes about elderly people."[59]

Aging makes us nervous. It generates all sorts of images, few if any are positive. To avoid the pain we deny, we use humor. Saturday Night Live recently did a skit with a few of my favorite comedians about older people trying to use Alexa, the Amazon Echo personal assistant. [60] "But the technology is not always easy to use for people of a certain age." You can Google this, but here is the link: https://www.youtube.com/watch?v=YvT_gqs5ETk. "Well, I don't know about that." I admit this made me laugh, still does, but I also recognize that my response is largely because of my conditioning – and my subconscious acceptance of our materialistic, youth-focused, consumer culture's stereotypes even when they affect me at sixty-seven.

Now, replace the circumstances of this skit with overt sexism or racism, and no one will, or should, be laughing – there would be outrage, lost advertising, incredulous media pundits pontificating. And here is a small dose of reality based on attitudes produced by the ageism of our society and how they affect people – in real life. "Adults aged 65 and older have a high rate of suicide. Those 85 and older have the highest rate of suicide among adults." [61] Still laughing?

Granted, dealing with inevitable physical limitations and illness can be debilitating, but depression in older adults is not a normal condition – we are doing it to ourselves. Other factors that increase risk and rates of suicide among so-called "seniors" include: (1) social isolation, including from death of a spouse or divorce; (2) substance abuse, especially alcohol and more recently opioids; (3) gender disparity, including the finding that middle-aged white males have the highest suicide rates and accounted for seven of every ten suicides in 2015 (men of all ages die by suicide something like three and a half times more often than women, and this typically occurs not long after their retirement); (4) poor sleep quality, apnea and having trouble falling asleep; and (5) a previous diagnosis of mental illness that accounts for more than 90 percent of suicide deaths, regardless of age.[62] Yikes!

Becca Levy, professor of psychology at Yale, conducted a study of older adults and found those who held positive beliefs about aging were less likely to develop dementia, even for those with a genetic predisposition. However, in our society, it is difficult to achieve that awareness. She reported, "Children as young as three or four have already taken in the age stereotypes of their culture." "These age stereotypes," she said, "are communicated to children through many sources, ranging from stories to social media. Individuals of all ages can benefit from bolstering their positive images of aging."[63] Same with early sexism indoctrination. I have a clear memory from about age four or five sitting in the back seat of a car and thinking that "all men were older than all women." Ignore the fact that this is a child's illogical statement and see it for what it is – a child assessing the environment by observing and learning the restricted roles of men and women in the early 1950's. So it goes also with ageism – it starts early.

Gerontologist Dr. Bill Thomas wrote on aging, "Every day we all wake up one day older and further removed from the epicenter of adult power."[64] In our youth obsessed consumer culture, it is not easy to overturn old social conventions about the aging process. Early in our history, older people were respected and integrated members of society, contributing in many ways. But according to Marc Freedman in his book *How to Live Forever*,[65] "That all changed in the 20th century. American society began to recognize childhood as a distinct life stage. Later life went from being considered 'divinely blessed' to being deemed a medical condition. … Institutions like nursing homes sprang up to warehouse these human artifacts on the periphery of society … the enactment of Social Security in 1934 hardened the definition of old age." Freedman continues with an observation, "In a single century we'd gone from one of the most age-integrated nations on earth to its mirror opposite. … In the end, culture and institutions lined up to radically reroute the river of life." America may now, to a large extent, be characterized as age-segregated; we live in an "age apartheid."

In his 2019 article, "The Truth About HR Hiring Practices," David Stewart reveals techniques of age discrimination used in the workplace. In analyzing some common HR practices in America, Stewart asks the questions, "Was ageism being practiced? Why would a highly skilled worker our age not be hired? What are the reasons candidates are not being hired, or even considered, for the jobs if they have the skills? Is it as simple as discrimination based on age?"[66] Stewart discusses several HR hiring problems: (1) "the candidate seems skilled, but culturally out of touch;" (2) "younger manager does not want an older hire, fearing a competitor;" (3) my personal favorite: "the hiring team sees the candidate as over qualified;" (4) "hiring team pre-supposes the more experienced candidate will want more salary, and not wanting to waste their time, they pass the candidate over for a younger one;" (5) "your resume and cover letter subtly indicate you are not current;" (6) "unconscious bias, on both sides;" and (7) "it is not your skills, it is your self-awareness". Read the article; it's very revealing – and disturbing – but nothing we hadn't already suspected. These are important considerations, situations we face when trying to stay employed or embark on a new career, an issue further discussed in Chapter 9.

As Ashton Applewhite, anti-ageism activist and author and *This Chair Rocks: A Manifesto Against Aging* told me after her talk at a Bioneers conference, age discrimination is typically the first time a privileged white male faces serious, impactful discrimination. Oh, I knew that, duh, but suddenly I realized (more like a blinking back into consciousness) that she was talking about me. So, imagine now, for example, what a woman faces – and a woman of color – her entire life and how that gets all amplified when they become "of a certain age." Most men seriously just do not get that … until.

Applewhite has further written, "It's not the passage of time that makes it so hard to get older. It's ageism, a prejudice that pits us against our future selves – and each other. … Aging is not a problem to be fixed or a disease to be cured," she says. "It is a natural, powerful, lifelong process that unites us all. So how come so many of us unthinkingly assume that depression, diapers, and dementia lie ahead? That the 20th century's astonishing leap in life expectancy is a disaster-in-the-making? Underlying all the hand-wringing is ageism: discrimination that sidelines and silences older people."[67]

It is important to understand the myths and violence of ageism and how we have internalized them. Jonathan Rauch is a senior fellow at the Brookings Institution in Washington. In his book, *The Happiness Curve: Why Life Gets Better after 50*, Rauch wrote that by telling people "their best years are behind them at age fifty, we make them gloomy about the future. In all of those ways, by telling the wrong story about adult development, we bait and set the midlife trap."[68]

Applewhite continues, "People are happiest at the beginnings and the ends of their lives. The vast majority of Americans over 65 live independently. Older people enjoy better mental health than the young or middle-aged. The older people get, the less afraid they are of dying. Why don't more people know these things? Because ageism – internalized and in the culture at large – obscures all but the negative aspects of life after 65 (or 50, or just aging past youth). The personal and social consequences are disastrous. In the 20th century, powerful movements emerged to challenge racism and sexism. It's high time to mobilize against discrimination and stereotyping on the basis of age."[69]

During my forty-year career as a consultant, I had the great fortune to have worked in many countries, mostly in Asia but also in East Africa and the Caribbean, for durations ranging from a month to several years in any one country. Not once in any of those countries did I ever hear anyone ruminate or complain about the burden of living with or "taking care of" their parents or grandparents. On the contrary; older adults or "elders" were treated as respected members of the family and community, bringing their wisdom to the "youngers." This is the way it used to be everywhere. Families were typically extended, in multigenerational households and cooperative communities. The older adults lived at home and, if no longer working outside, contributed to the family's welfare by cooking, cleaning, looking after and tutoring the children, or managing household finances.

They were contributing; their life had purpose and meaning – and they felt secure.

However, the situation has become quite different in the United States. For the most part, older adults are seen as invisible, innocuous, and irrelevant – many of us see them that way and, sadly, many see themselves that way. I suspect most Americans accept and view the aging process as a gradual increase toward diminishment and disengagement from life – and with a dose of inevitable dementia, "senior senility." And that's depressing. We have internalized as truth many dysfunctional messages heard all our lives. We clearly have an "aging problem" unlike a more natural way of sharing and caring in many other countries. Americans to a large extent have bought into the disempowering ageist and patriarchal messages of our alpha-male, productivity, youth-centred, sexist, and materialistic consumer culture. Hey, I mean let's call it for what it really is. Most of us live in urban areas and rarely experience nature or are cognizant of the planet's cycles of birth, reproduction, aging, death, and recycling. We have mostly tried to protect ourselves from the "terrible realities of nature" and are terrified to really look at two significant natural realities – aging and death.

If not careful, we know we will wind up at the metaphorical mercy of "A Place for Mom" and its spokeswoman, who appears to be *Leave It to Beaver*'s mom in pearls and perfect hair, forced to leave our home for "the Home" for physical or financial reasons. Oh, thank you, "A Place for Mom," for taking her off our hands at last. Whew! And what ever happened to Dad? Or we may fall prey to the "reverse mortgage" people. And do you really have any reason to trust the TV people, Joan Lunden or Tom Selleck? I mean, seriously?

It is hard to accept being ignored and disrespected when our life experience and hard-earned wisdom are not valued – to be seen as "overqualified" yet powerless, innocuous, invisible, forgotten. Because of this, we may become reluctant to engage with social and environmental issues, to take a stand, However, it is now, with our experience and hard-earned wisdom, that we are most needed to repair failing social systems and an unhealthy planet – to mentor the young and calm down the adults. Many of us entering retirement are afraid of being disenfranchised, institutionalized, dependent on others for financial support. We have seen the Walmart greeters, pushing shopping carts, or the good "senior volunteers" stuffing envelopes, and it can be scary.

But you don't have to stand for this; you can fight back. Individually we are weak, easily manipulated, but when part of an advocacy organization we can be strong. The early Gray Panthers network is well-known, formed by Maggie Kuhn in response to her forced retirement in 1970 at age sixty-five. Kuhn has famously said, "Old age is not a disease – it is strength and survivorship, triumph over all kinds of vicissitudes and disappointments, trials, and illnesses."[70] But there are many other organizations. For example, The Radical Age Movement, founded by Alice Fisher and based in New York City, confronts the prejudice deeply embedded in our culture as manifested through ageism and other social justice issues. They help organizations and individuals establish Radical Age Chapters for local action.[71]

There are many illuminating videos on YouTube that talk about aging and ageism, including several TED talks. One by Kim Eng in 2018 on conscious aging is part lecture, part meditation and teaches about "our attachment to the physical body and the anxiety that we face as we age and contemplate death."[72] Another is by Joyce Hawkes, a biophysicist who "discovers new life after death."[73]

Ashton Applewhite's TED Talk, "Let's end ageism," given in April 2017, is a realistic and humorous look at what ageism means and does to us.[74] She said that when she was a teenager and couldn't find her car keys, she never once thought to call that a "junior moment." So why would we use that common but disparaging and hurtful term "senior moment" when it happens today? It's not true. It's not you. So, stop saying that!

We live in a patriarchy, or rather, a society shaped by the male dominance of a patriarchy. Ageism is intimately linked with all other "-isms" supported by the patriarchy. So, what exactly is the patriarchy? Patriarchy is a society or government system where men hold the power and women are largely excluded from that power. But it is more complicated and even more damaging than that. We tend to think of any discussion of the patriarchy having solely to do with sexism, but it has wider-ranging negative impacts on all cultural groups, ethnicities, and genders, including men themselves. "Yes, things have gotten better," you say, but it's still with us. And how does the impact of this patriarchy become amplified as we age, especially for women?

A woman "who steps outside the rules of patriarchy and threatens its authority can expect to be hated and feared by men and those women who find their source of power in men."[75] As women age, they can be viewed – by society and by themselves – as diminished in a variety of ways that are not experienced by men. They become compared with younger, "prettier, sexier" women in the workplace. Jean Shinoda Bolen, a Jungian psychotherapist and author, has said, "In a youth-oriented patriarchy, especially, to become an older woman is to become invisible: a nonentity."

A 2015 study by the National Bureau of Economic Research (NBER), based on what was perhaps the largest experiment to test the pervasiveness of age discrimination in hiring, showed that older women's resumes received far fewer callbacks from potential employers than did those of older men and of younger applicants of either sex. According to the NBER researchers, "We find robust evidence of age discrimination in hiring against older women, especially those near retirement age. But we find that there is considerably less evidence of age discrimination against men after correcting for the potential biases this study addresses."[76]

An overt and very common example of differential age discrimination was the story told to me by a client, a retired business executive in her seventies, who was forced to retire several years ago by her male boss in one of the most transparently ageist and sexist ways imaginable. She had been told outright by her male boss that it was time to retire and let the younger people take a greater role. There was nothing wrong with her work performance; in fact, it was exemplary. But it was clear to her this was about her sex accentuated by her age and appearance, which when approaching retirement has a much greater influence on women than men. As she told me, "I feel like I've done something wrong. I've gotten older." That is real pain. It then became very hard for her to stay motivated on anything; there was too much despair – and shame. So, the alternative was to just muddle through; forget the dreams, get by.

Much has been written and accepted about the overt and subtle impacts of a sexist male-dominated power system on the development of women and girls. But the damaging impacts of this system on men and boys in our society may seem surprising.[77] Not to me. Jungian analyst James Hollis and author of *Under Saturn's Shadow*,[78] has written about the psychologically and spiritually wounded men born of the patriarchy and reveals secrets that many men share but rarely admit to others and to themselves. Listening to the revealing interview with James Hollis by Lourdes Viado would be well worth your time.[79] Hollis has written, "When we remember that patriarchy is a cultural contrivance, an invention to compensate for powerlessness, we realize that men, contrary to widespread opinion, are more often the dependent sex. ... He is driven by his childhood experience of the power of the feminine." It is perhaps unfair of me to stop this exploration here, with a statement such as that, but there are space limitations – and you have the resources to follow this up on your own.

Author and activist bell hooks has written about men and the patriarchy: "The crisis facing men is not the crisis of masculinity, it is the crisis of patriarchal masculinity. Until we make this distinction clear, men will continue to fear that any critique of patriarchy represents a threat. ... The first act of violence that patriarchy demands of males is not violence toward women. Instead patriarchy demands of all males that they engage in acts of psychic self-mutilation, that they kill off the emotional parts of themselves. If an individual is not successful in emotionally crippling himself, he can count on patriarchal men to enact rituals of power that will assault his self-esteem."[80]

As previously stated, "every man has an appointment with himself." If not now, then later, an inevitability – so when? Might as well be now. But that's another story, an important one, one that needs to be understood.

My focus here is on how the patriarchy, in league with ageism, affects us – men and women – as we age and disempowers us when making decisions about somehow living through this thing called "retirement." The negative messages we have absorbed, as though they reflect truth, hold us back as we age and try to move into a comfortable, happy, and secure retirement.

Bettina Aptheker, an activist, feminist, and history professor, spoke of older people, especially women: "We're either invisible, or we're in the way."[81] Clinical psychologist Doris Bersing lamented, "After fighting for equal rights and against negative stereotypes, baby-boomer women find themselves in a society that obsessively worships youth and relegates its seniors to second-class status. Baby boomer women grew up around the fighting of the feminist movement in the sixties and seventies; many were feisty revolutionaries."[82] What then does the future hold for you? What role do you see yourself playing in our society as you age? For us baby boomers – women and men – who spent much of our adult lives trying to make a difference, new limits placed on our identities can be very disturbing. But I am not under any illusions of a level playing field.

As she autographed her book for me, Ashton Applewhite wrote, "Wake Up! Cheer Up! Push Back!" But privileged, educated, American, WASP man that I am, please, I've had it easy with my own private internal struggles, real though they may have been – are. But I can recognize this; at least I can try to understand, without judgement, and help others.

We can begin to confront our society's myths about ageism and the patriarchy and overcome their effects on our mind-set and ability to find new work, financial security, and purpose as we age. As these messages have been internalized, they have held us back from our full potential, but these myths can be released through self-exploration and action.

Understanding how ageism affects you is critical to your well-being, your happiness, and even your financial security, as well as your ability to thrive, not merely survive, in your remaining years. Question our consumer media narrative and barrage of advertising. We can make ageism as unacceptable as any other form of prejudice – and dismantle it. What can you do about it? How can you overcome this? How can you dismantle its effects and mobilize against the hold this "last socially acceptable prejudice" has on you? Now, reflect and ask yourself some more specific questions:

- What ageist and other disempowering messages am I hearing and have taken in as truth over the years?
- Where did those messages come from?
- What purpose have those messages served or continue to serve – am I using them to protect myself in some way?

The two articles by Ron Pevny in Appendix 2 argue that many older people are questioning the validity and viability of conventional models of aging, which assume our energy and productive capacities begin to diminish somewhere around an arbitrary age of sixty. On the occasion of the not-so-magical moment that was my sixtieth birthday, I did not suddenly feel particularly diminished. Nor did I feel that way later. Did you?

IONS, in its conscious aging program,[83] has prepared the following exercise, questions for you to begin reflecting on how you feel about getting older – how aging is changing the way you view yourself. The IONS program asks workshop participants to reflect on several questions about ageism:

- Have current cultural views of aging been detrimental for you personally? If so, in what ways?
- Can you think of a personal experience that indicated to you that as an elder you might not be considered as useful as a younger person? How did that make you feel?
- On the other hand, can you think of an experience where you felt you were honored as an elder? What was that like for you?

"Pevny states that life expectancy has dramatically increased and that as we age, it's becoming more and more important to find ways to bring meaning to our lives beyond the limited options that have been available to us in the past. Those options usually focus on the outer and not the inner; they don't recognize how vibrant and meaningful a life can be in one's later years."[84] You can ask yourself two more questions:

- In the years to come, how do I see myself finding this fulfillment?
- What, if anything, am I doing now in this regard?

And we are not alone. We can resist while "our shells begin to crack." Katherine Thanas, late Buddhist abbot of the Santa Cruz Zen Center, reminds us of our shared illusions and how we must transform individually and thereby collectively. "One of our deeply shared convictions about ourselves," she wrote "is that we are unworthy. It is a separating experience. You feel everybody else is more worthy than you, going someplace and doing something, and you're isolated by your sense of aloneness. The truth is that probably our isolation and separation is our deepest, most common experience. … Such a feeling is deeply shared, and we are embarrassed to talk about it. The community awakens together. As soon as one person comes out of his or her shell, all of our shells begin to crack, and possibilities previously unknown become available to us."[85]

With gratitude, I am reminded of Lyla June Johnston, who said during her talk at Bioneers in October 2018, "You are sacred, you are good, you belong, you have purpose … and every time you raise your hand, you help other people know they are not alone."[86]

So, we do not have to accept ageism or any patriarchal nonsense as givens. We are better than that. There are alternatives! You can resist. For example, Rabbi Zalman Schachter-Shalomi, writing about conscious aging and spiritual eldering in his book, *From Age-Ing to Sage-Ing: A Revolutionary Approach to Growing Older*, said, "The model that I'm proposing does more than restore the elder to a position of honor and dignity based on age and long life experience. It envisions the elder as an agent of evolution, attracted as much by the future of humanity's expanded brain-mind potential as by the wisdom of the past. With an increased life span and the psychotechnologies to expand the mind's frontiers, the spiritual elder heralds the next phase of human and global development."[87] Nice.

This is the focus of the next chapter, embracing conscious aging, an understanding of which is the second step in our REWIREMENT process – to take back your power, authority, and dignity – to rise above the myths of ageism and your inner critics, monkey chatter self-talking you into depression or apathetic numbness. In Chapter 5, we will examine the inner work of conscious aging. But first, reflect on some of the topics of this inner work in Appendix 2, as defined by Ron Pevny:

- Life review
- Healing the past
- Recontextualizing
- Deepening spiritual connection
- Accepting mortality
- Creating a legacy
- Letting go

Your initial reflections on the issues and questions posed to you in this chapter will set the stage for exercises in the next chapter that focuses on the challenges and opportunities of conscious aging.

Chapter 5:
Touch of Grey

"Generally, by the time you are Real, most of your hair has been loved off, and your eyes drop out and you get loose in the joints and very shabby. But these things don't matter at all, because once you are Real you can't be ugly, except to people who don't understand."
~ **Margery Williams, *The Velveteen Rabbit***

"So live as if you were living already for the second time and as if you had acted the first time as wrongly as you are about to act now!"
– **Viktor Frankl, *Man's Search for Meaning***

Step 2: Embrace Conscious Aging

In 1992, Omega Institute sponsored a conference in New York City on "Conscious Aging," the first of its kind on aging. Speakers included Ram Dass, who had just turned sixty; Rabbi Zalman Schachter-Shalomi; and others from fields that included spirituality, transpersonal psychology, and consciousness research. That same year, Sounds True produced a two-CD set, a collection of learning lessons, featuring Ram Dass's lectures from the Omega conference called "*Conscious Aging: On the Nature of Change and Facing Death.*" With insight and humor, Ram Dass tells conference participants the purpose of conscious aging is to "open your heart to a life filled with abundance and wisdom and free of the fear of death." He tries to convey a message that "when you lose your fear of death, you have the ability to gain a love for life."

Aging is natural. Anne Lamott, writer and progressive political activist, has said, "We contain all the ages we have ever been." It is a powerful, lifelong, and totally transformative process. Much experience and wisdom has been gained, but we are also facing new challenges, mostly physical. However, it is well-documented from hospice workers that the most common emotion for many on their death beds is regret, regret for a life not lived more fully or aware, more "conscious." So many regrets.

So, what is "conscious aging?" From Latin *conscius* (to know), conscious means to perceive with some degree of controlled observation, to be aware, especially of something within the self. Aging is all about getting older and showing the effects characteristic of increased age. Conscious aging is concerned with acceptance of the present moment and the positive aspects of growing older. We age consciously "by facing our fears, uncovering the wisdom of life experiences, healing wounds, forgiving ourselves and others, and charting a path forward that involves passing on a legacy, serving as an elder committed to healing the planet, and facing mortality with dignity and grace."[88]

Michael Singer, in his book, *The Untethered Soul: The Journey Beyond Yourself*, further elaborates on what it means to be more centered, more conscious, more fully aware: "What differentiates a conscious, centered being from a person who is not so conscious, is simply the focus of their awareness. It's not a difference in the consciousness itself. All consciousness is the same. Just as all light from the sun is the same, all awareness is the same. Consciousness is neither pure nor impure; it has no qualities. It's just there, aware that it's aware. The difference is that when your consciousness is not centered within, it becomes totally focused on the objects of consciousness. When you are a centered being, however, your consciousness is always aware of being conscious. Your awareness of being is independent of the inner and outer objects you happen to be aware of."[89]

"Becoming conscious," wrote Ron Pevny, "means becoming aware of the emotional baggage and encumbrances we are carrying as we move beyond mid-life adulthood, such as unhealed wounds, unfelt and un-processed grief, grudges, and heart closing attitudes that require forgiveness, and stories of unworthiness, or victimhood we have constructed over decades to define our lives." [90] The Buddhist monk Thich Nhat Hanh has said awareness is "like the sun. When it shines on things, they are transformed." Thus, through the process of conscious aging, becoming more fully aware in the present, we are transformed.

A common question I hear, or a variation thereof and one that has concerned me, is, "How can I overcome my depression and feelings of isolation during retirement?" In this chapter, we will consider what can be done to address the scourge of ageism vis-à-vis our natural aging trajectory. We will find ways to change our minds and take action to avoid its debilitating impacts, impacts of mind-set that affect our ability to find purpose and cope with our finances, for example. Our aim is to be secure, fulfilled, and happy as we age. Most "senior citizen" or so-called "successful retirement" or "successful aging" programs focus on admonishing us to stay young, "young at heart" whatever that means, and stay in the game as though nothing has changed, fighting physical changes with plastic surgery and vitality with pills – and lots and lots of the exhausting and self-serving smart-money-boy advice on investing and saving, saving for retirement and life on the beach, maybe a boat, definitely golf.

Harry Moody, former vice president and director of academic affairs for AARP, has written that conscious aging, "as an emerging cultural ideal, represents a genuinely new stage and level of psychological functioning. As a way of life and a level of consciousness, Conscious Aging has appeared at a distinct moment in history. Yet the holistic path of late-life development is not a new idea but a possibility long familiar in the spiritual traditions of the world, which depict later life as a time for the growth of consciousness and wisdom." Moody further asserts that conscious aging has "emerged as a social ideal at a specific moment in history, in the first decade of the 21st century. This historical moment reflects the convergence of two historical trends: the evolution of psychology to include humanistic, transpersonal, and lifespan development theory; and the widening impact of population aging in all post-industrial societies."[91]

The late Robert C. Atchley, a gerontologist, provided us with these thoughts on conscious aging: "The vision laid out by the early framers of the 'aging with consciousness' movement involves developing and nurturing a contemplative life and engaging in service rooted in the higher levels of consciousness that a contemplative life makes available. Aging with consciousness is neither quick nor easy. It requires that we come back over and over again to our intention to be awake as we age. It requires that we practice compassionate listening and look at the world from a long-term vantage point that transcends our purely personal desires and fears."[92]

The conscious aging, or spiritual eldering, movement has been built to a large extent on the inspiration and recommendations of the pivotal and inspiring book by Rabbi Zalman Schachter-Shalomi and Ronald S. Miller, *From Age-Ing to Sage-Ing: A Revolutionary Approach to Growing Older,* published in 1995, a few years after the Omega Institute conference. I know, for me, their book, and the insights of Reb Zalman, had a great impact and helped me put my aging life, at a critical turning point, into positive perspective with the realization that I need not be a victim, subject to whatever seemingly inevitable wind may blow. I could take back my power.

According to Reb Zalman, "The model of the spiritual elder is an appropriate one for individuals experiencing an extended lifespan. This process can be facilitated through the application of transpersonal and humanistic processes. A major part of this work involves an examination of one's life and an understanding of how apparently negative events often lead to positive outcomes. Inner work is also essential to relieve oneself of the burden of resentment and anger that can accumulate over a lifetime." The principles and practices of spiritual eldering described and put into practice in his book are "to age consciously by facing our fears, uncovering the wisdom of life experiences, healing wounds, forgiving ourselves and others, charting a path forward that involves passing on a legacy, serving as an elder committed to healing the planet, and facing mortality with dignity and grace."

Reb Zalman founded a conscious aging support organization that today has become known as Sage-ing International (SI), which works to fight ageism and promote conscious aging, intergenerational mentoring and "eldering."[93] SI is a resource for those seeking purpose, service, and continual growth in their later years. SI's mission is to transform "the current paradigm of aging to 'sage-ing' through learning, community building, and service."

SI's objectives include:

- "embracing new paradigms for aging to realize our potential;
- recalling important people and events and how they have shaped us;
- harvesting the wisdom learned through life's triumphs and challenges;
- finding solace in forgiving others and ourselves;
- making peace with death, taking spiritual and practical steps; and
- creating a legacy through service, mentoring and activism."

We are reminded by Ram Dass that "just because you are old doesn't necessarily mean you are an elder." An "elder," then, is an older person, an "older," valued for their extensive life experience and wisdom. We all know some narrow-minded, thick-as-a-brick, fundamentally conservative older people who really have little to offer in the way of imparting wisdom to younger people, people they do not understand and continually criticize. Key topics of conversation, for whatever reason, seem to be mostly about their ailments, the ailments of others, and small-minded criticisms and complaints about just about everything as though they are no longer a part of this world – angrily identifying problems with no hint of offering solutions. A retirement home resident friend of mine in New Hampshire, a true elder, commented that to a large extent she is surrounded by "walking corpses" whose days revolve around dining hall meal times, possessing few interests, living in the past, and seemingly just on a holding pattern for the inevitable, which cannot come soon enough. I find this extraordinarily sad. And when younger people encounter such older people, it is much too easy for them to generalize incorrectly about what it means to "be old". The young need to engage with and learn from true elders.

For some, growing older takes on new meaning, not all negative. Terrence McKenna has joked, but not really: "Culture is a con-game designed to bewilder you for 35 to 40 years." (or usually a lot more!) "And then if by some miracle you can outlive that span of time, a strange realization will begin to dawn as you sit at the poker table. You realize, 'This is a bunch of crap. I've been had.' Well, up until very recently only a very few people in any society lived into those ages and then that was called wisdom: 'You know, he just sits on his porch and rocks and occasionally chuckles.'" [94]

A good definition of an elder has been provided by Barry Barkan, director of Live Oak Institute in Berkeley, California, and co-founder of the Pioneer Network, a national association of leaders in the field of aging. This definition – to me – best captures this post-adulthood stage achieved by some, not all: "An elder is a person who is still growing, still a learner, still with potential and whose life continues to have within it promise for, and connection to, the future. An elder is still in pursuit of happiness, joy and pleasure, and her or his birthright to these remains intact. Moreover, an elder is a person who deserves respect and honor and whose work it is to synthesize wisdom from long life experience and formulate this into a legacy for future generations."

Mentor was the friend of Odysseus and the wise elder who remained in Ithaca to watch over Odysseus's son, Telemachus, while his father battled during the Trojan War, described in the *Iliad*. In English, the word now refers to any wise adviser. Marc Freedman, in his 2018 book, *How to Live Forever: The Enduring Power of Connecting the Generations*,[95] stresses the importance of mentoring, intergenerational support, and collaboration where an aging population helps the younger generation in desperate need of guidance and encouragement from authentic mentors. This is a role of the modern elder. Freedman indicated we can choose one of two paths forward; "one path characterized by scarcity, conflict, and loneliness; the other by abundance, interdependence, and connection." Which path we take "will determine not only our collective ability to navigate the multi-generational world already upon us, but also our individual ability to find the keys to happiness and fulfillment in the second half of life."

Recently, the moniker "modern elder" has become popular. In his 2018 best-selling book, *Wisdom @ Work*, Chip Conley defines this role.[96] He describes a modern elder as being part mentor, part intern – a "mentern" – someone who shares wisdom and experience while at the same time remaining curious and open to learning, with the dual roles of "wisdom keeper and seeker." After all, he wrote, "wisdom is most powerful when it is exchanged freely across the generations."

Conley has said being a modern elder is no longer so much about reverence (for an elder) as it is about relevance. This new role can be about taking the wisdom gained over a lifetime and applying it to modern-day problems, juxtaposing a lifetime of wisdom with curiosity in the present moment to creatively discover new solutions. The term is useful and appealing as it places an older person, rather than an "enlightened elder," very much within and not apart from society and with much potential to still contribute. It stresses the benefits in the workplace, communities, and home of intergenerational cooperation and collaboration. Conley has identified five criteria that may be demonstrated by a modern elder; namely, "stewardship, emotional intelligence, holistic thinking, unvarnished insight, and good judgment," and these are defined and discussed in *Wisdom @ Work*.

The Institute of Noetic Sciences (IONS),[97] an international nonprofit organization based in Petaluma, California, was founded by Apollo 14 astronaut Edgar Mitchell in 1973. IONS has been at the forefront of research and education in consciousness and human potential. The mission of IONS is "to reveal the interconnected nature of reality through scientific exploration and personal discovery, creating a more compassionate, thriving, and sustainable world."[98]

I am certified as a workshop facilitator for the IONS Conscious Aging program.[99] The program objective is "to transform your expectations of aging from self-limitation, lack, isolation, and fear toward expansiveness, inclusiveness, wholeness, connection, and compassion." The program was developed by IONS over a four-year period of testing and refinement and based on research and practices described in two important books on consciousness and transformation.[100]

The IONS program is designed as eight facilitated workshop sessions; namely, (1) introduction to conscious aging, (2) self-compassion, (3) forgiveness, (4) life review, (5) transformative practices, (6) death makes life possible, (7) surrender or letting go, and (8) creating a new vision of aging. Each session provides activities that include "listening to one's inner wisdom and guidance, integrating inspirational ideas and best practices, sharing in intimate conversation circles, and harvesting the collective wisdom of the group." From the workshop introduction, expected workshop outcomes enable participants to:

- "explore unexamined, self-limiting beliefs and assumptions about aging and learn to make better choices about how to age more consciously;
- develop the skills of self-compassion to cope more effectively with the stresses associated with aging;
- discover what has given heart and meaning to your life and how that can enrich your intentions for a healthy aging process;
- identify and heal the regrets, sufferings, and negative self-concepts that may have kept you from more fully appreciating yourself and the life you lived;
- minimize any feelings of isolation you may be feeling and deepen your relationship with the world around you;
- learn to manage your fears and those of your loved ones in the presence of death through the transformative power of surrender and acceptance; and

- cultivate a personal roadmap for your own aging journey by deepening your spiritual life and learning to make each moment matter." [101]

Again, conscious aging, self-compassion, forgiveness, life review, transformative practices, death makes life possible, surrender or letting go, and creating a new vision of aging are the eight elements covered in the IONS Conscious Aging workshops. The full course of workshops is designed to cover about twenty hours over eight weeks. I am not able to provide the content here and will not attempt to summarize it. Having gone through the course myself, and now qualified to facilitate it, I can say it can be a life-changing experience.

Buddhist *roshi* Joan Halifax has worked with people for many years in hospices and on death row, as well as in village clinics. In her 2010 TED Talk, she spoke about compassion, the nature of empathy, and what she has learned about compassion assisting the dying during the process of death. "Compassion is comprised of that capacity to see clearly into the nature of suffering," she said. "It is that ability to really stand strong and to recognize also that I am not separate from this suffering. But that is not enough because compassion … means that we aspire to transform suffering."[102]

Kristin Neff has designed a "Self-Compassion Scale" (SCS) to measure levels of self-compassion across several parameters or aspects of our lives.[103] You can take her online test to assess your own levels of self-compassion: https://self-compassion.org/test-how-self-compassionate-you-are/. Interpreting your score (from the testing site): "Average overall self-compassion scores tend to be around 3.0 on the 1-5 scale, so you can interpret your overall score accordingly. As a rough guide, a score of 1-2.5 for your overall self-compassion score indicates you are low in self-compassion, 2.5-3.5 indicates you are moderate, and 3.5-5.0 means you are high. Remember that higher scores for the Self-Judgment, Isolation, and Over-Identification subscales indicate less self-compassion, while lower scores on these dimensions are indicative of more self-compassion."

I took the test at a time when I was not feeling particularly strong about anything (!) one way or the other, and here are my results:

- Self-Kindness: 4.40
- Self-Judgment: 2.60
- Common Humanity: 3.75
- Isolation: 3.25
- Mindfulness: 3.25
- Over-Identification: 3.00
- Overall score: 3.43

But try – and this is important – try not to get too hung up on this, on the "scores" you got or what the scores mean. Just use the process as one more tool for self-reflection. You could also make a list of the experiences, mistakes, or perceived imperfections that trigger your inner critic. Over time, you could pay attention to what you say to yourself when such experiences occur. Do you think they might be trying to teach you something if you would only listen? When you become aware of these musings by your inner critic, reflect on your feelings, your emotions. What might be underneath? Can you begin to ease off on the suffering, the painful emotions, your own personal critic is creating?

"Forgiveness," according to psychologist Frederick Luskin in his book *Forgive for Good*, "is the moment to moment experience of peace and understanding that occurs when an injured party's suffering is reduced as they transform their grievance against an offending party. This transformation takes place through learning to take less personal offense, attribute less blame to the offender and, by greater understanding, see the personal and interpersonal harm that occurs as the natural consequence of unresolved anger and hurt."[104]

Lyla June Johnston, at the 2017 Geography of Hope Conference, spoke powerfully about forgiveness. As an indigenous woman, a Diné or Navajo, she has experienced or inherited much that could never be forgiven, a genocide of native peoples. She has had to learn forgiveness in the face of great adversity and discrimination. She stated, "They say that forgiveness is the most powerful medicine on earth. … This is not to say what has happened is OK – but to say that through that process I am going to love the people who are hurting me. And through that process I am going to love the people who are pawns of a system. And so, we really work to do forgiveness. … they say that if you do not forgive, you become the oppressor. … Forgiveness is something we must not only administer to others but to ourselves. … But if you practice forgiving it will become as natural as breathing, and you do it in the moment, as it's happening"[105]

It is important to recognize several misconceptions, several errors, about forgiveness. We often fall into these traps, these pitfalls, such as:

- forgiving an offense means you condone the offense;
- forgiveness means you must reconcile with someone who treated you badly;
- forgiveness depends on whether the abuser or lying person apologizes, wants you back, or changes his or her ways; or
- forgiveness means that we forget what has happened to us.

Here is something you could do now. Write a letter of forgiveness to someone you have harmed or who has harmed you (or write to yourself forgiving yourself). Then, burn the letter, release the person, the issue, the guilt or the pain – and give up your resentment. Not easy, I know. But does it feel better? What's the point of holding on to this never-ending punishment of self and others? Are you jamming a sword through your belly to get to the guy behind you? Can you even laugh? But at some point, your forgiveness may – someday, just may – turn into gratitude – gratitude for these powerful lessons you have learned.

There is some measured empirical evidence, if not already intuitive, that gratitude can rewrite – rewire – your brain.[106] Gratitude, as observed through positive psychology research, is deeply and reliably associated with greater happiness. "Gratitude helps people feel more positive emotions, relish good experiences, improve their health, deal with adversity, and build strong relationships."[107] Practiced on a regular basis and with a recognition that the source of past, present, and optimistic future gratitude lies at least partially outside of yourself, gratitude will help you connect to all that is beyond and greater than your individual "monkey mind" ego.

In *The Pastures of Heaven*, John Steinbeck wrote, "After the bare requisites of living and reproducing, man wants most to leave some record of himself, a proof, perhaps, that he has really existed. He leaves his proof on wood, on stone, or on the lives of other people. This deep desire exists in everyone, from the boy who scribbles on a wall to the Buddha who etches his image in the race mind. Life is so unreal. I think that we seriously doubt that we exist and go about trying to prove that we do."

Now, would you write your own obituary? Someone will. Would it be a brief review of a life lived well or a chronology of where you were born, your degrees, where you worked, and who you left behind? Does it highlight your strengths and accomplishments only? Are you still trying to impress from "beyond the grave?" What about your core values? What was the degree to which you lived them? Do these values come through when people read your obituary? Is it all "happy, happy, did stuff, got married, did some more stuff, died" or does it show some of your flaws; does it show that you were a human who lived and breathed, made mistakes, had failures but learned from those failures and then succeeded in something? Would it read as something sad and boring or would it be an inspiration to others to lead a better, more conscious life? My measure of a successful obituary is if it makes someone laugh, as in, "oh, yeah, me too." So, I challenge you now – or later – to write a tribute to your own life, what we call an "obituary." And how would you write this? Is it the summary of what you've done so far, your life up to now? Or would you place it somewhere in the future, at a time when you expect to have achieved some current goals?

Nan Phifer in her 2010 book, *Memoirs of the Soul: A Writing Guide*,[108] offers a structured, organized process to follow when writing a "soul memoir," including useful exercises. This is a huge topic, and there are many guides out there – some good, some not so good. Some, such as *Memoirs of the Soul*, will help you with writing your memoir and organizing a review of your life and then turning that into a legacy, a harvesting of experience and wisdom. Two other excellent books to help you in this process are *Legacies of the Heart: Living a Life that Matters* by Meg Newhouse[109] and Rachael Freed's *Your Legacy Matters: Harvesting the Love and Lessons of Your Life,* "a multigenerational guide for writing your ethical will."[110]

But what if you have no interest or ambition to write a memoir? I get that. But at least consider conducting a life review, looking back and reflecting on your life. "So when I refer to life review," said Tom Meuser, director of Gerontology at the University of Missouri in St. Louis, "typically I use that phrase to denote a general process of looking back to bring an understanding" and integration "to the present and the future."[111]

A life review can help you understand more about what you did, when you did it, how you did it, and who you did it with, such as identifying those people who most influenced you along the way. In this way, you can begin to integrate the past with the future. This gives us the opportunity to examine and learn from our life experience. It is quite normal to look back on our lives as we age. Has it been overall a good life? Do I have regrets?

Ron Pevny, in *Conscious Living, Conscious Aging,* asserts that the inner work of conscious aging is based on first conducting such a life review. He has provided a method for doing this in as much or as little detail as you wish. Conducting a focused life review can be powerful, and Pevny provides the following process:

- "Break your life at the seven-year segments. For each segment, reflect on and write about your strongest memories; most influential people in your life; the most difficult or painful experiences; the most joyous or enlivening experiences; and how this life chapter may be impacting your life now. Some people like to integrate artistic expression into this process. An especially impactful way to do this is to imagine your life as encompassing the cycle of a year, with January being your first seven years; February, ages eight to fourteen; October, ages sixty-four to seventy and December, seventy-eight plus.

- "Look at your life thematically. Reflect on and write about the important people in your life; the development and use of your talents; the evolution of your spiritual life; the wounds and losses you experienced; the biggest challenges and how you dealt with them; the people, things, and experiences that brought you the most joy and made you feel most alive; and the values you have come to hold most dear." [112]

When I did my life review, I designed it as a table with the life stages (in seven-year increments) running down vertically on the left side of the page. At the top of the page, running horizontally, I made columns such as places I lived, main activities, work, accomplishments, struggles or obstacles, and people who were most influential to me during that stage. You can make up your own table with whatever column headings suit you. The end result will be nothing if not interesting. You may begin to see patterns and influences that shaped you along the way. What's done is done, and you can live without regrets with a daily focus on the present and planning for the future.

"Some people live as though they are already dead," said the Zen Buddhist monk and mindfulness meditation leader Thich Nhat Hanh. "There are people moving around us who are consumed by their past, terrified of their future, and stuck in their anger and jealousy. They are not alive; they are just walking corpses."[113] Yikes! But you know it's true. I was just shopping at Walmart this afternoon. But that's not fair. And there are people who spend their lives resisting change, those I like to call the Beginners (Chapter 3) and for whom transformation, of consciousness or otherwise, is just so much woo-woo.

In their book, *Living Deeply: The Art and Science of Transformation in Everyday Life*, authors Marilyn Mandala Schlitz, Cassandra Vieten, and Tina Amorok state that "conscious transformations are profound internal shifts that result in long-lasting changes in the way you experience and relate to yourself, others, and the world." Their book is the result of a ten-year research program conducted through IONS. They further assert,

"Your behavior, attitudes, and ways of being in the world are changed in life-affirming and lasting ways only when your consciousness transforms, and you commit to living deeply into that transformation."[114] According to the authors, consciousness "includes your own internal reality. It includes self-awareness, your relationships to your environment, the people in your life, and your worldview or model of reality. Simply put, your consciousness determines how you experience the world."

After all that, what exactly is transformation? "Transformation is a process of profound and radical change that arises from deep awareness and leads to fresh orientation and new direction. ... Transformation is the process of moving from limitations to full creativity and full expression." It is the change that happens when someone comes into greater alignment with themselves, their purpose. Alignment is "finding congruence between the inner and outer experience. ... The sense of coming home to oneself awakens vitality and full engagement."[115]

If we operate within a worldview that is basically unconscious, then how can we become conscious, aware and alert, to the possibility of coming into this alignment – this transformation? Thich Nhat Hanh underscores the power of mindfulness to transform our lives, writing in his book, *You Are Here: Discovering the Magic of the Present Moment*, that "mindfulness is not an evasion or an escape. It means being here, present, and totally alive. It is true freedom – and without this freedom, there is no happiness."

The authors of *Living Deeply* and the IONS Conscious Aging workshops on transformation ask, "How do consciousness transformations – the kind that make a long-term difference in your life – begin?" They provide examples of the "many doorways to transformative experiences, both painful and awe-filled." These include several possibilities or doorways, explored in detail during IONS workshops, including intense suffering or crises, realizing your life has diverged from your values or purpose, "hitting bottom,"[116] noetic experiences,[117] "non-ordinary" states of consciousness,[118] meeting a teacher, peak experiences, and being immersed in nature.

You can rewire for creativity; creativity is like building muscle strength – through exercise it is enhanced, through practice it is amplified. There are many ways to rewire your brain to accentuate your innate ability to create new ideas and positive actions. Conferences, seminars, workshops, books, books, and more books can show you ways to do this. But a rather good and brief summary of ways to rewire your brain for creativity was prepared by Deep Patel for the online site, "Entrepreneur". These include, but are not limited to, (i) mindful observation, (ii) change your environment, (iii) take a creative stroll, (iv) recharge your curiosity, (v) try some blue sky thinking ("free your mind and brainstorm without limitations … freeing yourself of constraints, assumptions and self-limiting beliefs"), (vi) practice creating, and (vii) take time to daydream.[119]

Soon after undergoing surgery for pancreatic cancer, Steve Jobs told the Stanford graduating class of 2005, "No one wants to die. Even people who want to go to heaven don't want to die to get there. And yet death is the destination we all share. No one has ever escaped it. And that is as it should be, because death is very likely the single best invention of life. It is life's change agent. It clears out the old to make way for the new."

Earlier in his commencement address, Jobs had said, "Remembering that I'll be dead soon is the most important tool I've ever encountered to help me make the big choices in life. Because almost everything – all external expectations, all pride, all fear of embarrassment or failure – these things just fall away in the face of death, leaving only what is truly important. Remembering that you are going to die is the best way I know to avoid the trap of thinking you have something to lose. You are already naked. There is no reason not to follow your heart." After reflecting on his own mortality, he urged the graduating class, "Your time is limited, so don't waste it living someone else's life. … I have looked in the mirror every morning and asked myself: 'If today were the last day of my life, would I want to do what I am about to do today?'"[120] Jobs continued to do what he wanted to do – with great creativity – and six years later died at age fifty-six.

As part of the conscious aging process, it is important to explore the concept of death, your ideas and feelings about it, and how accepting death would influence your choices and life priorities. Thich Nhat Hanh reminds us that death is an ongoing process. "If there were not birth and death in every moment, we could not continue to live. In every moment, many cells in your body have to die so that you can continue to live. Not only the cells of your body, but all the feelings, perceptions, and mental formations in the river of consciousness in you are born and die in every moment."

Death and dying are inevitable, we know this, but all our lives we have shied away from our own death even though we have seen it all around us. It is something so remote, even uninteresting perhaps, especially for the young. This is a matter that is very emotional and confusing and frightening also. But facing our death, recognizing it and realizing it will become our reality one day, should be a very meaningful and transformative procedure. I have lived in several cultures where death is more accepted, an integral part of life, not necessarily the tragedy and loss many of us in America view it as. We scold at nothing in particular; we want to "not go gentle into that good night, Old age should burn and rave at close of day; Rage, rage against the dying of the light." So that particular view, from Dylan Thomas's poem, is largely accepted in the West, maybe even viewed as a sign of good mental health. However, I suggest that an alternative could be to just calm down, accept the inevitable, face it as a natural part of life, this transition and transformation. Stop the fight, the denial. Healthy traditional rituals in many other parts of the world help those dying and those who remain, but in America we seem to have lost these healthy rites of passage. After all, a funeral is always such a sad thing, isn't it? Too early. Tsk. Tsk.

The *Tibetan Book of the Dead* includes this passage, to be read at the moment of death: "Oh, Nobly Born, Now is the moment. Before you is mind, open and wide as space, Simple, without center or circumference. Now is the moment of death." Now imagine you have only three months to live. No question. The doctor got it right. This ship will sail. No turning back. How would you spend your remaining time? Where would you place your focus? With whom would you want to be over those days and then with you at the moment of your death? Are you feeling regretful and resistant or content and accepting?

Now, you could ask yourself several questions about your beliefs around your mortality:

- What are my fears about dying and death?
- What are my beliefs about death?
- How did I develop my beliefs about death?
- How has the death of someone close to me had an impact on my beliefs?
- Have I ever been with someone right at the time of their death? How did it feel?
- What do I imagine when I think of my own death?
- Have I prepared my own advanced directives in preparation for death?

Eckert Tolle has given a lecture on acceptance and surrender that may be found easily on YouTube. Tolle stresses that we are unconsciously creating a futile conflict, "an inner state of war," between the inner and outer, a battle between external circumstances (as they are) and our thoughts and feelings about those circumstances. It is painful "to stand in opposition of what is." He asks, "What does it feel like to not want to be where you are? … But you are here, always. Is it so hard to accept that?" [121]

We can ask ourselves, as urged by Tom Pinkson, "What is the state of consciousness I want to be in as I age and when I die? Whatever that state of consciousness is, if that's what I want to manifest under those trying conditions, or whatever the conditions might be, and they certainly can be very trying, I need to practice it now. Because if I wait until I'm aging and dying and then try to manifest those aspects of consciousness, my chances of doing it are not going to be as successful as if I practice it. If I want to be peaceful, if I want to be calm, if I want to have a sense of equanimity as

I'm going through my final years, then I need to work and cultivate those qualities in my life with the challenges that come up in daily living now."

Pinkson asks us to consider, "What state of conscious awareness do I want to cultivate now as I age and when I'm facing my final hours?" You can create an intention statement as your vision of conscious aging. Here are three examples of intention statements from his book, *Fruitful Aging*.[122] Obviously, you will want to make your intention statement your own.

- "I am a sacred, worthy, luminous being. I am love and my love is for giving."
- "I am a joyful, kind, patient, fluid-flowing, peaceful man of light and love. I am one with the universe."
- "I am a profound, courageous life-force, talented in loving myself and benevolent to all."

He continued, "One of my favorite sayings is, 'When the going gets tough, you get what you practice.' Another favorite saying is from Huston Smith who wrote, 'It's relatively easy to experience an altered state of consciousness through different methodologies such as meditation, chanting, or psycho-spiritual technologies. But can you change that altered state into an altered trait?' The only way that is going to happen is with conscious applied work with your intention and attention."[123]

Consider now some rites of passage that could relate to aging consciously. Rites of passage that have helped us move from one life stage to another, still prevalent in some cultures, are largely missing from our modern society. In an Appendix 2 article, Ron Pevny asserts that these healthy rites of passage are now needed if we are to be initiated into a new meaningful life stage that some may call "elderhood."

- Can you imagine what a rite of passage into elderhood might look like?
- Have you experienced a vision quest or other ritual of initiation or passage?

- How might our society be different if we honored, embraced, and integrated the wisdom of our elders?
- What are you doing or see yourself doing in the future in terms of service and sharing your own wisdom?

In this chapter, you have gained an understanding of conscious aging by reflecting on your attitudes about aging, In the context of your current situation, you can begin to apply what you have learned to improve your wellbeing. You can even take on the attitude of wise elder Emma Knight, age 7, who wrote for a class assignment, "When I turn 100 years old I will be tired of everything and everyone. So I will tell everyone I'm going to Canada but actually go to the Bahamas. I'll live in a tiny hut with my tiny dog. I will order fish tacos when I'm hungry and live my best life with no crap."[124]

The next chapter is all about Step 3 of the REWIREMENT process – waking up to and discovering your core values and character strengths. Identifying your uniqueness, your gifts, will inform your decisions and enhance the trajectory toward rediscovering your purpose and moving toward such goals as greater happiness and financial comfort as you consciously age.

Chapter 6:
Beat It on Down the Line

"Personal leadership is the process of keeping your vision and values before you and aligning your life to be congruent with them."
- Stephen Covey, *7 Habits of Highly Effective People*

"Don't let your special character and values, the secret that you know and no one else does, the truth - don't let that get swallowed up by the great chewing complacency."
- Aesop (ca. 620 – 564 BCE)

Step 3: Wake Up to Your Values and Strengths

What are your values and greatest strengths of character? Have you ever really examined these characteristics, the combination of which only you possess? Can you identify and define your values and strengths? In this chapter, you will take the next step in REWIREMENT by continuing to look inward for self-reflection and discovery. This will require identifying your needs, values, strengths, and personal gifts in the context of aging and retirement so that you may live your years to the fullest, including with improved finances and general well-being.

Needs and Values

One approach to alignment that supports deep transformation is exploring your needs and values. "When you become conscious of your underlying needs, your core values can come into focus." Our emotions or feelings directly relate to and inform our needs. Have your needs been met or unmet? Your self-criticism or inner critic can be a guide to identify unmet needs. This includes the habit of harshly judging yourself and others. Ask yourself a few questions. What do I really need? What do I really want in this (relationship, job, partnership, opportunity)? What motivates me toward that need? What is it that is so important that keeps me from fulfilling that need and creating what I want? Do I, in truth, really want something else? What is that?

For example, let's say you want a new job. Your underlying needs, in this case, may include a desire to contribute, inspire, be challenged, and be more secure financially. Or you might want to get some particularly toxic or annoying person out of your life. The needs here may be obvious, such as protection from pain, increased independence, or even safety. Rarely, if ever, is it a single need. And if you feel down and disconnected, out of touch, this is a sign to you that some critical needs are not being met. One of the major causes of depression, for example, is a blockage to creativity, a basic human need; creativity puts us in alignment with our purpose. Without it, not being able to act on our creative impulse, we feel rootless, cast adrift on an uncaring sea – and so on.

Fulfillment of our basic human needs, such as safety and shelter, is the foundation of a life well lived. Humanistic psychology maintains that each person has a driving desire to realize their full potential, that is to reach a level of "self-actualization." The theory of self-actualization and the hierarchy of needs, a principle of psychological health, is well worth considering. Self-actualization was first advocated in 1954 by the transpersonal psychologist Abraham Maslow, who described it as "becoming actually what you are potentially," a promise and need to actually become everything you are capable of becoming. Maslow maintained that the average person is already whole but with "dampened and inhibited powers and capabilities." He wrote, "I think of the self-actualizing man not as an ordinary man with something added, but rather as the ordinary man with nothing taken away." In fact, he is implying that we are all "hardwired to self-actualize."[125]

Central to Maslow's theory of self-actualization is the idea that people live within a hierarchy of needs. A "deficit" need is perceived as something we lack. The image of a pyramid was used to describe this hierarchy of needs with the more basic needs at the bottom.[126] In theory if not in fact, when all of one's basic needs are met, a person can move to self-actualization or a higher level of human consciousness. First, at the most basic level, fundamental to your survival, are your physiological needs. This will include food, water, air, and sleep to keep your physiological processes in good working order so you can address your higher needs. When your physiological needs are deficient, you will need to devote all your energy to meet these most basic needs. Next come the basic needs for safety, a security that ensures our environment is predictable. Our next higher basic need is based on belonging and love. Loneliness and feeling as though we are unwanted or worthless result from our need for love and belonging not being fulfilled. When these needs are fulfilled, we feel a sense of being whole. Needs for self-esteem and earning the respect of others, when we value ourselves and are recognized for our achievements, boost our confidence and feelings of self-worth.

But of course, reality is – and humans are – never quite so simple. An additional viewpoint presents a more dynamic view of the hierarchy of needs in which the different needs overlap at the same time and to different degrees over a lifespan.[127] When all these most basic needs are met, recognizing a person's self-actualization can come into being with a heightened sense of confidence, creativity, and sustainability.

An individual's first realization of self-actualization, or more precisely of the process of self-actualizing, can seem like an epiphany, an amazing grace, that can last weeks, months, hopefully years if honored. Self-actualization includes honoring your creativity and striving to reach higher levels of consciousness, happiness, and wisdom, to potentially become a fully conscious human. This may also be viewed as a state of consciousness that comes through discarding all outward self-definitions, not allowing others to define or label you. Self-actualization may be achieved within a single lifetime, but a higher level within his "hierarchy of needs," recognized by Maslow later in life, is self-transcendence, when a person is motivated by values that transcend the impermanence of personal self or ego and thus enters a connection with Spirit not unlike enlightenment as envisioned in the spiritual philosophy of Buddhism. More on that in Chapter 12.

Emotional awareness of your needs helps guide you when making decisions. When you become aware of your needs, what is being fulfilled and what is not and what motivates you, you can create powerful action plans (if carried out!) that are driven by your core values and lead to getting things done (imagine that!). But what do we mean by core values?

Your values are your principles or standards of behavior you desire to be important and that shape the way you view the world, your place in it, and how you live and work. If recognized and embraced, your values guide you to identify priorities toward living the life you want, in the way you want it, fulfilling your purpose. And when your actions, or vibration, are not in alignment with your core values, you will know it – something is wrong, something just does not feel right – and this will make you unhappy and confused. So, just as it is important to be aware of your needs, it is critical that you be conscious of your core values. When a goal is not being met, then it is likely to be because of not linking it to a core value. When a value is being honored and expressed, then you can be in alignment with the goal and be invigorated.

A value may be viewed as a need no matter where you go, perhaps connected to your spirit or soul somehow. What's most important to you? Your core values determine how you will answer that question. Our core values highlight what we stand for. They will guide our behaviors, decisions, and actions. When you have a conviction of what you value, you will begin to live in alignment with your own values, not somebody else's, and will experience greater fulfillment. Without knowing your values there will be internal conflict, which can then trigger destructive habits, addictions, and unproductive behavior.

One pathway used to bring a person into alignment is to explore and clarify needs and values. One of my clients, a mid-career professional, was frustrated with her career and was considering leaving her job for something new. The reason was to increase her opportunities for advancement in her field, but the ultimate concern was having to confront overt and implicit sexism among some colleagues in her workplace. She felt this would continue to hold her down and impede her advancement. She felt that if she could, in her own words, express herself more, stand up more for herself, "then I will be able to bring more of myself, my skills and gifts, to work, to be a bigger player and advance in my career." During the coaching session, we first explored what she was longing for and what motivated her. From my notes, she responded something like this, "I want my voice to be more authentic, but I don't know if this is even possible. I really am sort of set in my ways. I am motivated to do my best work and to advance my career in the organization, but I see so many obstacles, mostly from the attitudes of some of the men in my office, some of them key decision-makers." She then began to look at what she needed and explored some of her values, some that were being met and some that were not. She responded that she needed to be heard, be seen, be recognized, be valued for what she can bring to her company. She said, "I don't really feel appreciated now. I feel demeaned and belittled. Sometimes I think my outward appearance, my weight and face, are all that they see. And I don't see how I can advance my career if things stay the same in this job." She was having some difficulty identifying specific values, so I asked her to identify a time when she felt passionate and fully energized about something in her life or some aspect of her job. She recalled a specific time when her integrity and honesty were recognized; she felt appreciated. This enabled her to identify some other values that made her feel aligned with a purpose embedded in her job. I then helped her to connect to these values and identify what was being honored and not honored in her current position with this company.

When asked what she had learned, she responded, "All my life society has conveyed to me some very disempowering, negative messages. But I do have a choice to buy-in or not. I do have voice, and my voice is important." She came to realize that her emergent, powerful voice would allow her to override these external and internal messages and to stand confidently, whether in this job or the next. After all, with a disempowering mind-set, the same situation is likely to arise in the next job. We closed the session with her identifying some exciting intentions, even some wild dreams, she had for her future career, and some actionable first steps that she could take.

Find a list of core or personal values. You can Google around to find a list to give you an idea of some common values.[128] But to prioritize and focus on your values, you could select seven or fewer from a list on the Internet; values that particularly resonate with you. Personally, if I must choose, I resonate most with these core values, among others: authenticity, creativity, kindness, trustworthiness, spirituality, happiness, and wisdom. I can't tell you why; I just do.

To gain greater insight into the process of identifying your primary core values you could ask yourself several questions, such as the following:[129]

- When was a time I felt passionate about my life or work?
- When was my life or work particularly meaningful or fulfilling?
- When was a time when I felt fully energized about my life?
- What were the greatest lessons I learned from adversity?
- What insights do these times reveal about my life purpose?
- What do I stand for?
- What legacy do I want to leave?
- What are three intentions I have for your future?
- What is a purpose I feel called to fulfill?
- What does it feel like without that value present?

Think of a "peak" experience, a time when everything was in place, everything was fine, and all was right with the world, in the flow. I remember one such experience in April 1986. I was holding my eight-month-old daughter while sitting on the curb next to my rented U-Haul truck in the parking lot of the Vince Lombardi Service Area on the New

Jersey Turnpike. All was perfect, sitting there in the sun, on the curb. I felt blessed and full of gratitude amidst the warmth and truck stop smells of diesel fuel and fast food. OK, sorry, no waterfalls or rainbows. But I could have given you another story that involved beautiful mountain vistas, a bottle of wine, and camping at Lake Tahoe, but that would have been too obvious. Now, think of your own peak experiences and find what qualities really stand out and made you feel so fulfilled in that moment. What was it about that experience that made it so special? What values were being honored or expressed in that experience? If you knew you wouldn't be laughed at or couldn't care less, what would be a core value you would like to hold and express throughout your life?

What are your top seven core values? It doesn't matter if these came from a Google search or a deep soul search. Can you assess roughly how much you are currently honoring each on a quick scale of 1-10? What could you do to honor your top three values more deeply today? Is that important to you? If so, you could write down the ways in which these values appeared to you during the day. Over several days, you may begin to see a pattern.

So, what's the point of all this? When you are clear on your needs and values, you can take action to change your situation, to make long-lasting sustainable change, to live a values-centered life. Identifying a problem or an issue is nice, but behavior does not change until action is taken. This is alignment, when your life is in line with your needs, values, and purpose. When you're in alignment, you can make the change you want to see in yourself and in the world. So, ask yourself, "How much of my life choices actually align with my values?" "How can I close any gap that I see between the values I say I have and the values I am actually living?" And finally, "What steps can I take toward living my core values more fully, living an honest life with integrity, and in ways that get me what I want out of this life?" That's pretty much it.

Character Strengths

Now let's turn to identifying your character or signature strengths. One of Yale University's most popular undergraduate courses is on well-being and happiness and is taught by Dr. Laurie Santos.[130] I completed the accelerated online version of this course offered by Yale in 2018 called "The Science of Well-Being." The course presented an overview of what psychology and biology say about happiness. The purpose of the course was to not only learn what psychological research says about what makes us happy but also to put those strategies into practice. An important issue is the need for us to stop trying to fix our weaknesses and instead begin to leverage our personal strengths. I offer some modifications of the content of that course to you here.

The first part of the course included testing for signature or character strengths. The objectives of this testing were to assess my current level of well-being, produce a baseline measurement of well-being, and to discover my signature (character) strengths and apply them in my daily life. The first assignment was to measure my current level of happiness, my "baseline happiness" using a validated psychological survey. The happiness measure is from the Authentic Happiness Inventory developed by Christopher Peterson at the University of Michigan. The inventory is a quick set of twenty-four questions that provide an overall measure of your happiness levels. You can take the Authentic Happiness Inventory survey online by registering at the University of Pennsylvania's Authentic Happiness website.[131]

Once you get your score (should be a number between 1 and 5), write it down to keep track of it. What is your Authentic Happiness Inventory Score?

You can also explore other subjective measures of your well-being beyond the Happiness Inventory. To do so, you can take another survey available on the Authentic Happiness website, called PERMA,[132] an acronym for the first letters in Positive emotion, Engagement, Relationships, Meaning, and Accomplishment, the basic dimensions of psychological flourishing and well-being.

Now you can identify your Character (or Signature) Strengths. To identify your strengths, take the online Character Strengths Survey available on the VIA Institute of Character website.[133] The VIA Character Strengths Test is an online questionnaire that comprises 240 questions. There are no right/wrong, no better/worse answers, and the key is to be authentic and spontaneous in your responses. You could encourage your coworkers, friends, and family to also take the questionnaire.

From the VIA website: "Character strengths are viewed as our positive personality in that they are our core capacities for thinking, feeling, and behaving in ways that can bring benefit to us and others. ... The VIA Survey of Character Strengths is a simple self-assessment that takes less than 15 minutes and provides a wealth of information to help you understand your core characteristics. Most personality tests focus on negative and neutral traits, but the VIA Survey focuses on your best qualities. Created under the direction of Dr. Martin Seligman, the 'father of Positive Psychology' and author of *Authentic Happiness and Flourish*, and Dr. Christopher Peterson, distinguished scientist at the University of Michigan and author of *A Primer in Positive Psychology*, and validated by Robert McGrath, Ph.D., the VIA Survey is regarded as a central tool of positive psychology and has been used in hundreds of research studies and taken by over 5 million people in over 190 countries resulting in better workplaces ... schools ... teams ... LIVES the world over."

Your participation will result in a personal profile that ranks your twenty-four-character strengths according to the VIA Classification. Pay most attention to your top five strengths. According to Seligman, "What is unique about your profile is the position of each strength. The strengths listed at or near the top are likely to be those that are most representative of the 'real you'." He theorizes that the twenty-four VIA character strengths are the pathways to each of the five elements of well-being (PERMA). Your strengths underpin each element, and he states that deploying your highest strengths leads to:

- more **P**ositive emotion
- more **E**ngagement

- better **R**elationships
- more **M**eaning
- more **A**ccomplishments.

Furthermore, you will see from the VIA website that each character strength falls under one of six broad "virtue categories" that appear to be universal across diverse cultures and nations. These Core Virtues are wisdom, courage, humanity, justice, temperance, and transcendence.

You can use your character strengths by getting into the practice of doing intentional activities that will boost your own happiness. You could try this (from the Yale course): "Each day for the following week, try to use your selected strength in a new way. For example, if curiosity is one of your strengths, enroll in another course on a topic you know nothing about; if kindness is your strength, perform an anonymous favor for someone; and so on. Try to use your strengths at least once per day all week long." You can note down in your journal what you experience over the week. You can also learn more about how to use your strengths on the VIA website.

In addition, you may be interested in taking a more comprehensive test to determine your personality type. One popular and well-accepted option is the free online Myers-Briggs personality test or the Jung Typology Test, based on Carl Jung's and Isabel Myers-Briggs' personality type theory. You can access the test at the Humanmetrics.com website.[134] Over the years, I consistently test out on Myers-Briggs as an ENFJ (Extraversion, Intuition, Feeling, Judgment), one of sixteen distinct main personality indicator types explained on the site. The Jung Typology Test goes further to place me in the Protagonist archetype. Take the test. It is fun and can be illuminating.

- What is your Myers-Briggs personality indicator type?
- What is your Jungian personality archetype?

In the next chapter, we will explore ways to identify your personal vision and begin to establish some goals that are most aligned with your core values and character strengths. This will help to inform the process of aging consciously, furthering your REWIREMENT, and happily living your purpose.

Chapter 7:
Sugar Magnolia

"When I dare to be powerful, to use my strength in the service of my vision, then it becomes less and less important whether I am afraid."

- Audre Lorde[135]

"The greatest danger for most of us is not that our aim is too high, and we miss it, but that it is too low, and we reach it."

- attributed to Michelangelo Buonarroti (1475 - 1564)

"I can teach anybody how to get what they want out of life. The problem is that I can't find anybody who can tell me what they want."

- Mark Twain

Step 4: Identify Your Vision and Goals

There is a famous quote of great relevance to almost anyone, but I am thinking most about we who are aging (consciously) and facing retirement. Sometimes incorrectly ascribed to Nelson Mandela, the quote was made by Marianne Williamson, who wrote, "Our deepest fear is not that we are inadequate. Our deepest fear is that we are powerful beyond measure. It is our light, not our darkness that most frightens us. We ask ourselves, 'Who am I to be brilliant, gorgeous, talented, fabulous?' Actually, who are you not to be? … Your playing small does not serve the world. There is nothing enlightened about shrinking so that other people won't feel insecure around you. We are all meant to shine, as children do. … And as we let our own light shine, we unconsciously give other people permission to do the same. As we are liberated from our own fear, our presence automatically liberates others."[136]

In this chapter, you will continue the REWIREMENT process by understanding the importance of identifying your main focal areas for desired improvement. This involves identifying your vision for your life overall or for something specific. You will also identify your main goals and commit to taking action to achieve those short and long-term goals in the context of conscious aging, retirement, and financial security.

Vision

What is vision? The *Oxford Dictionary* defines it as "the ability to think about or plan the future with imagination or wisdom." But how can you arrive at a vision for yourself? Martha Lasley, a founder of Leadership that Works, including the Coaching for Transformation training program, has identified and recommended seven steps to explore your vision through what she calls the "Tell Your Vision" process.[137]

Lasley says that developing a powerful vision is easy if you take one step at a time. Going through the steps in her "Tell Your Vision" process, or guide, you will explore your values, environment, action, identity, and contributions that lie ahead. The process begins with a look at the past and ends up with a story about your future. The first two steps of the process will enable you to identify the best of what exists now. The subsequent five steps help you envision a compelling future. You begin with your history, examining where you have been. The end of the process is your vision story, where you have identified where you want to be. The following seven steps to explore and identify your vision are adapted from Martha Lasley's book, *Courageous Visions*, and used here with permission from the author.

Step One: History – Identifying Milestones and Possibilities. Chart your history by writing down important milestones in your life or making simple sketches that illustrate your journey to date. If you prepared your Life Review chart in Chapter 5, then you can use that here. Include high points, low points, and milestones from the past. Reflect on the following questions:

1. What empowering traditions do I want to keep?
2. How does respecting the past help me embrace the future?

Step Two: Values – Clarifying What Matters Most. Values are not wishes, morals, or "shoulds." Your values are your intrinsic beliefs about what is important in life. If you made a list of values that you currently live by in Chapter 6, then you can use them here. Determine what values you deem most important, that you would like to honor more fully. Reflect on the following questions:

1. What was a peak or otherwise exceptional experience that best reflected my values?
2. What personal values do I cherish that people I care about also value?

Step Three: Environment – Choosing What You Want. This is a big one; do not skip it. Picture your ideal future environment and every aspect of your surroundings in as much detail as you can. Picture your home, your community, and the place where you will work or volunteer. Don't limit yourself to what's practical. Dream big. Get a feel for your ideal environment and notice what it looks like. Consider your ideal possessions, climate, living space, artwork, people, music, scents, and ambiance. Reflect on the following questions:

1. Describe your environment in the perfect future. What surrounds me that is most important to me?
2. Visualize the ambiance I want to create.

Step Four: Action – Shaping Behaviors and Capabilities. Continue to think about your ideal future and your behavior. Notice what you do in this ideal world. In your ideal future, determine what capabilities you have mastered. Build your awareness about what you especially enjoy doing. Reflect on the following questions:

1. What personal capabilities do I already have that I will use even more in the future?
2. What new or strengthened competencies do I hope to master within the next five years?

Step Five: Identity – Honing Your Image. Narrowly focus in on what's special about you. In an ideal world, imagine the short phrases people will typically use to describe you. Determine the unique strengths and talents you offer that others find particularly valuable. Reflect on the following questions:

1. What is unique about me?
2. While thinking about your ideal future, brainstorm the identity or nicknames you would like to earn. Imagine you overhear people talking about you in a positive way. What do you want them to say?

Step Six: Contribution – Serving Your Purpose. Think about how you wish to serve. Imagine your ideal contribution. Picture yourself in balance with giving and receiving. Envision that you take care of yourself so that you can contribute fully. Reflect on the following questions:

1. Identify all the potential ways that you would like to make a contribution. What do I contribute in the short term? In the long term?
2. What do I consider the most important contribution that I could make in my lifetime?

Step Seven: Vision – Picturing Your Future. Again, further describe your ideal future, choosing words or phrases that energize you. Notice what's exciting or compelling about your future. Write your personal vision story in a way that is clear, brief, and comes from the heart. Reflect on the following questions:

1. What headline introduces the cover story?
2. You are quoted in the article. What do I have to say about my success?

You can now pull it all together to prepare a "personal vision statement" about the ideal future you would like to live, depending on your needs, strengths, values, and priorities. Probably the best way to approach this is to handwrite your statements in the first person. Having written goals increases the chance of them coming to fruition. The physical act of writing seems to give more power and a greater commitment to achieving that goal. Make sure you write the statements as if they have already happened.

Step into the future; get wild and crazy, dare to dream big. It doesn't matter how many words it takes, there is no limitation, so long as you can clearly articulate your vision of the ideal future in your own words – not someone else's. Be detailed and the more specific the better. Susan Heathfield wrote, "When people live and experience the components of their personal vision frequently, they can feel inner peace and joy that knows no bounds. Your personal vision statement can have the same impact on you."[138]

Goals

Having established your vision for transformation, you can move into the process of goal setting and taking action to make the sustainable changes you want to see. Four factors will condition your success in meeting the challenges of transformation. You will need to:

- clearly see and agree on your *need for change*,
- develop a *vision* of your objectives of specific changes and a broad *strategy* for reaching those objectives,
- identify your *capacity to change*, and
- define your *actionable first steps*.

One of the main challenges facing you will be to develop all four of these factors to achieve your desired outcome. Four undesirable outcomes may follow if, on the one hand, any one of these factors is lacking. On the other hand, a strong foundation for sustained transformation will be enabled when all four are present. This simplified approach to change (see figure), addressing all success factors, will avoid you making low priority interventions, suffering from false or haphazard starts, and arriving at ineffective outcomes.

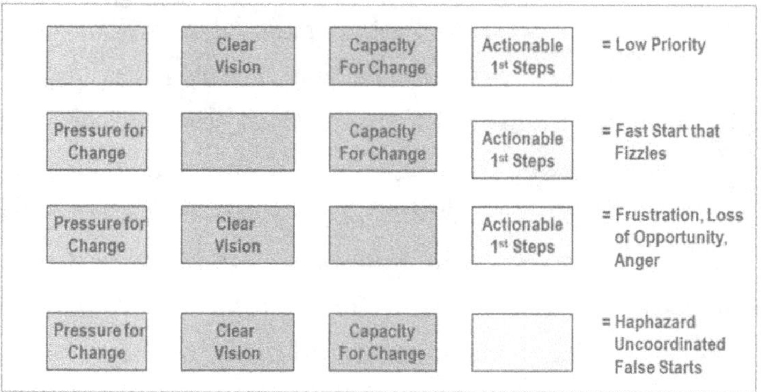

Four success factors required for you to create sustained, effective change [139]

I coached remotely with a client living in Bangladesh (I will call him Samjith). Samjith clearly exhibited these four success factors, leading him to create sustained and effective change in his life. There was pressure for change, a clear vision of where he wanted to be, his capacity for change, and finally the identification of actionable first steps that, when carried out, helped him reach his goal. He had some very specific desired outcomes that included identifying his most important personal (family situation) and professional (freelance consulting business) challenges and the goals he wanted to set for himself over the next twelve months to create certain changes. We agreed to start small and to break up his desired outcomes into smaller chunks. Samjith was clear on the importance he placed on goal setting and increasing his business. Procrastination was not an issue for Samjith; neither was any unusual amount of stress. However, staying focused and on track with what was most important was his priority, i.e., managing his time and opportunities. He expressed a willingness to take risks to stretch himself and achieve his goals. In this way, for designing action, some needs and values were established prior to action planning. He wanted to focus on increasing his consulting business, participating in training workshops and seminars, and finalizing his PhD dissertation. Moving from these overall goals, we began to focus on an immediate and measurable short-term goal, to finish his PhD dissertation, which was close to completion. He felt this was holding him back from advancing further in his career and earning potential.

I then asked Samjith several empowering questions, for example, "How are your goal choices aligned with your needs and values?" "Which action can you choose first?" "What is a first step you can take now toward finalizing your PhD thesis?" and "What resistance or obstacles might come up for you?" One actionable first step was to finalize the edits and comments of one important chapter he had recently received from his advisor. To support his progress and structure accountability in a way that enabled him to take full ownership, we identified what he wanted to be held accountable for; namely, completing the edit in three days from the session and notifying me by email when that was completed. In that way, I was able to support him to fulfil his commitment and move closer to completing his dissertation.

Another client in Connecticut (let's call her Karen) was seemingly disturbed by the perceived inadequacy and negativity of everything around her; she believed no one supported her, all were against her, and nothing was her fault, her doing. Karen was an argumentative "victim," and when there was a shift in mind-set for the better, it did not last long. I could have just listened and responded with "Tsk. Tsk. I know. That's just terrible. I know. You're so brave," but that would not have served her, and I would not be doing my job as a transformation coach. When I pointed out that her negativity may be holding her back from achieving her main goal of finding a better job, she quickly reverted to her disempowered and debilitating story, like a broken record. Karen had no clear vision of where she wanted to be and appeared to be unwilling to create one. She seemed unwilling to take the actionable steps she identified that could improve her situation. She could not get out of her story long enough to make any real change, and we unfortunately had to end our sessions. Karen may very well have had some good reasons for saying and doing what she did. Her internal protectors may have been activated to keep her "wounded child" from upsetting the system or to protect her from further pain or shame. While those psychological mechanisms may have worked in the past, in response to a painful experience, for example, they were now, when faced with new circumstances, holding her back. As Karen was depressed, what she really needed was psychotherapy, beyond my capabilities and training, and I recommended she see someone specifically for that. Coaching can certainly complement psychotherapy; it is not a replacement in this case.

If you too are attracting negativity, inviting chaos into your life, ask yourself some questions. Is it serving me? Is it protecting me? Is it keeping me safe? What is it costing me to stay like this? And, after all, do I really want to change? But "'Cheshire Puss,' asked Alice. 'Would you tell me, please, which way I ought to go from here?' 'That depends a good deal on where you want to go,' said the Cat. 'I don't much care where,' said Alice. 'Then it doesn't matter which way you go,' said the Cat.'"[140] And if you honestly compare where you are now with where you want to go, you can then begin to close the gap.

If you are out of alignment, saying one thing but doing another, saying you want something but seeking something else, you are not trusting yourself; you're not trusting your intuition. You must find the root, the story that is causing the misalignment. Otherwise you keep staying in the cycle of victim and blame. Ask yourself, what do I need to do to create a new story? You are your story; your beliefs and your thoughts create your reality. So what story are you living now? When you take action to change the cycle, you are disrupting your story, disrupting your dysfunctional world and your pain. That should be a good thing. Right?

When working with new clients, I first give them a questionnaire, to be completed as briefly or as detailed as they choose, to discover more about them and their concerns before our first session. We then arrange for our first coaching call, a Discovery Session. From my point of view as a coach, this initial session aims toward a deeper understanding of the client and serves to establish four elements in the relationship, one that will be served or held throughout all remaining sessions. In addition to agreeing on logistics, important elements of the Discovery Session include (i) making an empathic connection with the client, (ii) creating a conscious relationship between coach and client, (iii) clarifying some of the client's values, and (iv) beginning to establish a focus of coaching and clear desired outcomes of the client.[141] A conscious coach-client relationship is important to me because I want meaningful and sustainable transformation to occur for the client. For this outcome to occur, the ongoing focus is on creating and sustaining the relationship through my awareness and deep listening as well as establishing a safe space that is confidential, nonbiased, and nonjudgmental – and free from any advice. The session may also begin to identify or provide hints to a transformation agenda, a way forward toward alignment.

From discussing responses to the client questionnaire and narrowing down topics, we then proceed to a coaching focus that is likely to eventually include goal setting and action planning. The following questions are posed, and you could ask them of yourself now:

1. Are there any significant dates during my life? What is important about those dates?
2. What is the greatest personal or professional change I would like to see in the coming year?
3. What book, movie, play, song, poem, art, plant, animal, landscape, person or something else has recently touched my core or essence? Why?
4. What are some of my greatest accomplishments?
5. What goal(s) would I like to accomplish through coaching?
6. What are five things I have procrastinated? Do I know why?

7. When was life especially meaningful? What was I doing? Who was I with? What was I feeling?
8. What is most rewarding in my life right now?
9. What is an image or metaphor that best describes my life right now?
10. What do I particularly dislike, resist, or avoid?
11. How can I be my own worst enemy? What are the worst things I say to myself (e.g., negative self-talk, internal critic)?
12. What risks have I taken? What motivates me to take risks?
13. What is most stressful in my life right now?
14. Have you ever worked with a therapist, psychiatrist, or other mental health professional? If so, how was the experience?
15. Describe your current support system. Which people in my life believe in me, encourage me, challenge me, and are with me through difficult times?
16. Who inspires me?
17. What do I want to do before I die? Or more specifically, if you wish, imagine you are otherwise in perfect health, but you knew you would die in three days, what would you do? How would I then spend my time and with whom?

So first, it is essential to have clarity on your goals, being as specific as you can. You can close the gap between where you are and where you want to be by designing your goals, action plans, and support systems to create an ideal transformed life. Sounds good to me.

One way to identify and set realistic goals that are also in alignment with your values and strengths is to use the SMART acronym as described in the book, *Coaching for Transformation: Pathways to Ignite Personal & Social Change.*[142] When narrowing in on a goal, ask yourself these SMART questions:

*Is it **S**pecific*? The more specific the goal, the easier it is to implement and enlist support from others. The clearer the goal, the more powerful it becomes. Start by asking yourself, "What is the desired outcome?" and then refine it until it is concise, simple, and clear.

*Is it **M**easurable*? Measurable goals establish concrete criteria for determining progress and completion. Not only do you have the data to support staying on track, but you can celebrate the achievement of milestones, building momentum along the way. If you want to "become a better leader," which is quite vague, then ask yourself, "How will I know I have achieved my goal?"

*Is it **A**live*? When you have a goal that is energizing, you are far more likely to put it into action. If a goal is accompanied by a feeling of dread or serious unease, then reassess your goal. Set the bar high, but ensure the goal is doable. Unrealistic, complicated goals can de-motivate rather than inspire us. Goals that inspire us are not a burden but are enjoyable to accomplish.

*Is it **R**elevant*? Without a sense of what makes your goal important, it is human to rarely commit to or realize that goal. Ask yourself, "What values does my goal honor? What will this goal get me? What meaning does the goal have? How does this goal make a difference for me or others? What impact will it have?"

*Is it **T**ime-Bound*? A useful and motivating goal is grounded within a time frame and answers the question, "By when?" Without a completion date, there is no sense of urgency and no real commitment to your goal. A timeframe will set a clear intention of the desired completion date (I hate to say deadline). A goal of increasing sales by 5 percent, for example, is meaningless without a date attached to it. "Let's increase our offer," works very differently from, "Let's expand our offer by 5 percent by March 26."

Here are two examples of personal SMART goals to help you write your own. Try not to be overly ambitious, and never beat yourself up if a day or two are missed in a meditation routine or if you fall off your diet, for example. The important thing is to keep moving forward, without regrets or recriminations; just pick yourself up and keep at it.

- "I will improve my health by losing twenty-four pounds over the next twelve weeks. To achieve this goal, I commit to exercising aerobically for thirty minutes every other day; cutting out carbohydrates from bread, potatoes, and rice; and eating more fresh fruits, vegetables, and lean meats. I will keep a daily food, exercise, and weight log for the twelve weeks to monitor my progress."

- "To help reduce my procrastination, I will deepen my inner awareness and calm my mind by meditating in silence for twenty minutes each morning before work over the next month and journal my insights and success with accomplishments each day."

Another very simple but useful exercise I do with new clients is have them complete a *Life Balance* or *Discovery Wheel*, sometimes called a Life Pie or Wheel of Fulfillment,[143] to identify areas for improvement and then design goals associated with those areas. The purpose of this exercise is to quickly and subjectively measure your satisfaction with a variety of key areas in your life. Action plans naturally evolve from identifying values, strengths, vision, goals, and balance wheel work. The balance wheel is a tool to activate and support your whole life strategic planning and will give you a snapshot in time of your life. This will allow you to determine your level of satisfaction for several areas of your life and will serve as the basis for further developing your goals and strategic planning. It will be easier to make changes in an area of your life, step-by-step, if you examine that one area of your life and explore both short-term and long-term actions to achieve your goals.

***Instructions*:** This exercise provides a visual representation of where you are, relatively, in several areas of life. Print out or draw the wheel, then shade in the area after you have assigned your rating. Rate your Level of Satisfaction in each area of the wheel, with a 1 (closest to center of the circle) = Not Satisfied and 10 (at the outer edge of the circle) = Completely Satisfied. Then, think about what actions you could take to improve your scores.

Unsatisfactory or struggling	1 - 3
Maintaining or surviving	4 - 7
Fulfilled or thriving	8 - 10

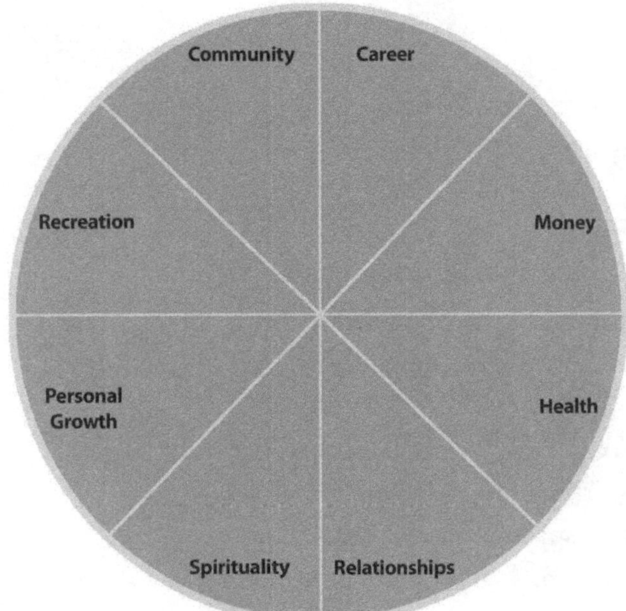

Your Life Balance Wheel (Life Pie)

A description of each category of the balance wheel follows, but feel free to create your own balance wheel categories and descriptions based on what matters most to you.

Career

- My work stimulates and fulfills me.
- My career path makes good use of my talents.
- I am proud of my contributions at work.

Money (Finance)

- I have enough money to meet my basic needs, and I plan for future financial security.
- I regularly contribute to a savings account.
- I am free of money worries.

Health

- I exercise regularly.
- I eat nourishing food.
- I manage stress well.

Relationships

- I enjoy my friends and family.
- My support network nurtures me.
- I have meaningful connections with people I care about.

Spirituality

- My spiritual life is rich and fulfilling.
- I have a spiritual practice that supports me.
- My inner path and outer connectedness are sources of inspiration.

Personal Growth

- I continuously deepen my self-awareness.
- I actively seek personal and professional growth opportunities.
- I am moving toward living the life of my dreams.

Recreation

- I regularly enjoy leisure time.
- I have hobbies or other activities that stimulate me.
- Fun is an integral part of my life.

Community

- I belong to a community that is based on mutual respect.
- I contribute to and receive support from my community.
- I have an emotional connection with people who share my values.

What three main areas on the wheel are you looking to change and/or improve?

1. Write down your Focus Area #1.

2. Write down your Focus Area #2.
3. Write down your Focus Area #3.

Ask yourself, focusing on a main area on the wheel:

- Where am I now?
- Where do I want to be?
- What am I willing to do to get there?

Consider the SMART goal establishment process described earlier in this chapter. Is each goal Specific, Measurable, Alive, Relevant, and Time-bound?

Identify one goal you have for each of these areas

1. Write down your Goal #1.
2. Write down your Goal #2.
3. Write down your Goal #3.

What has been holding you back or preventing you from making progress?

1. Write down your Goal #1 Blockage.
2. Write down your Goal #2 Blockage.
3. Write down your Goal #3 Blockage.

What will your life look like if you don't make these changes? What is the cost to me for not making these changes?

1. Write down your Goal #1 If Business as Usual.
2. Write down your Goal #2 If Business as Usual.
3. Write down your Goal #3 If Business as Usual.

How will your life change if you achieve these goals? What are the benefits to you for making these changes?

1. Write down your Goal #1 Transformation.
2. Write down your Goal #2 Transformation.
3. Write down your Goal #3 Transformation.

What is one action or step you can take today toward committing to achieve each of these goals?

1. Write down your Goal #1 Action.
2. Write down your Goal #2 Action.
3. Write down your Goal #3 Action.

Now, reconsider how you identified and set your goals. Ask yourself first if these really are your own, self-identified goals or have they been instilled in you by a lifetime barrage of advertising and culture, by a consumer conscious society? Are they someone else's goals for you or are they your own? You have several barriers that are holding you back from achieving the success or change you want to see. With a bit of rewiring, you can break through those barriers and reach a whole new level of success. You can follow a goal-setting program, but I think you already know what to do. You know there can be more to life – if you envision a goal achieved and then act on it.

You will benefit from opening yourself up to new opportunities, techniques, perspectives, and actions that will help you feel more fulfilled in all aspects of your life. You can develop and pursue goals that are aligned with a vision of the life you want, goals that relate to your values and strengths. This can support a sustained cycle of creativity and abundance. Go back to your intentions, and ask yourself, "What do I want? What is it that I really want in my life?" Something that is nonnegotiable. And then, just do it – chart your course and take action based on your beliefs. Create your own reality. Is it simple? Yes. Is it easy? No. But you need to start somewhere.

In the next chapter, you will begin to identify, examine, and gain an understanding of purpose and how to begin its rediscovery and "re-firement." This will be critical to your well-being and fulfillment during the process of REWIREMENT for conscious aging.

Chapter 8:
Ripple

"To everything there is a season, and a time to every purpose under Heaven."
– Ecclesiastes 3:1

"The purpose of life is not to be happy at all. It is to be useful, to be honorable. It is to be compassionate. It is to matter, to have it make some difference that you lived."
– Leo Rosten[144]

"Those who have a 'why' to live, can bear with almost any 'how'."
– Viktor Frankl, Holocaust survivor and author of *Man's Search for Meaning*

Step 5: Re-Fire Your Purpose

What do we mean by purpose? We all are, to some degree, on a search for meaning. That is what everyone really wants – meaning, purpose, a reason to get up in the morning. Shakti Gawain, author of books on personal growth and consciousness, wrote, "Every one of us comes into this life with lessons to learn and gifts to give. The more we learn and grow, the more we become capable of developing and sharing these natural gifts." And we long for a sense of connection – with ourselves, with others, and with Spirit, however we may envision the numinous, the Great Mystery.

You might say your higher-level purpose goes pretty much something like this: "The purpose of my life is to live with integrity and authenticity and to experience it as fully as I can, to learn and grow and become all that I can be. My purpose is to grow spiritually, to love myself and others, to serve my community and respond according to my abilities. My purpose is to use my gifts to make a positive impact on my well-being, my prosperity, my family, my community, and the planet."

OK. Something like that. Nice, idealistic, but suitably vague, and could we get off the crystals for a moment and be a bit more specific? One thing does seem crystal clear; your purpose is not to sit in front of the TV for hours watching the news, angrily identifying obvious problems, and making random exasperated comments to no one in particular. Your purpose is not to continually make plans, have vague dreams, and then do nothing but complain about your lot in life. You're getting old? Oh, how sad. Me too.

But perhaps it's better if you begin to ask yourself, "How can I open to and align with a purpose that best addresses my needs, values, strengths, and abilities to achieve my goals?" Still too vague? Lily Tomlin, the comedian, once said, "All my life, I always wanted to be somebody. Now I see that I should've been more specific."

In the previous chapter, we examined your values and strengths. Now we will examine your purpose. This step is about rediscovering, reimagining, and re-firing your purpose. The philosopher Alan Watts has famously said that our life is more like a song or a dance than it is a journey; the purpose is in the living, the experiencing, not the end. Influenced by this, Wayne Dyer wrote, "When you dance, your purpose is not to get to a place in the floor. It's to enjoy every step along the way." In this chapter, you will continue to look inward for self-discovery, envisioning or rediscovering your purpose – a purpose that's always been there but perhaps is not yet fully expressed, not utilizing your character strengths and personal gifts in ways that will expand the positive process of your conscious aging and retirement.

Author and entrepreneur Ajit Nawalkha said that his mother's annoying comment was, "*Log kya kahenge*," Hindi for, "What will people think?" "The random thoughts and opinions of others must not go into any recipe for designing your life, envisioning your future, or reimagining your purpose. You get to choose your purpose, not your mother." And furthermore, Nawalkha wrote, "Purpose isn't about how big you go; it's about how real it feels. It's about being aligned. It's about what's true for you. And always know that it's not your job to save us all. Please, don't try to save us all. Don't suck the joy out of living your purpose. If saving the world gives joy to you, go for it. More power to you. But don't do it just for us. First, do it for yourself."[145] If you say your purpose is to create a positive transformation of consciousness in the world, that's all well and good, but something a bit more down-to-earth might be to help your customers regain their financial independence. Now that's a worthy purpose.

Ron Pevny (see his two articles on conscious aging in Appendix 2) said that today's definitions of elderhood, and what it can be, are intimately connected to important questions such as how, as "elders," we will meet our needs for purpose, meaning, and service to our community and the planet. Meeting these challenges is not necessarily easy after a lifetime of negative and disempowering programming. One could say we have thousands of years of programming to get over! We will need to take some action, make conscious preparations at our physical, psychological, and spiritual levels. [146]

Author and explorer Dan Buettner traveled the world with a team of researchers in 2004 to examine five communities, the so-called Blue Zones, in the United States, Costa Rica, Italy, Greece, and Japan that exhibit unusually high percentages of people living into their hundreds.[147] They identified several universal healthy habits these communities shared, despite their many cultural differences: namely, a healthy diet, frequent exercise, focus on family/community, and – a common thread across the

Blue Zone communities – having a real and fulfilling sense of purpose. According to Buettner, "Knowing your sense of purpose is worth up to seven years of extra life expectancy. … The Okinawans call it '*ikigai*' and the Nicoyans call it '*plan de vida*'; for both, it translates to 'why I wake up in the morning.'" Buettner's findings and the Blue Zones research have shown the many benefits of having a purpose in life: it gives you direction, reduces mortality risk, increases your resilience, improves quality of sleep, helps you achieve success (on your own terms), and cultivates a positive outlook.

Dan Buettner and the Chopra Center's Mind-Body Medical Group have identified some ways you can uncover, put into action, reassess, and live out your purpose and benefit from it.[148] To discover your purpose, your *ikigai*, you can ask yourself four questions; where they overlap in a sort of Venn diagram is called your *ikigai*:

- What do I love?
- What am I good at?
- What does the world need from me?
- What can I get paid for?

And that's basically it! Caroline Myss said during an interview, "If you have life, you have purpose. It can't be otherwise."[149] I must admit I am a huge admirer of Caroline Myss, medical intuitive and author, with her characteristic clarity of thought. In 2009, she wrote, "If you don't appreciate what you have in life right now, whatever it is, you will never realize your purpose. Without appreciation, you will never become strong enough to respect yourself."[150]

Holocaust survivor Viktor Frankl wrote about our freedom of choice: "Between stimulus and response there is a space. In that space is our power to choose our response. In our response lies our growth and our freedom. … When we are no longer able to change a situation, we are challenged to change ourselves. … Everything can be taken from a man but one thing: the last of the human freedoms – the ability to choose one's attitude in any given set of circumstances, to choose one's own way."[151]

But following your purpose, or purpose itself for that matter, appears to not be an option; not something you design or otherwise create. Purpose is not a choice, it is something you already have, you were born with it. So, "finding" your purpose makes little sense. You cannot find something you never lost. You don't get to choose, only uncover or rediscover your purpose! According to Myss, "I cannot take you out and say you are separate from the whole. If someone says to me, 'Well, how do I find my life purpose?' I first say, 'You've never lost your life purpose.' Number two, I say, 'Have no judgments about your life. No expectations. Give up the need to know what happens tomorrow. Just be fully present and appreciate all that is in your life right now.'"[152] This is important to understand as part of any transformation. After all, there are no guarantees of a successful outcome for anything, but that should not stop us from moving forward and taking action – as if!

Meg Newhouse, life coach, author and founding member of the Elders Action Network (formerly, Conscious Elders Network), has developed a life planning program and a corresponding toolkit with a focal point of discovering our "passion and purpose." [153] This is the spark that can motivate us to express ourselves more meaningfully and purposefully. Her approach assumes that many of us will be fortunate to have the opportunity of using our later years to self-actualize. We must, therefore, ask ourselves, "What do I want, and where will I be most fulfilled and productive?" A good question; I think most everyone asks themselves this. But the trick is to then make it happen. Focusing on your passion and purpose is all about doing the hard work of visioning, creating, and sustaining activities that keep you busy and keep you fulfilled during that thing called "retirement."

If you fully engage with your vision, you can be pretty much guaranteed to come into alignment with a greater purpose for your life. Your dreams and desires may seem simple at first but then can take on a greater dimension as they transform yourself and the world. Reawakening to the purpose of your life, recognizing that changes over your life, may seem like a calling if you are so fortunate to realize this. Something that is greater than yourself may begin to emerge. Envisioning your future, as a method to align with your values, does not have to be a struggle. Here are some questions that may help you to consciously connect with your life purpose.[154]

- What are the most compelling elements of my vision? (from Chapter 7)
- What areas of my life do I envision changing?
- What matters most to me about my vision?
- What impact can my vision have on others?
- How will my life change once my vision is real?
- What is the difference I see myself making in my life, community, organization, or in the world once I realize my vision? (Discussed further in Chapter 13)
- What legacy do I long to leave as a result of the seeds planted by my vision?
- How will I further explore my vision and keep it alive?

Richard Leider, once ranked by Forbes magazine as one of the "Top 5" most respected executive coaches and author of the best seller *Repack Your Bags*, has written, "What if a life purpose is something you are born with, but you also have full control over how and when you act on it? … Choice is the power in purpose. Each of us is an 'experiment of one.' Each of us has an embedded destiny – gifts to add value to the world. And, we were born with free will to choose how we think, act, and react."[155]

Leider has formulated seven reflections to begin unlocking your purpose. These initial seven reflections can be used to formulate a personal purpose statement. He has written, "There are no rigid formulas for how to write your purpose statement, but there are many helpful techniques to assist you. Here are seven mind-changing ideas that have brought powerful results to many people over the years." Use Leider's reflections, reproduced here with his permission, to see what you can discover about yourself and your dreams: [156]

1. Think about this sentence for a moment: From family and friends who knew me when I was very young, I have heard that my "special gift" is … How have these "gifts" persisted in my life?
2. Imagine being on your deathbed, still clear and coherent, when your best friend drops in to visit you. Your friend asks, "Did you give and receive love? Were you authentically you? Did you make a small difference in the world?" How would you answer these questions?
3. Take a calculator and do some "life math." Multiply your age by 365. Then, subtract that number from 30,000, roughly an average American life expectancy in days. Finally, divide that number by 365. Once you get clear that you have this many more years to wake up, it might inspire you to live more courageously now. How do you feel about how you are spending your most precious currency – your time?
4. Now ask yourself, "How did I wake up this morning?" Did you resist getting up or did you get out of bed with energy and purpose? Think about the way you wake up, these days, and you will learn something about your life's purpose. How is your "mood" getting up most days?
5. Write the question, "What are my gifts?" on five index cards. Give them to five people who know you well and ask them to write their response to the question on the card. Put them all together in a place where you can see them. What theme or thread do you see?
6. Are you curious? What are you most curious about, these days? Here are some clues that will help you answer: (i) Time passes quickly when you're exploring this. (ii) It's so interesting, you can't help spending time on it! (iii) A bad day doing this is better than a good day doing most other things.
7. Look around you for potential models and mentors. Ask yourself, "Who is really leading the kind of life and doing the kind of work that I envision in the next phase of my life?" Initiate a courageous

conversation to find out what they like "most" and "least" about their work?

Based on these questions, you can prepare and reflect on your draft purpose statement. You can now write a single sentence expressing your "reason for getting up in the morning." That's all, just one sentence, one that is general enough to cover most mornings. This could be your *raison d'être*, your reason to be. So, ask yourself, "I get up in the morning to ..."

Remember those questions posed by Dan Buettner earlier in this chapter? – those four simple questions to help you discover your purpose, your *ikigai*? Did you reflect on them? No? Why not? If you want to uncover your purpose, if this is an issue for you, something that is keeping you stuck, then I suggest you look deeply into these questions and find the answers that resonate most for you. Once again, so you need not flip back, ask yourself these questions to envision your future and rediscover purpose. Where your answers overlap, this is your *ikigai*:

- What do I love?
- What am I good at?
- What does the world need from me?
- What can I get paid for?

In this chapter, you have gained an understanding of your innate purpose, your "reason to be," and how to begin its rediscovery and consider its strengthening or re-firement. Up to you to take this step further. Helping you to gain clarity on opportunities and envision meaningful work to undertake during your conscious aging REWIREMENT is the subject of the next chapter. This "work" may be a new occupation that is more in alignment with your values, character strengths, vision, and goals – to strengthen your re-fired purpose and support your financial needs.

Chapter 9:

Uncle John's Band

"Half of life is lost in charming others.
The other half is lost in going through anxieties caused by others.
Leave this play; you have played enough!"
– Rumi

"You can't get there by bus, only by hard work and risk and by not quite knowing what you're doing. What you'll discover will be wonderful. What you'll discover will be yourself."
– Alan Alda

Step 6: Envision Your Work

An old man walked to a neighboring village and came upon a group of workers carrying heavy stones up out of a quarry. He sat down to watch, first seeing one man struggling under the weight of a heavy stone, grunting and having a very hard time with the job. The old man asked him, "What are you doing?" The man grumbled, "Carrying stones, duh," and went on with his work. Then the old man saw a second worker, carrying a stone not unlike that which the first worker carried, but he made the work look easy and he was smiling enthusiastically. He asked the second man the same question to which the man replied, "I'm building the greatest cathedral ever."[157]

This parable about two laborers who viewed their work very differently shows that their attitudes about their work differed only in their viewpoints. When you recognize your current viewpoint is just one way of seeing, then you can begin to become liberated from any self-imposed negative thoughts and inner critics that have kept you stuck in a rut, on the couch.

In this chapter, you will envision meaningful work that is in line with your values, character strengths, purpose, and gifts, as well as your financial and other goals. When you expand your view from one based on limiting beliefs, you can begin to explore and embody a much wider range of alternative viewpoints. This approach will help you release those disempowering viewpoints and embrace new possibilities – but recognize that it has taken a lifetime of monkey-mind negativity to get to this point. But you can envision a new future using methods of visioning that will help you open to new possibilities and opportunities by first visualizing and then creating a future in alignment with what you really want.

Énouement is a word I just discovered in *The Dictionary of Obscure Sorrows*. It means "the bitter sweetness of having arrived in the future, where you can finally get the answers to how things turn out in the real world … where your choices would lead you," seeing how things turned out but not being able to tell your past (er, your present) self![158] Yeah, I know. It's a word. My new word.

The desire to reinvent yourself, redefine the work you will do, may be the result of having come out of an unsatisfactory career and the need to now be engaged in work that has greater meaning for you, with the potential for greater impact. This quote or a version of it, sometimes attributed to Thomas Merton or Stephen Covey, sometimes others, maybe Confucius (!), resonates with many as they enter their later years: "You spend your life climbing up a ladder only finding that when you reach the top, you discover you have laid the ladder against the wrong wall."

Envisioning the future is an alignment pathway that can help you get clarity on what you want to see in your life, a life of improved relationships, community, service, comfort, financial security, and new work in line with your values and purpose. And "one of the things that sets coaching apart from therapy is a focus on the future,"[159] not the past. You can envision your own new future using visualization methods to help you open to new possibilities and opportunities. And you can do this by first visualizing, then creating a future in alignment with what you really want. I have taken myself and clients into visualization meditations where they meet their future self and seek guidance. For some unknown reason, present self and imagined future self typically like to meet each other on a tropical beach. Must have coconut palms. No explanation for that.

"Your thoughts create your reality,"[160] or more precisely it is your thoughts about your reality that create your experience of that reality, but I nitpick here. What is important is that you have a choice, and you have that ability to choose every day. Envisioning the future is empowering and can help you imagine the life you want, your "dream come true" even. As journalist Connie Schultz declared in her 2016 TEDx talk, "But I am too old to do that. Well, you're going to be sixty someday anyhow. You might as well be a (doctor, painter, fill in the blank) when you're sixty."[161]

Now that you've retired, are considering it, or expect it will soon be forced on you – well, er, congratulations? But for many of us, the main concern is how to find new work, appropriate to our experience and lifestyle, so that we can stay active and be financially secure. It appears that most boomers do not want to retire – we really don't want to stop working, stop contributing. We want to stay active, appreciated, engaged with our work. Giles Andrews, CEO of Zopa, a UK online personal finance peer-to-peer lending company, has said, "Retirement is no longer about clearing your desk on your 65th birthday." And it does appear "older adults are working longer. By 2014, 23% of men and about 15% of women ages 65 and older were in the labor force, and these levels are projected to rise further by 2022, to 27% for men and 20% for women. The poverty rate for Americans ages 65 and older has dropped sharply during the past 50 years, from nearly 30% in 1966 to 10% today."[162]

Now, some thoughts about "retirement" – even though everyone seems to know what that's all about. Wikipedia succinctly informs us that "retirement is the withdrawal from one's position or occupation or from one's active working life." Hmm. Over the next twenty years or so, an average of ten thousand people each day will reach age sixty-five. Since the mid-1930's, this has traditionally been the beginning of retirement in the United States and now many other parts of the world. And when they finally do retire, their requirements for healthcare and assisted living for some are likely to alter the appearance of retirement living arrangements.[163]

Retirement is a word generated by modern Western society and – to be pessimistic – its relentless appetite for commercial consumer exploitation and productivity (I'd throw in capitalist but that's too much alliteration). Clearly, you say, that is why I used the word *retirement* in my book title – to sell books. Brilliant. But once we appear to no longer serve that commercial machine, and our role in it, we are told it is time to "retire." And we have bought into that all our lives; now it's our turn. What goes around comes around.

Official, institutionalized, universal retirement is a recent phenomenon, only appearing as US government policy around the end of the nineteenth and beginning of the twentieth centuries. Previously, people could expect to live an average of twenty-six to forty or so years; longer than this was rare in most places. Life was hard; health care was weak. So only a small percentage of any population reached an age where they were unable to work for physical reasons due to age. This low life expectancy and absence of pensions meant most workers continued to work until death unless they could be cared for at home by their children. In 1880, for example, 78 percent of American men over age sixty-four were still officially working.[164] Then in 1889, under Chancellor Otto von Bismarck, Germany became the first country to introduce universal "retirement" and financial benefits for all. But it was not until 1935 that America introduced an official retirement age and began providing social insurance, following the German system that initiated sixty-five as the retirement age.[165] By 1990, only 30 percent of men over sixty-four remained in the US workforce.[166]

In December 2013, the Bureau of Labor Statistics made a ten-year projection of the entire US workforce, foreseeing more people working longer into their older years. In 2002 and 2012, 20.4 percent and 26.8

percent, respectively, of those aged sixty-five to seventy-four were in the workforce. The Bureau has predicted that by 2022, a rise to 31.9 percent of this age bracket will still be working.[167] Don't ask me; it's statistics.

Now the world of work is changing. It's no longer what it once was, even as recently as ten years ago. There are no assurances, no guarantees. While writing this, I came across a book review in the *Washington Post* with the ominous heading, "Instead of feeling secure, many retirees feel betrayed." Katherine Newman, author of *Downhill from Here: Retirement Insecurity in the Age of Inequality*, wrote, "A pension was once regarded as something of a sacred bond between an employer and loyal employees. … The more immediate problem for Social Security for most of Newman's subjects," wrote the reviewer, "is that monthly benefits, though reliable, are too low to allow most retirees to make ends meet. So most Americans count on a combination of employer-sponsored pension benefits and private savings (like a 401(k) plan) to supplement their retirement income. Both are voluntary, and that is part of the system's vulnerability."[168]

And that "sacred bond between an employer and loyal employees" is rare today in America, replaced by betrayal and anger. For example, many retirees thought their employer, General Electric (GE), would take care of them forever. It didn't. Oops. Despite its earlier promises to its employees, GE cut retiree healthcare benefits and slashed the dividend their former employees once relied on as guaranteed income. Mary Anna Feitler, who is seventy-five and worked at GE's plant in Indiana for nearly twenty-seven years, told a Bloomberg reporter she had seen her medical expenses growing by about $5,000 a year to $22,000! "We're doing OK," she said, but "I don't know whether to anticipate that it's going to get worse."[169] And that's an optimistic, hopeful story? There are horror stories everywhere as retirement planning with guarantees are not what they used to be. Maybe you have a story. I do. So does my wife. It happens.

More and more, we want to keep working past this traditional retirement age because we feel a need to continue contributing to society and for economic reasons. But we also want to find meaning and purpose in our own lives, and work does that for us. According to a Gallup survey published in January 2004, due to insufficient savings or fears of being socially isolated, boomers are showing a reluctance to retire. The average age at which American retirees say they retired has increased steadily from fifty-seven to sixty-one years of age over the past twenty years, but nearly half of those still working (49 percent) say they do not expect to be able to retire until they are sixty-six or older; one in ten predict they will never retire.[170]

Most of us also rely on a sustained income stream just to survive; savings just won't do it for us. This goes against our parents' – the Greatest Generation's – old norms and stereotypes of "work hard and then you can just relax," lie on a beach somewhere, play bridge or golf or whatever. We are no longer defined by the old expectations of what we should or should not do at a certain age, and that means we need to reimagine, reinvent, reboot, and rewire our lives, specifically our mind-set about what it means to age.

The transition that comes with retirement is rarely a simple one, even for those who've been economically successful and have plenty of savings, either through their own effort or through investments or inheritance. Without some preparation, transitioning from full-time work to full-time retirement can cause depression and other negative health effects. For most retirees, their identity and self-worth had been tightly woven to their work. They spent most of their working lives perfecting a persona that no longer functions and will now need to change in a variety of ways. Peter Greeman, an advertising executive and nonprofit leader, has advised those going through this transition: "Recognize that your fears of retirement are really fears of change – which may not be bad – they get to them before they get to you. Giving up your career identity can be very scary. It's a lot like giving up smoking – but you feel so much better in the end."[171]

Many of us have very little understanding of what may be involved with this transition or what we will need to do as we march or waddle straight into a vision of retirement that may no longer exist. Consider this relevant musing by Carl Jung when writing about four archetypal stages of a human life: "Thoroughly unprepared, we take the step into the afternoon of life. Worse still, we take this step with the false presupposition that our truths and our ideals will serve us as hitherto. But we cannot live the afternoon of life according to the program of life's morning, for what was great in the morning will be little at evening and what in the morning was true, at evening will have become a lie."[172] Some rethinking, reconsidering, rewiring, and reinvention may now be in order.

Some form of meaningful alternative work becomes even more important. Steve Langerud, a workplace consultant in Iowa, has said, "Following a path that's not deeply engaging, even when you succeed, can lead to dissatisfaction and, in extreme cases, depression. This is a theme among my boomer clients – 'I went to the right schools, I got the right job, I bought the right things and I'm still not happy.' … The good news is it's never too late. As we live healthier and longer lives it's easy to leave dissatisfaction behind, and craft a new life of meaning, significance, and service."[173]

There's an impulse to express who we are through what we do, and this is important at every point in our lives. When our sense of meaning and fulfillment is tied to our work, and then we lose that work, it gets complicated; it can be traumatic. It's important to be engaged in projects that allow us to express our character strengths and gifts, in support of causes we are passionate about, with people who share our values and aspirations. It's important we now develop a clearer sense of the kind of work that gives meaning and purpose to the remainder of our lives. I hope this will help you take your own gifts, passions, and values, and then clarify some direction, so you can envision and reimagine your work, work that is meaningful and fulfilling.

There are lots of books out there on so-called "successful retirement" and continuing to work, some good, some horrible. Some are just insulting; "senior citizens" living their "Golden Years," fighting anything having to do with age or else settling for much less. But a practical and comprehensive overview of working during retirement is John Nelson and Richard Bolles's book, *What Color Is Your Parachute? For Retirement: Planning a Prosperous, Healthy, and Happy Future.*[174] This useful book can help you get ideas and clarity about opportunities and possibilities of living with new meaningful work. You never know; something might click!

Elizabeth White is an author and aging solutions advocate for older adults facing uncertain work and financial insecurity. In her excellent and resource-rich book, *55, Underemployed, and Faking Normal,*[175] and her no-nonsense 2017 TED talk,[176] White speaks of the reality of limited financial resources and despair that many people encounter in their later years. Given how our society is structured, it has become increasingly common for people to come to this point even after many years of hard work and faithfully following the system. She notes that "millions of baby boomers are moving into their senior years with empty pockets and declining choices to earn a living." She offers some practical advice for "smalling up," facing our situation, not denying it, and developing a strategy to "live a richly textured life on a limited income." For many, she says, this will require an end to magical thinking, that something will happen to save us, make it all go away. If necessary, we must "come down off our throne," take the initiative and act to change our work and financial circumstances. And this may require taking work we may consider to be "beneath us" to survive, work that is not in line with our years of experience and specific skills. White calls this taking on "bridge work," which "is what we do in the meantime while we figure out what's next." She recommends people in similar circumstance connect through "resilience circles" to share and support one another to get through difficult times.

More and more people are freelancing several part-time jobs with flexible hours and cobbling together a multi-stream income. This so-called gig economy has been defined somewhere out there on the Internet as "a labor market characterized by the prevalence of short-term contracts or freelance work, as opposed to permanent jobs."[177] Not for everyone, but great for entrepreneurs, this approach to work can be rewarding, drawing on your creativity and abilities, but it may not give many the security they so desire. Many people do appreciate and benefit from the flexibility, including complete control over when they work, how much time to work, and juggling with other priorities that are important to them.

Or if you want to become more entrepreneurial, there could be a negative marketing or selling mind-set that you may first need to address and overcome. With a more positive attitude, you can find certain time-tested steps to follow and much guidance all over the Internet and in bookstores. Thanks to South Park, you can even begin to think about your new entrepreneurial marketing plan. But in one episode, Tweek has a problem. It seems his underpants are going missing. Annoying. We discover this is because the underpants gnomes, who work late into the night, remove his underwear and sometimes socks. When confronted by the boys, the gnomes try their best to explain why they are stealing Tweek's underpants. Our enthusiastic gnomes proclaim that they only have three simple steps to their business model:[178]

1. Step One: Collect underpants
2. Step Two: ? ? ?
3. Step Three: Make profit

Easy, right? Don't be an underpants gnome. Have a clear Step Two. You clearly need to make some profit, to be financially stable during your retirement, and you know how to do something, if only how to collect underpants. And you may have some more fundamental questions. Can I do that? Can I do it the same way I've always done it before? Will it be profitable? Here's the kicker: "I'm too old to do that." Will they still let me do that? Will anyone hire (or buy from) me? Selling is icky. Do I even want anyone to hire me? After a lifetime of working for a boss, can I be an entrepreneur? Or if I'm already an entrepreneur, and now want to expand that or do something new, can I? And my personal favorite, "Why bother?" Do I have the *chutzpah*, the *cajones*, the audacity and stamina to pull this off? Uh, yes you do, oh, inner critic. Of course you do – "necessity is the mother of invention,"[179] said Frank Zappa never.

So, when the need is there, when the gaining of something becomes imperative, you will force yourself to face your fears and find ways of getting it. And you will overcome those troublesome inner critics, those protectors who may have served you so well in the past, kept you safe, but now are just messing with you and holding you back. But you can take heart. As an older adult contemplating something new, taking a leap, a risk to start something new, profitable, and meaningful, you can feel encouraged by the many advantages older adults bring to first-time entrepreneurship. "Instead of counting your years, count the advantages those years have given you. … The fundamental principle of successful entrepreneurship isn't doing something completely new. It's doing something that makes customers so happy that they're willing to give you money in return. That's true whether you're offering software or sandwiches. You don't have to come up with a dazzling breakthrough; you just need to solve a customer's problem. Opportunities are everywhere."[180] Especially for someone such as yourself, who has a lifetime of experience, conflict resolution, and dot-connecting integration skills.

Overcoming a negative mindset about marketing and selling as well as starting something new is one thing, and it is essential. Once that is out of the way, prospects for older people who want to start-up new work, be their own boss, is encouraging. The U.S. Bureau of Labor Statistics found that for workers 65 and older, the self-employment rate is the highest of any age group in the country at 15.5%; for ages 25 to 34 it is only 4.1%. Encore.org, a nonprofit promoting older generation second careers "focused on improving communities and the world," conducted research into older people and start-ups. Findings revealed about two in five Americans between ages 50 and 70, roughly 20 million older people, would like to start-up nonprofits or businesses ventures within the next five to ten years. And we can take heart from the findings of the Kauffman Foundation, which discovered that over the past ten years or so, the highest rate of entrepreneurial activity is found among the 55 to 64 age bracket. Perhaps you thought it was those 20-something Silicon Valley techies in hoodies? Nope. And older entrepreneurs are clearly more successful. While only about 28% of start-ups initiated by younger entrepreneurs lasted more then three years, those established by older entrepreneurs were vastly more successful, with a whopping 70% of their start-ups still ticking away after three years.[181] Why? Experience? Wisdom? Perhaps a willingness to take risks and typically with more capital to invest?

In her 2019 book, *Never Too Old to Get Rich: The Entrepreneur's Guide to Starting a Business Mid-Life*, career, retirement, and finance counselor Kerry Hannon wrote, "Longer lives and fear of outliving their money are motivating many people to keep on keeping on in the working world. The frustrating reality of ageism bias by employers is alive and well, which is why being your own boss has become the default for droves of older workers who are shut out of the workforce by employers who see their expiration date and view them as lacking stamina, up-to-date skills, or perhaps simply being too expensive in terms of salary demands." Reality check.

One eye-opener is Chip Conley's 2018 best-selling book, *Wisdom @ Work*.[182] Conley discusses workplace ageism and maintains we should treat age as we would any other type of diversity. He asserts that people who have been forced to make mid-career changes, retire, or else choose to work past "retirement age" need help. In early 2018, Conley, founder of Joie de Vivre Hospitality and strategic advisor for hospitality and leadership at Airbnb, founded the Modern Elder Academy as the first "midlife wisdom school" to "navigate midlife transitions."[183] Academy program graduates, who have the dual roles of "wisdom keeper and seeker," receive a "certificate in Mindset Management."

The academy, situated in El Pescadero on the coast of Baja California Sur in Mexico, seeks to abolish our society's outdated model of a simplistic and disempowering three-stage life of "learn, earn, and retire." Instead, older participants come to understand "how to repurpose a lifetime of experience for the modern workplace" while remaining active and working. He has observed that leadership, for example, requires and most benefits from "age diverse teams" and that when we remain curious and engaged, we lose track of age – it then becomes unimportant and uninteresting. After all, it appears many boomers really do not want to "retire" but rather continue working in ways that take advantage of their years of experience and skill. Why, after all, at the peak of our abilities and influence, do we stop and "retire," remove ourselves often willingly from the game, from contributing? I have never quite understood that.

Your current objective may well be to find work that aligns with your goals, needs, values, purpose, passions, and requirements for an adequate income. If you are anything like me, this can require a reinvention of new work during this process of aging consciously. You will become aware of various alternative strategies for creating vision and goals that can make dreams come true. This can mean discovering a new or refocused passion, dream, or work direction – a reinvention, a rewiring. In Chapter 2, I painfully described some of the angst and transformation of my own personal conscious aging story. This was (still is) a process of reinvention, moving from my *Iliad*, being a consultant who traveled all over the place, to entering my *Odyssey*, becoming a transformation coach and staying mostly in one place, at home. This was also a change in professional focus from getting others to believe in me to helping others believe in themselves. From being like a passionless "commodities broker" to becoming a hopeful agent of change.

In conclusion, Richard Leider, in his book, *Work Reimagined: Uncover Your Calling*, has written, "It is the end of work as we know it. … We commonly identify work as something that is a chore, or which we only do to get paid. When we operate from a powerful sense of what we are called to do, then we are not, as the saying goes, simply making a living, we are making a life. In order to live the life we imagine, we must continually reimagine that. In order to do work that makes such a life possible, we must regularly rediscover and reimagine our calling." [184]

In this chapter, you have gained an understanding of "working beyond retirement" and that aging consciously can entail doing work that is more in alignment with your values, character strengths, vision, goals, and purpose. You have the resources to envision and make the change you want in your work and to begin securing your financial future – this only requires that you settle on a plan and then take action! But you are going to have to "just pick a darn movie and see it all the way through;"

find what inspires you, pick a strategy, and go for it. No endless debate or analysis. And, finally, I think it is quite important to take to heart what Dr. Jim Fadiman has said about any important activity, "Don't wait until you are ready to start. Start and learn what you need to do to continue."[185]

The next chapter will help you identify ways to approach financial security and prosperity while recognizing the many myths we hold about money and how we can overcome a mind-set of scarcity, shame, and fear.

Chapter 10:

Ship of Fools

"Shame is like everything else; live with it for long enough and it becomes part of the furniture."
– Salman Rushdie

"You can only become truly accomplished at something you love. Don't make money your goal. Instead, pursue the things you love doing, and then do them so well that people can't take their eyes off you."
– Maya Angelou

Step 7: Manifest Your Prosperity

To me, there is great truth in the quote by Salman Rushdie and great beauty in the quote by Maya Angelou. But, know this; this is perhaps the most important yet most difficult chapter for me to write. It's personal. Money shame. I know it. An ache in the pit of my stomach, a cavity that fills up in measure to my bank balance. We live thoroughly in a materialistic money culture, but we don't really talk about money, certainly not about the pain and shame of it. Money seems to be a taboo subject. "Many people would rather talk about their sex lives than about their bank balance."[186] We want it; we don't want it. We don't think it's important; we think it's important. Sell something and you are creepy; provide a service and maybe you're not. Really confusing. This book's original subtitle ended with "*And Stop Worrying About the Money*," but I dropped that – maybe because I just can't stop worrying about the money. It's important, sounds easy, but it's not. But it can be done. Many of us need to get honest about money and get over this confusion.

A few years ago, money coach and author Tammy Lally lost her middle-aged brother, Keith, to suicide – on the day he was served a foreclosure notice. He left behind his ten-year-old daughter; his eighteen-year-old son, just a few weeks before high school graduation; and his loving wife of twenty years. How did this happen? Lally said her brother was "caught in our family's money shame cycle." I find it impossible to listen to her 2017 TEDx talk without tearing up.[187] It's too intimate, too close to home. She notes her brother's case is not uncommon.

In her 2018 book, *Money Detox: Your Invitation to Liberation*, Lally reported that adult suicide rates between the ages forty and sixty-four have risen almost 40 percent since 1999. Job loss, bankruptcies, and foreclosures were present in nearly 40 percent of these deaths, with white middle-aged men accounting for seven out of every ten suicides. Lazy, crazy, stupid, or just "bad with money?" – this is "money shame." According to Lally, money shame arises from an intensely painful experience of believing we are flawed and therefore unworthy of love and belonging. A painful shame that is based on our bank balance, our debts, our possessions, and our job titles (or loss thereof) – equating our bank accounts, our net worth, with our self-worth.[188] This can keep us from falling asleep at night and from waking with a positive outlook in the morning. I get it.

In this chapter, you will continue the REWIREMENT process by understanding how our materialistic society's consumer myths have been internalized to create our disempowering money mind-set – and how this is holding you back from the financial security you need and deserve. This mind-set, produced and continually reinforced by our TV advertising and youth-oriented consumer culture, can be released and altered through self-exploration. It is this gnawing financial insecurity, feelings of lack, that keeps us from fully embracing our conscious elderhood and fully living our potential because this basic need that is so tied to security is not being met. If such basic needs as security, love, and belonging are left unmet, we cannot free our minds and grow into our self-actualized life in our later years. Instead, we remain stuck in a land of baser pursuits, unfulfilled, with our inherent creativity and potential blocked. The inevitable result – depression, clinical or otherwise – becomes a continual battle. But by taking action, you can face these issues and improve your feelings of financial security.

A big concern for many of us as we age is how we will be able to stay in our own home and not go into The Home, and how we can afford either of those options. "When boomers require more attention than can be effectively provided by family members, nursing homes and extended care facilities will need to be considered. For families already challenged due to the economy and demands of raising a family, this can be brutal. Assisted living facilities that provide hands-on personal care for those who cannot live alone, but do not require the full-time coverage provided by a nursing home, cost an average of $3,261 per month, according to a Genworth Financial survey. Nursing homes with semi-private rooms are $5,790 per month, while those with private rooms ring in at $6,390 monthly."[189] Yikes! My wife, a registered nurse, has worked at the same assisted-living facility, aka "nursing home," for the last fifteen years. The stories I have heard, the indignities, the incompetency even, make me want to have a plan to shoot myself in the head before I lose all control and move into a place like that. But that's just me.

Whether you realize it or not, you're probably going to be reliant on Social Security for a portion of your income at some point in retirement. "According to data from the Social Security Administration (SSA), 62% of current retirees lean on the program for at least half of their income, with just over a third reliant on Social Security for virtually all (90%-plus) of their income. This more or less corroborates surveys conducted by Gallup of retired and non-retired individuals. Of the retirees, just 1 in 10 aren't reliant on their Social Security income in any way. Meanwhile, more than 4 out of 5 non-retirees expect to lean on their retirement benefit as a major (30%) or minor (54%) income source."[190]

There are politicians with very questionable motives who are continually creeping around the halls of Congress trying to cut back on "entitlement benefits" or even eliminating them altogether. Not part of the government budget, social security pays for itself through a dedicated tax that everyone pays into and would be in excellent fiscal shape if Congress had not borrowed heavily on it to pay for foreign wars and adventures that the country could otherwise not afford. Now they don't want to pay it back and want to "balance the budget" by eliminating it. How some of these people get elected is astounding to me. But "never underestimate the power of stupid people in large groups." Well, maybe not so stupid, just easily manipulated by masters of power. Anyhow. So, what's my point? You might just want to do something to earn supplemental income and be less reliant on Social Security and the slippery whims of Congress.

Now, facing such possible scenarios in addition to struggling monthly to budget and manage money is not uncommon. But money is too often a taboo subject, and we hide our problems around money. This must be faced and not denied. Lally states that our self-destructive and self-defeating financial behaviors are not driven by our rational minds. Instead, they are the product of our subconscious belief systems rooted in childhood and are so very deeply embedded that they shape the way we view and deal with money as adults. She maintains all of us experience some form of money shame to some degree, irrespective of our relative poverty or wealth, "because we give money all of our power." She contends that each of us can break through the money shame cycle; not changing can be debilitating if not fatal.

By now you have come to the clear realization that this is not a book about money in retirement or giving you a magic pill to stop worrying about it. It's not at all about directly achieving financial security and certainly not a get-rich-quick scheme so you can have your boat in retirement. No knight in shining armor on a white horse to save you here. But in this chapter, we do search for the root of our angst. We dive (or more accurately dip our toes) into this money shame and its concomitant disempowering scarcity mind-set. In that way, once these are addressed, overcome even, you can start to take control over your finances and ensure, or at least dramatically increase, the likelihood of a comfortable "retirement" and a degree of freedom in your later years. This should, after all, be a time of comfort and reflection without undue worry about future financial uncertainties. And you already know there are no guarantees of a positive outcome for anything. That is just reality – but that should never be a reason for you to not begin or aim toward your goals – to act at any time in your life and, yes, regardless of age.

You know that denial can also be a very powerful tool, even your best friend, keeping you comfortable and safe. If you deny a thing, then it's gone, and you don't have to do anything about it – for now. You may even say it is someone else's problem; "they" will fix it in time. At least you've accomplished something, you forgot about it, just denied it. But somebody somewhere said, "Denying what you feel will not make it go away. It ensures that it never gets resolved." Then one day something happens, a trigger that forces you to blink back into consciousness. You recognize this thing needs to be examined and fixed, some action needs to be taken – by you. Because you know you can't keep floating down this same river. Denial will just keep you from what needs to be done. You know this. But now comes the fear. Fear can boil up when facing truth and facing the unknown, and it's not a lot of fun; it can keep you paralyzed. And fear, the avoidance of pain, can make us slip back into denial. Denial might be your friend for a while, but fear is an enemy forever. Like Cheese of the Month, it's that "gift that keeps on giving" until you face it and stare it down.

"Ever more people today have the means to live," wrote Viktor Frankl, "but no meaning to live for." And Johann Wolfgang von Goethe wrote, "Many people take no care of their money till they come nearly to the end of it, and others do just the same with their time." OK, so enough with the lofty, "pithy aphorisms".

How do you use this time? Do you procrastinate over matters pertaining to money and finances? Is procrastination a symptom of low self-esteem? I don't know; some say yes – maybe. But for whatever reason, we put things off. Years can fly by and we wonder, duh, why we still haven't become that person we dreamed about, realizing who we know we can be – who we really are. If you are like me, you will stand on the scales a few times a week and if – oops! – you've gained a couple of pounds, you will then do something about it – exercise more, hold off on the carbs. Or you might feel powerless and go eat more cake, but I doubt it. It is most likely you will make course corrections, adjustments to either comfortably maintain or lose even more until you achieve your weight-loss goal or at least stabilize. That's another story, a complicated one also having to do with self-worth and childhood and so on. But do you also do that with your finances? Do you even check them regularly, set goals, make course corrections when it looks like there may be danger ahead? Is it just too unbearable to face, not wanting to see what you know you are likely to see? This is a choice you must make, to either face the situation or not. You're not going anywhere – well, not yet.

We experience a "cultural condition of scarcity," a psychic or psychological environment that creates within us a feeling of lack, of need, of not having enough, not being good enough. A goal is to rise above that mind-set of thinking that there is always something missing, this lack, a scarcity in your mind. This goal is about having a healthier relationship with money. I am not going to delve into the well-known law of attraction[191] and a subcategory, the law of abundance, the belief or truth that "there is ample money for everyone who knows how to acquire it and keep it," [192] but I will touch on its foundations. If this resonates with you, then it is important that you recognize some of the emotions and values you are holding around money and gain a better understanding of how they either help or hinder your financial situation and ability to live comfortably without worry.

Nancy Levin, an integrative coach and author of *Worthy*, wrote about the relationship between net worth and self-worth: "The state of our net-worth is a direct reflection of our self-worth."[193] She asserts that creating your financial freedom is not so much about changing what you do, such as how and where you invest, but rather in changing your limiting beliefs.

The root of the problem, these feelings of unworthiness, can be replaced with the recognition and solidity of your own inherent value. She discusses the many excuses we use to avoid creating a life that we really want and that in taking back our financial power, we see ourselves as being worthy of having abundance.

Deborah Price, money coach and author of *Money Magic*, has an interesting take on how people come to view money. "Whatever your personal history with money is," writes Price, "your story must be told so that you can witness it objectively and consciously."[194] She has identified eight main types of relationships people have with money. She uses the metaphor of archetypes to describe these relationships. She provides exercises on how to identify your "money archetype" and then address issues you have about money within the context of your archetype. She describes these archetypes and their characteristics; namely, the Innocent, the Victim, the Warrior, the Martyr, the Fool, the Creator/Artist, the Tyrant, and the ideal money type, the Magician. Many of these archetypes overlap; we can identify ourselves as hybrids, and rarely does someone have a single money archetype. Her approach is a fun and insightful way to begin examining your money mind-set through metaphor.

The late Joseph Campbell, literature professor, student of comparative mythology and religion and author of *The Hero with a Thousand Faces*,[195] wrote that "money is congealed energy, and releasing it releases life possibilities." Money can be seen as a form of energy, you receive it in exchange for your contributions and you give it on the basis of your needs. *The Energy of Money*, a book by Maria Nemeth, is, according to medical intuitive and author Caroline Myss, "a new approach to working with energy that can free your spirit, expand your vision, and help you achieve your purpose. A soulful guide for financial success."[196] Nemeth views our relationship with money as a Hero's Journey, described in Joseph Campbell's classic book. She wrote, "The main goal of the hero's journey is to make your dreams a physical reality – and to learn from all the challenges along the way. In doing this, we see and appreciate our own true nature more clearly – which is where our dreams come from – and we share ourselves and our accomplishments as a contribution to others. I believe that this is the purpose of being human." She asserted that, as the hero, you can bring forth your natural strengths and values to improve your relationship with money. Nemeth, who leads a "You and Money" course, addressed the causes and solutions to the problems we have in our relationships with money, with each of us on our own hero's journey.

You can become energetically blocked when you have a money shame mind-set. Your inner connection to the heart, your intuition, can be obscured by thoughts of fear and want. Lynn Twist, author, founder of the Soul of Money Institute and cofounder of Pachamama Alliance, asks, "What blocks us?" The Soul of Money Institute enables people to discover how to make these mind-set shifts and learn new tools and practices to create abundance and lasting financial freedom. Their programs also take you beyond yourself by considering your community and the planet.

In her book, *The Soul of Money,*[197] Twist encourages us to understand that any problems, habits, or panic you have about money are not entirely your fault, but you do have responsibility, a choice. She asserts that what you think, say and do, your life energy, becomes focused on overcoming lack when you think your world is characterized by scarcity. She maintains that this mind-set or block can be transformed if you maintain an "attitude of gratitude." If you are feeling thankful without resistance, the heart connection will open. Your state of mind and energy focus then shift toward happiness. This attitude of gratitude, according to Twist, will unleash a power of receiving abundance in many forms. And like a magnet, you then begin to attract what reflects this gratitude.

Our current individual, environmental, social, and spiritual crises, according to Twist, are interconnected, the result of our collective unhealthy relationship to money. Messages about money, abundance, and scarcity have us behaving inconsistent with our humanity and with our desire to live in a healthy biosphere. Instead, our society, through its relentless consumer culture, has created a world in which we consume resources beyond a sustainable capacity and are seriously damaging the biosphere upon which all life depends. This is the core problem when nature is seen merely as a commodity, resources to exploit without consequence.

According to Lynn Twist, all this is caused by an underlying cultural condition, what she calls our "scarcity consciousness." The root problem is that a scarcity consciousness and the unhealthy relationships with money it causes are the biggest obstacles standing in the way of you being able to achieve the levels of wealth and financial security you want to reach. The lie of scarcity, within a society characterized by debt and deficit, says you don't have enough, you are not enough, and there is always something more you need to get or be if you are to become successful, happy, and worthy of respect and love from others – and yourself. Yikes! In a culture that emphasizes outer appearances and profit over people while devaluing and trivializing our inner resources and shared humanity, it is not such a great leap to say this has fueled the high amount of mental illness and substance addiction we now see in most communities.

This cruel cultural condition of scarcity catches all of us in its net. In *Soul of Money*, Twist identified three toxic money myths, in our own affluent society, that comprise this consciousness of scarcity. The first toxic myth is the subconscious belief "there is not enough to go around." You behave as if there is not enough of anything – money, time, sleep, you name it – and assume someone will always be left out. This myth legitimizes an incessant accumulation way beyond what is needed so that we are confident we are not being left out or behind. This accumulation is at the expense of other people and nature; it is human exploitation that is damaging to all of us and to the environment. The second toxic myth is that "more is better" – of anything, of everything – and continuous advertising is always telling you that you need more and more or must replace whatever you have with the latest. It is not surprising that, according to Twist, the storage industry in America is growing tremendously to warehouse what we cannot keep in our house, what we are not using but cannot part with – all our stuff. And the third toxic myth is the worst. It tells us that all this is normal, and "there's nothing we can do about it" – that there is not enough, more is better, and that's just the way it is. "It's just progress," and we would be crazy to question that. By not questioning this subconscious mind-set of scarcity, we buy into the consumer culture that is driving behavior that is out of alignment with who we are – or should be – as human beings and with the requirements of the natural world, the biosphere, upon which we ultimately depend for virtually all resources. And we wonder why we feel anxious, get depressed.

I participated in an excellent seven-week online course about financial freedom, "True Prosperity," presented by Lynn Twist and Tammy White. The course has been described as a "transformative journey as you shift into Prosperity Consciousness and become a reflection of what's possible for everyone – an active, engaged culture that honors people and leverages money in a way that serves the highest good of humanity." Something you can do is to see what the Soul of Money Institute offers that could be of benefit to you on your own Hero's Journey toward financial freedom.[198]

When honestly facing down your financial fear, having wrestled it to the ground, I assume you will want to begin doing something to seriously improve your situation and increase the likelihood of a successful outcome. You will first need to recognize and accept your financial past and present, then create some SMART goals (Chapter 7) around money, and I expect you then would like to also put some time-tested systems in place that will give you the financial security you desire and "stop worrying about the money." That's pretty much true for me. I want to be comfortable, to be free, to give back even. I'm not interested in a yacht, a home in Monaco overlooking the azure sea, or a gold Lamborghini Aventador LP-700-4. No judgments here; that's just me.

A transformation coach I am. A financial advisor I am not. I have a PhD in monkeys and trees. I perceive myself as being incapable of ever getting a degree in economics or anything having to do with finances. I know my limitations. But fortunate we are that there are those among us who are adept at this subject. They are all over the place, giving advice on wise investing and "location, location, location" – some very good, some very bad. We are usually on our guard; we don't want to get fooled again. Just the subject of money is painful enough.

Someone whose books and programs are extremely popular (so she must be doing something right) is financial advisor Suze Orman. Orman has written that "getting ahead" is "about taking charge of our finances so that we can experience personal freedom, provide for those we're responsible for, and help the less fortunate." In her best-selling book on financial freedom, Orman presented nine steps, which are only listed here.[199] You can follow up on these if you are so inclined. Her nine steps are:

1. "Seeing how your past holds the key to your financial future
2. Facing your fears and creating new truths
3. Being honest with yourself
4. Being responsible to those you love
5. Being respectful of yourself and your money
6. Trusting yourself more than you trust others
7. Being open to receive all that you are meant to have
8. Understanding the ebb and flow of the money cycle
9. Recognizing true wealth."

Sounds pretty good to me, but we have read books, even made notes, and then done nothing. Oops. Others spend tens of thousands of dollars getting financial advice, going down rabbit holes of seminars and implementing the latest "smart money boy" strategies. But they still struggle, "rearranging the deck chairs on the Titanic." Oops. And all of this, getting the financial freedom you want, you can do on your own – you know this. But it's true that the process and systems to achieve your money goals can be quicker and much less expensive with a personal advisor or coach. I personally know of one professional, time-tested example for entrepreneurs and small business owners. Financial executive, host of the "Cash Flow" podcast, author, and money coach Pam Prior has helped entrepreneurs and "normal people" with their money mind-sets and financial planning. Her clients come to understand the tools for assessing their financial picture and how best to use them to get where they want to be financially. Her book, *Your First CFO: The Accounting Cure for*

Small Business Owners,[200] has become a best-seller with entrepreneurs, and you can find her through her website[201] – https://pamprior.com – again, if you are so inclined.

In this chapter, you have gained an understanding of myths and shame that underlie a disempowering money mind-set of scarcity, immediately setting you up for defeat. So, the real reason for this pain, this insecurity over your money, is not really poor financial planning or investments gone wrong or any other excuse you can think of; it's all about your mind-set, including money shame. This shame and negativity surrounding money can be released and altered through self-exploration. There are tools around to do this. And you can then go further to learn how to manage your finances, additional tools that will enable you to improve your financial security and freedom.

I conclude this chapter with a quote from author Julia Cameron, who wrote about an ideal energetic scenario: "What we really want to do is what we are really meant to do. When we do what we are meant to do, money comes to us, doors open for us, we feel useful, and the work we do feels like play to us."[202] You can keep that in mind. In the next chapter, you will learn about ways to expand your consciousness through a variety of experiential means, a REWIREMENT in line with a re-fired purpose and a more empowering mind-set.

Chapter 11:

Turn on Your Love Light

"Every life is many days, day after day.
We walk through ourselves, meeting robbers, ghosts, giants, old men, young men, wives, widows, brothers-in-love, but always meeting ourselves."
– James Joyce, *Ulysses*

"Keep walking, though there's no place to get to.
Don't try to see through the distances.
That's not for human beings. Move within,
But don't move the way fear makes you move."
– Rumi (1207 –1273)

"Whoever travels without a guide
needs two hundred years for a two-day journey."
– Rumi

Step 8: Expand Your Consciousness

The Greek equivalent of the familiar Latin phrase *Nosce te ipsum* ("know thyself") was inscribed in the forecourt of the Temple of Apollo at Delphi during the fourth century BC. The phrase was later expanded on by Socrates, who taught that "the unexamined life is not worth living." We, on our journey, think somehow our effort and all its challenges and manifestations are outside of us. But then we come to realize our journey is within, a journey of exploration and personal development without end. Rainer Maria Rilke wrote, "The only journey is the one within." This is the only journey that really matters.

Chinese philosopher Lao Tzu supposedly said, "The key to growth is the introduction of higher dimensions of consciousness into our awareness." Ron Pevny, in his book *Conscious Living, Conscious Aging*, wrote, "From an even broader perspective, growing in consciousness means growing in awareness (experientially as well as conceptually) of our connectedness. We are one with all of humanity and the living planet that supports a vast web of interdependence. This is where, as theologian Frederick Buechner described: 'Our deepest gladness and the world's hunger meet.' From that knowing we can make our most fulfilling and important contributions as elders. And at yet another level, higher consciousness – lies the experience of the Great Mystery itself, the source and essence of all."

In this chapter, you will continue the REWIREMENT process by learning how to "change your mind," expanding your consciousness through a variety of experiential means and to integrate these experiences to effect sustained transformation for the better. A chapter on consciousness can go in many directions. Expanding consciousness is all about transformation, and there are many tools and methods for that. It has taken many years of intensive consciousness conditioning to get where we are now, both positive and negative, and some might correctly say it has taken thousands of years. Most of the effects of conditioning over which we have some degree of control began when we were very young. This is about an expansion of awareness, not succumbing to illusion, moving into areas that can be uncomfortable and fearful, sometimes embracing the shadow side of our personalities. But if we have the courage and the determination to change, an effective rewiring of consciousness can lead to sustainable transformation of our mind-set on aging, retirement, work, money, how we view the world, the cosmos, and our place in it, and our attitudes about what it means to be alive.

Rabbi Zalman Schachter-Shalomi, known as the spiritual father of the Jewish Renewal movement, favored the term "spiritual elders" for older adults who are aging consciously (Chapter 5), those I called the Wizards in Chapter 3, those who are self-actualizing, those who will come to transcend themselves, their egos, and serve others. He has written about consciousness, spirituality, and aging and wrote that "spiritual eldering has benefited from all this exploration. It draws liberally on the breakthroughs in consciousness that we have made in the past three decades. It also depends on the shift from the old, otherworldly spirituality to the new celebrational spirituality that heals the split between spirit and matter and that affirms the sacredness of life on Earth. This attitude enables us to harvest our lives and to bequeath a legacy to the generations that follow us."[203]

Reb Zalman, in an interview with Jeffrey Mishlove, said, "I feel that the urgent question is for many people, when you have an extended lifespan, can you do this without having extended consciousness? It is so clear to me that without extended consciousness, the extended lifespan is a depressive thing."[204] He also wrote that "with an increased life span and the psychotechnologies[205] to expand the mind's frontiers, the spiritual elder heralds the next phase of human and global development."[206]

Like many so-called boomers, I experienced a profound expansion of consciousness through psychedelics when I was young, for me between the ages of seventeen and twenty-three. When I was seventeen, the summer of '69, I was taking a class at Corcoran School of Art in Washington, DC, and decided to go with some friends one hot August weekend to the Atlantic City Pop Festival, three days of music – and who knew what else to expect? If you Google that festival, there is scarce information, but it was huge and was held at the Atlantic City racetrack.[207] I still have my tattered, orange ticket stub for August 1–3 at $15.00 for all three days – not too shabby. "There is almost no existing film footage or audio from the entire weekend in circulation; a YouTube search yields a few grainy, silent clips and less than a minute of Janis Joplin singing. And relatively few still photos exist. But it definitely happened. I know, because I was there. … Due to the excessive summer heat, water trucks periodically doused those on the ground; the rest of us baked."[208] Most of the bands that played at Atlantic City then moved on two weeks later to a festival in upstate New York named Woodstock – but I missed my ride to that because of some questionable friends whose names I forget.

I don't know why – I was young and open to new experiences, a little foolish, naïve, desperate for some change perhaps, certainly curious – and it seemed like a good idea to try something I had heard about, LSD. Everyone else was doing it, or so it seemed. What could this innocuous little orange pill in the palm of my hand do, I wondered? So, I began my "long strange trip" sitting near the stage in the middle of a big, sweaty crowd of close to 100,000 souls at the Atlantic City racetrack on a hot day in August. Not ideal, but it happened. What followed was an unforgettable experience, certainly not a nightmare but a profound "rewirement" of how I experienced the five – or six – physical senses and how my mind viewed the world and everything in it. I would never be able to view the world the same again. I depend on my senses and my mind to know what I know. When each one fell away in succession, becoming unreliable, I came to realize that I only think I know what I know; reality can be very different, and no longer could I depend on the truth of my senses. Like the fire that cast light and shadows on the walls of the cave, described in Plato's *Allegory of the Cave*, the reality of objects was seen to be misrepresented, incorrectly perceived. Plato's prisoners in the cave could never free themselves from their chains, constraints that never allowed them to see objects for what they really were. I understood my view of reality was based on these impressions, merely the light and shadows that could be perceived thorough my limited senses, filtered through my conditioning. I began to see these projections in my world differently, with new eyes, more innocently and from a strange new viewpoint. Now, for a brief time, I could see there was much more, and that can change a person's life. It did for me. But no one stays in this "strange new land" forever, and a glimpse of the illumination of mystical experience is fleeting; escaping our conditioned bondage is no easy feat.

It was a pivotal time, a peak experience, and a life-changing event. But the usefulness of integrating those insights into my life, at age seventeen, without any support, was not quite comprehended. On the verge of leaving the only home I knew and going away for the first time to college, psychedelic integration was the least of my concerns. Fifty years later, my memory of that day is vague. I do remember some events vividly, internally and externally, but for the most part, I am not going to try to explain or interpret them here. And I can never describe adequately the internal visions, the fractal patterns, the vivid colors. I remember not particularly enjoying the "Crazy World of Arthur Brown," imagining Procol Harum to be profound in some inexplicable way, wondering who that woman on stage was playing piano because she clearly was not Joni Mitchell, and finding Little Richard hilarious as he jumped up and down on his piano for some reason.

A year or so later, while sitting with a tree, an enormous white oak, on a hillside in Washington, DC's Rock Creek Park, I came to understand there was an ineffable consciousness possessed by this tree, not the same as mine, its own, and with an awareness of me and its environment. I saw this life form and myself and all others on the planet hurtling through deep space on a very large rock, no destination, just moving through the universe. A tree was no longer just a pretty prop in my environment. No longer something that was presumably alive – something to be used as needed – it was alive!

I saw my biological evolution and that of the tree took the same amount of time to get to this point. I was no better than this plant, just different. I knew I was not viewed by any divine entity as a superior being among all the other sentient beings. If anything, I was much less adapted to my environment, disconnected, because it was clear that I and my species, while thinking we were the pinnacle of evolution because we could build cars and cathedrals for our own amusement, were a serious threat to ourselves and to all other lifeforms on the planet. This may not sound so profound, but I cannot find any other way to explain it, this awe, an openness and connection to nature, this living biosphere, brought about by the simple ingestion a psychedelic substance. But this journey clearly led me "into intimate contact with the total reality of the moment."[209] Well put.

In October 2018, my daughter and I attended the annual Bioneers Conference in San Rafael, California. Monica Gagliano, research associate professor in evolutionary ecology at the University of Western Australia, gave a presentation on her research into plant intelligence and imagination in science.[210] This was followed later in the day by a panel discussion on "Plant Intelligence and Human Consciousness" with Michael Pollan, Monica Gagliano, and J. P. Harpignies.[211] They discussed some beliefs, definitions, and theories of consciousness and intelligence. If human consciousness implies a quality of "self-reflection," then perhaps this is not relevant for plants, in human terms. Maybe. But after all, I can only know my own self-awareness, never someone else's let alone that of a plant. If intelligence, which literally means "choosing between," may be defined as the ability to solve novel problems, then we can say plants have intelligence. It is a matter of understanding that consciousness and intelligence are diverse and unquestionably not the purview of humans alone.

A quote attributed to Bhagat Singh Thind, writer, scientist, and lecturer on spirituality, states, "A state of consciousness which has not been experienced by a person, cannot be conceived or understood by him. It is also an error to think that what we cannot imagine, is inconceivable and has no existence in fact." And it's just not possible for me to convey the richness, the depth of the experience of ephemeral connection with that tree and all life; anyhow, I have forgotten most of it and am just not that articulate. I cannot even recall whether it was LSD from ergot, mescaline from peyote, or psilocybin from so-called magic mushrooms that elicited the experience; it was a long time ago, and I tried all those at some point. But the essence of this mystical experience, for that is exactly what it was, sent me on a trajectory and a career in biodiversity conservation with a connection, curiosity, and appreciation of nature that has remained with me ever since.

At some point soon after Atlantic City, I began reading more about the psychedelic, or entheogenic, experience from those who were more articulate. When Aldous Huxley wrote the *Doors of Perception* in 1954 about his experiences taking mescaline the year before, he began a revolution in consciousness in our society. The title is taken from William Blake's 1793 book of poems, *The Marriage of Heaven and Hell*, and this, in turn, inspired the name of the 1960s rock group, The Doors. "If the doors of perception were cleansed," wrote Blake, "everything would appear to man as it is, Infinite. For man has closed himself up, till he sees all things thro' narrow chinks of his cavern." Again, a reference to Plato's cave.

The term "psychedelic" originated in 1956 with British psychiatrist Humphry Osmond and is derived from the Greek words *psyche* (soul or mind) and *delein* (to manifest). It, therefore, can mean "soul-manifesting" or "mind-manifesting," the implication being that "psychedelics can access the soul and develop unused potentials of the human mind."[212] The word later became intimately linked with the counterculture of the 1960's. Aldous Huxley, based on his experiences with mescaline, preferred the term *phanerothyme*, Greek for "visible soul." An alternative term, preferred by many is *entheogenic*, which underscores the use of medicinal plants in a religious, spiritual, or mystical context. The term *entheogen* was first used in 1979 by a group of ethnobotanists as a preferred replacement for "hallucinogen" and "psychedelic," largely because of the baggage, connotations, and mixed meanings of those two words to our drug-obsessed and fear-based society. Its meaning also comes from two Greek words, *entheos* ("full of the god, inspired, possessed" and root of the word enthusiasm) and *genesthai* ("to come into being") and thus can mean to cause one "to become inspired or to experience feelings of inspiration, often in a religious or 'spiritual' manner."[213]

An understanding of psychedelics can help us with entering conscious aging, or spiritual eldering, and living a life of greater passion, service, and focused intention. Rabbi Zalman Schachter-Shalomi, a founder of the Jewish Renewal Movement, left the Lubavitch movement and founded a new organization, *B'nai Or* (Children of Light) and helped many rabbis and other spiritual leaders understand the connection between psychedelic experiences and their faith. He has discussed the impact that psychedelics had on his being and his religious practice in his chapter and interview called "Transcending Religious Boundaries" in the 2005 book, *Higher*

Wisdom: Eminent Elders Explore the Continuing Impact of Psychedelics.[214] "The wonderful thing about psychedelics," he wrote, "was the 'mind move' that occurred – the recognition of the fluidity of consciousness. My reality maps were no longer absolute. With psychedelics, I could see how all cosmologies are heuristic, and it depends on what you want to do. I could get into various viewpoints; if I wanted to see the universe from a Christian perspective, I got it. That was a very important discovery for me. … So the experience only opens you up to a greater vision. When you have the vision, you have a burden to carry that vision out. In other words, it makes demands on you. But you can also ignore the demands, shut the doors again, and then the places that have become transparent become opaque. It's beneficial to have someone with you who will help you harvest the experience. … Another thing I learned was how important it is to do one's contemplative homework afterward."

When asked if psychedelics could be integrated today in a more "wholesome" way than the "unravelling of the psychedelic experience" for recreation in the 1960s, Reb Zalman replied, "Attitudes have indeed changed. I can look back at the times when people tuned in, dropped out, and blew their minds. But then came the time when those people with the blown minds dropped back in again. They became the people who worked on Wall Street and made their mint or went to work with Microsoft on the computer revolution and brought a new mindset to the whole business. Nowadays, these folks are coming into their elder years, and I have the sense that they will want to look at the spiritual use of psychedelics at this point in their lives in a much more serious way."

If you change your mind, your consciousness, your awareness, then you will take the action that is needed to transform your life. Do we need to be afraid of this transformation? What is our fear? Chögyam Trungpa Rinpoche has written, "Fear is nervousness; fear is anxiety; fear is a sense of inadequacy, a feeling that we may not be able to deal with the challenges of everyday life at all. We feel that life is overwhelming. People may use tranquilizers or yoga to suppress their fear: they just try to float through life. We have all sorts of gimmicks and gadgets that we use in the hope that we might experience fearlessness simply by taking our minds off of our fear."[215]And Pema Chödrön has stressed that "like all explorers, we are drawn to discover what's out there without knowing yet if we have the courage to face it."[216]

Caroline Myss points to the need for us to face our fear of knowing ourselves, to uncover our purpose, and lead a life of greater fulfillment. "People want their reason for living to be a singular thing, like a career or a relationship, because this makes an individual feel secure in the physical world. We don't fare well in the realm of the invisible – so telling someone that their purpose is multilayered and includes the arduous journey of discovering who they really are is not always the answer they want to hear. But consider the complexity of the question: 'What is my reason for living?' How can that question not include a journey into the depths of your own life?"[217]

Of course, in no way are psychedelics or plant medicines the only pathway to a mystical experience or consciousness transformation. There are other pathways to healing, including meditation, mindfulness, holotropic breathwork, qigong, emotional freedom technique (EFT) or tapping therapy, eye movement desensitization and reprocessing (EMDR) psychotherapy, vision quests, shamanic healing, drumming, and the many schools of yoga, to name a few.

The therapeutic use of holotropic breathwork, an alternative to ingesting psychedelic or entheogenic substances, was developed by Stanislav Grof, who has written several books on the subject.[218] Grof is one of the earliest and most accomplished researchers into the therapeutic use of both psychedelics and holotropic breathwork to access non-ordinary states of consciousness. As stated by Grof, "Holotropic states activate the emotional and physical and then link it to spirituality. … This is what ancient cultures thought about the breath – it connects the external world with the body, and it activates the psyche to take us to the spiritual domain."[219]

A client of mine, age seventy-eight, has been a Catholic nun, spiritual director, and student of spirituality and prayer her entire adult life. "We continue to learn," she told me. "We never stop improving ourselves, our personhood, expanding our consciousness and learning, until we are called home to God." I can think of few people I have met who are as present, in the moment. She listens without effort or judgment, and in that way holds space for another's awakening. Listening, really listening (not just "yeah, I know, I know. I hear you") requires a very high level of self-esteem and self-love. She has never taken psychedelics and is not inclined to do so, but her mystical experiences, while few and far between, have shaped the direction of her life. When I first met her, I realized I was in the presence of, by most definitions and my limited understanding, a person who has achieved self-transcendence, experiencing a life of selfless service.

How to Change Your Mind: What the New Science of Psychedelics Teaches Us About Consciousness, Dying, Addiction, Depression, and Transcendence is a groundbreaking and influential book by Michael Pollan, *New York Times* best-selling author and professor of journalism at the UC Berkeley Graduate School of Journalism.[220] In his 2018 book, Pollan has summarized in detail the fascinating history of psychedelics from antiquity to the 1950s with the beginnings of research using psychedelics to cure alcoholism and other addictions and in conjunction with psychotherapy, which was extremely popular with actors in Hollywood. He discussed the influence of psychedelics on technological innovations, particularly in Silicon Valley, and mentions the impact that it had on Steve Jobs and many other technology and social innovators.

Pollan also presented an excellent overview of the recent revival of controlled research on psilocybin and other psychedelics to alleviate and even cure cancer anxiety, PTSD, depression, opioid addictions, alcoholism, and anxiety over death. He noted that Bill Wilson, founder of Alcoholics Anonymous, used LSD in early experiments, and the knowledge he gained was instrumental in his approach to treating alcoholism, i.e., the AA twelve-step program and surrendering to a higher power.[221]

Psychedelics for medicinal purposes are now being taken seriously, after a more than 50-year hiatus, and being reconsidered by the US medical establishment. In the United States, recent research on psychedelics, especially psilocybin, and their beneficial medical use has largely been focused at Johns Hopkins University and New York University. A recent article in *Scientific American* featured Johns Hopkins clinical pharmacologist Roland Griffiths discussing psychedelics as promising therapeutic tools.[222] I personally know a former participant of the Johns Hopkins psychedelic research program on treatment for cancer and the anxiety surrounding this illness. She enthusiastically reported a very significant and sustained improvement to her quality of life and alleviation of long-term depression as a result of participating in psilocybin treatment trials, and her cancer is in complete remission, which may be a testament to "mind over matter." The future is optimistic for continued research and psychedelic-assisted therapy to treat depression, addiction, PTSD, and anxiety from cancer and approaching death.[223]

Dr. Ira Byock, a physician, is founder and chief medical officer of the Providence St. Joseph Health Institute for Human Caring in Torrance, California, professor of community health and family medicine at the Dartmouth Geisel School of Medicine, and former director of palliative medicine at the Dartmouth-Hitchcock Medical Center. As an advocate for palliative care of aging and end-of-life patients, he is opposed to older people "dying badly and too soon." He sees the benefits of extending psychedelic-assisted therapies to palliative care of the aging and dying. "I've had patients who have literally said to me that they'd rather be pushed down a flight of stairs than have to face a future of crap care in some facility at the end of their lives." Byock, who is sixty-seven, has said, "I'm a child of the '60s, and there are legitimate medical uses of psychedelics when we're talking about end-of-life wellbeing issues."[224]

Current medical research on psychedelics is supported by the Multidisciplinary Association of Psychedelic Studies (MAPS). According to Brad Burge, Director of MAPS Strategic Communications, "We believe that drug policy should be grounded in science and compassion, so MAPS' current policy priorities are eliminating barriers to psychedelic and marijuana research and promoting harm reduction. … MAPS' mission is to develop medical, legal, and cultural contexts for the careful and beneficial use of psychedelics. In these contexts, no one would be criminalized for the possession or use of psychedelics, or any drugs. People would have access to legal, regulated markets, both medical and otherwise, to safely benefit from intentional psychedelic use."[225]

Mushroom species containing psilocybin are currently FDA Schedule I drugs, a designation for drugs of no medicinal value, possession of which is a felony. In 2018, researchers at Johns Hopkins recommended psilocybin be reclassified as a Schedule IV drug, as are Xanax and many other prescription drugs. Denver, Colorado, and Oakland, California, have effectively decriminalized mushrooms containing psilocybin; Oakland has decriminalized all entheogens or plant medicines. Oregon and California may allow medical research and treatment using psilocybin in 2020 depending on voter outcome. However, federal reclassification of any psychedelic is likely to take several years.[226]

Lynn Twist, introduced in Chapter 10 and founder of the Soul of Money Institute, is described as a "visionary committed to alleviating poverty and hunger and supporting social justice and environmental sustainability." She is also cofounder of the Pachamama Alliance, which empowers indigenous people of the Amazon rain forest to preserve their lands and culture. The Pachamama Alliance also conducts "transformative travel immersions" in partnership with indigenous people, who traditionally and currently use spiritual medicinal plants, including ayahuasca, datura, and San Pedro, to teach participants about the deeper reality of our connection to nature.[227] Among this organization's offerings is an online course called Awakening the Dreamer, "a transformative educational program that explores the challenges facing humanity at this critical moment in time and the opportunities we as a human family have to create a new future."[228]

Tim Ferriss, podcaster, entrepreneur, and author of *The 4-Hour Workweek*, a *New York Times* best-selling business book, has revealed his own experiences with psychedelics. In a significant and influential interview with psychologist James Fadiman, author of *The Psychedelic Explorer's Guide*,[229] he reviewed the history, current use, and potentials of psychedelics. Fadiman is arguably the most respected authority on psychedelics and their use, and since the 1960s has been engaged in extensive research into the medical and psychological benefits of psychedelics. During this podcast interview, Ferriss discussed with Fadiman "the immediate and long-term effects of psychedelics when used for spiritual purposes (high dose), therapeutic purposes (moderate dose), and problem-solving purposes (low dose)." Fadiman gave an overview of "best practices for safe 'entheogenic' voyages learned through his more than 40 years of experience – from the benefits of having a sensitive guide during a session (and how to be one) to the importance of the setting and pre-session intention. ... Cautioning that psychedelics are not for everyone, [he] dispels the myths and misperceptions. He explains how – in his opinion – psychedelics, used properly, can lead not only to healing but also to scientific breakthroughs and spiritual epiphanies."[230]

Microdosing, said to be common for many years among technology innovators in Silicon Valley, for example, involves ingesting a subperceptual dose of a psychedelic, typically one-tenth of a full LSD or psilocybin "trip" dose, in an amount too low (ca. 10 μg or 0.25 g, respectively) to experience any "mind-altering" or other side effects but high enough to produce sustained impacts on mental focus, curiosity, creative thinking, problem-solving, and general well-being over time.[231] The Third Wave website, for example, provides advice, recommendations, precautions, and preparations for microdosing.[232] An overview of microdosing may be found in the *Harm Reduction Journal*, "Psychedelic microdosing benefits and challenges: an empirical codebook," which was based on qualitative reports from a sample of 278 microdosers.[233]

Author and law professor Ayelet Waldman, in her 2017 book, *A Really Good Day*, describes how over a month the transformative experience of LSD microdosing made a rapid and sustainable difference to her mood, marriage, work, and overall well-being. She was influenced by the recommendations and precautions for microdosing made by Dr. James Fadiman. When she apprehensively began microdosing and documenting her experience, knowing it was illegal and not knowing fully what to expect despite many assurances, she discovered that her "keyboard is not exploding in psychedelic fireworks, lightning bolts shooting from the letters." She felt "no transcendent sense of oneness with the universe and with the divine. On the contrary [she] felt normal." As she wrote in her book, "Well, except for one thing: I'm content and relaxed. I'm busy, but not stressed. That might be normal for some people, but it isn't for me." Despite her great academic and professional successes, Waldman had frequently been clinically depressed and at times passively suicidal, an ongoing malaise that affected her ability to live a life of full potential and enjoyment as a lawyer, professor, author, wife, and mother. She concludes her book with, "that day when I got out of my own head, stepped into the circle, and embraced the moment, in the rain – that was a really good day." [234]

Waldman took 10 μg of LSD every three days over a strict thirty-day period. I have used a different substance and protocol. I have ingested 0.25 grams of potent, dried, encapsulated psilocybin mushrooms (*Psilocybe cubensis,* Ecuador variety) from a very trusted single source every third day for a longer period.[235] One could expect the results would be similar, and from her writing it would appear they were. However, I was not struggling to overcome the intense bouts of depression and anxiety experienced by Waldman prior to her experiment – and did not go into my own experiment with the intention of relief. For me, it was to seek greater focus and creativity, even creative inspiration and more intense curiosity. I have not been disappointed. And one thing I learned, and continue to struggle with, is that it matters significantly where I put my focus. Focus will increase, concentration will be there, but am I focusing on what really matters most to me? In my curiosity, am I focusing on my intention for the day – my goals? Or am I going down rabbit holes to chase every interesting, worthwhile "shiny object" that pops up on my computer screen or iPhone and intrudes, demanding attention – now! Being in the flow is a wonderful place to be, especially when that flow is getting me closer to where I say I want to be – like finishing this chapter!

One day, I experimented by increasing the dose to 1.0 gram. What I then experienced for about four hours I can only describe as I wrote, "everything is normal, just more – enhanced" with complete control, inspiration, and great curiosity. I drove to my favorite labyrinth nearby – in a small wooded copse, a memorial garden behind a Presbyterian church – a simple seven-circuit classical labyrinth made of earth and stones. While there were no visual effects, this was a time of great mindfulness, being in the present moment, allowing any negative or trivial thoughts to easily slide out of the way, opening to insights. No buzzers, no bells, no kaleidoscopic bursts of colorful fractal patterns expanding and then receding into infinity. None of that. I can do without such entertainment. One interesting inspiration gleaned during this one-gram experiment (of no interest to anyone other than myself) was how to improve character dialog in a novel I am slowly writing. Little doses, little things, little insights. Several weeks later, I increased the dosage to 1.5 grams, returned to the labyrinth and wrote poetry. I don't write poetry! This amount also increased my sociability.

Now, at the time of writing this, I have not experienced anything too much stronger psychedelically since my early twenties, certainly no dose that may be termed "heroic". I am not looking to be entertained; I am not bored. But I do know – I remember – the great potential for self-discovery and reconnecting with a living nature, not a nature just here to decorate our landscapes and our front lawns, not nature as pretty pictures or a commodity to use and exploit as we see fit in a Trumpian dystopia – as though it was all made just for us to use as we wish. I do know that nature is not a commodity but rather a partnership.

I don't know when or if I will take that next step with a much higher dose leading to an understanding of brief ego dissolution, but when I do it will be different this time. This would not be just "dropping a tab of Orange Sunshine" with a bunch of friends on a Saturday and see what happens, awkwardly giggling throughout the experience, missed opportunities. Been there. Done that. This time there would be preparation with intention, guidance without expectation, and integration in a way that could bring the experience, its profound lessons and insights, back into my everyday apparent reality with focused action towards change.

Psycho-spiritual and psychedelic integration coaching as well as psychedelic-assisted psychotherapy are new iterations on ancient tools in our human quest for consciousness transformation and in support of mind-body-spirit alignment. Both tools have become more common, nearly mainstream, in the last few years. Psycho-spiritual coaching may be described as a "holistic approach to personal and professional wellness that unites traditional psychological theories and inclusive spiritual principles. Its purpose is to assist individuals on their personal path to wholeness and wellness, guiding them toward achieving their highest potential in all areas of their lives. This unique approach to coaching considers the mind, body, and spirit, aiming to unify them in the service of personal development and transformation. As everyone is unique, so is each psychospiritual coaching experience. Through the client-coach relationship, diverse ideas and approaches can be explored with the aim of supporting the client's journey toward personal fulfillment."[236]

Psycho-spiritual coaching alignment pathways that support deep transformation and moving into action include "experiencing the moment," to acknowledge the intuitive wisdom of the body and explore emotions, and "embracing the shadow." The latter examines the inner realm, exploring multiple parts of the psyche and embracing positive shadow-side intentions, thereby connecting to a deeper source of inner wisdom for long-term, sustained healing. The shadow refers to the unconscious parts of your personality that your conscious ego has neither recognized nor acknowledged. "The shadow," wrote Jung, is "that hidden, repressed, for the most part inferior and guilt-laden personality whose ultimate ramifications reach back into the realm of our animal ancestors and so comprise the whole historical aspect of the unconscious."[237]

Shadow work involves "pulling out" from the psyche a shadow personality, a previously unacknowledged part, to be confronted, accepted, and integrated into our awareness. "Only in facing the shadow can we harness its energy. Ignoring it will not make it go away and may well give it license to manifest in destructive ways."[238] However, the shadow, as representing unacknowledged parts of our psyche, does have positive features important for personality integration and mental health. In an interview, Caroline Myss discussed the meaning of shadow, and said, "Shadow is that which you have yet to learn about yourself. … The spiritual path is the path of self-knowledge." Our shadow aspects need to be faced; they are not evil, not wrong. Shadow is not a polarity of good or bad, right or wrong.[239]

Connie Zweig, a Jungian psychotherapist and meditation teacher, specializes in shadow work and spiritual counseling. She has written extensively on how the "shadow side" of our personality, rather than being seen only as dark or evil, something to be avoided, is instead a source of emotional richness and vitality to be used as part of a pathway to emotional healing and living a more authentic life.[240] Dr. Zweig is currently completing a book focused on the shadow and the aging process.

Psychedelic integration coaching has been described by Sherree Malcolm Godasi, a professional psychedelic integration coach in Los Angeles, as "the bridge between the mystical and ineffable psychedelic realm and our everyday default world [with] the dual aim of maximizing the profound insights gleaned in altered states while reducing potential harms from challenging experiences related to returning to a standard state of consciousness. Through integration, the lessons turn into sustained healing, knowledge into personal and communal mastery, and visions into reality. Psychedelic substance engagement may impact the journeyer on a multitude of levels: cognitively, emotionally, spiritually, and physically. … Through integration, the visions turn into practice – turning into habits, into a lifestyle, and into healing, growth, and self-actualization." [241]

There are three standard components of a therapeutic psychedelic experience:

1. *Set* has to do with the mind-set and personality of the individual undergoing the experience. Critical to the experience is having a clear intention before beginning but without expectations. What is important is the individual's mood and attitude toward the

experience at the time of ingestion, and this would ideally be in accord with intention.

2. *Setting* includes the social and environmental surroundings at the time of the experience. The physical setting must be safe and free from disturbances and interruptions. Depending on the weather, many people prefer at least part of the experience to be in a safe, natural setting outdoors.
3. *Support* begins immediately and continues throughout the experience. The trusted sitter or coach must have an established skill set and follow clear guidelines and rules that are time-tested.

Psychedelic integration sessions occur both prior to and after the experience itself. The first session, or several sessions, is called the *pre-psychedelic preparation coaching* session. This phase (Preparation or Release) may be accomplished over several sessions prior to ingestion of a psychedelic. Time is spent preparing for the experience to ensure maximum benefit. This is when the individual identifies exactly why they are taking the psychedelic and what their specific intentions are going into the experience. The individual is likely to want to gain some insight into a problem. However, it is important to not go into the experience with any expectation. Depending on set and setting, the same person can experience very difference responses on different occasions given the same psychedelic and even the same dosage.

After the psychedelic experience (the Navigation or Receive phase), comes one or more *post-psychedelic integration coaching* sessions (Integration or Return phase). These third phase sessions are a time for recovery, reflection, processing, and taking action – all elements of integrating the experience so that it has the capability for long-term, sustainable transformation of consciousness through action. Integration may occur soon after the experience but more than likely over a period of several days. This is the time for processing any insights discovered during the experience and for integrating the experience into the individual's life. Understanding the experience, messages that may have been received or interpreted, are integrated in view of the original intention established during the first Preparation phase. Aided by the therapist or coach, the individual stays in the process to allow for "continued and deeper self-reflection, integration of the insights and wisdom, and application of strategies, skills, and tools to enable deep healing and awareness for inner guidance, spiritual awakening, and actualization. It is recommended to book 3 - 5 Integration Sessions following the entheogenic experience for optimal benefit."[242]

Deborah Servetnick, a psychedelic integration coach near Baltimore, Maryland,[243] emphasized the importance of these two pre- and post-psychedelic phases, allowing for adequate time to prepare for the experience and intensive follow-up reflection as soon as possible. However, "integration is as transformative as the trip," she told me, "and as an integration provider, I am aware of the 'recreational' user who doesn't understand the insight and reconnection integration offers. Lack of preparation can also lead to a disappointing or even negative trip experience. Integration is the way to sustain and optimize your trip."

Exploring your consciousness, how it can be expanded or enhanced through a variety of experiential means, is clearly not for everyone. I get that. But not all methods require the ingestion of an illegal psychedelic substance, to be sure. The subject is not to be taken lightly, and I am not so cavalier as to advocate this for everyone. Finding effective ways to strengthen your mindfulness, however you choose, such as through breathwork, yoga, or meditation, should be the goal.

This chapter has discussed how consciousness expansion techniques and experiences, if undertaken, may be integrated into your life to effect sustained transformation. All the REWIREMENT steps you've gone through to get to this point may be considered preliminary to being here right now, a consideration of this step. If you opt to dive more deeply, your intention-setting pre-psychedelic preparation sessions will draw from what you have experienced and learned about yourself in the earlier steps.

"The things which are seen are temporal, but the things which are not seen are eternal."[244] St. Francis of Assisi wrote in the thirteenth century,

"There are beautiful wild forces within us. Let them turn the mills inside and fill sacks that feed even heaven."[245] And Carl Jung has written that "the dream is the small hidden door in the deepest and most intimate sanctum of the soul, which opens to that primeval cosmic night that was soul long before there was conscious ego and will be soul far beyond what a conscious ego could ever reach."[246]

In the next chapter, we continue examining the inward journey, focusing on understanding how spirituality and maintaining a spiritual practice are supportive of conscious aging, transformation, and living your purpose in a creative life.

Chapter 12:
China Cat Sunflower

"While we recognize a God, it is really only the Self that we have separated from ourselves and worship as outside us; but all the time it is our own true Self, the one and only God."

– Swami Vivekananda

"The first peace, which is the most important, is that which comes within the souls of people when they realize their relationship, their oneness with the universe and all its powers, and when they realize that at the center of the universe dwells the Great Spirit, and that this center is really everywhere, it is within each of us."

– Black Elk, Oglala Lakota (Sioux) medicine man

"To experience our path, is to acknowledge the possibility that 'something greater' is attempting to live itself out through our lives."

– Lauren Artress

"At any rate, the point is that God is what nobody admits to being, and everybody really is."

– Alan Watts

Step 9: kNow the Numinous

I stopped going to church when I was fourteen. Nothing particularly objectionable or wrong with it really. I just lost interest; it never made any sense to me. But I did love the pageantry, the rituals, the history, and the musty, woody smells of the place, an Episcopal church in Alexandria, Virginia. I got confirmed, was an acolyte, sang in the choir, carried a flag and sometimes the cross in procession, and helped the priests with Holy Communion. Now there were good people there to be sure, and there were famous people (Gerald Ford was an usher before he moved on to greater things) and some rich people, privileged white people – WASPs. But it really did seem to me that Holy Communion for most adults of that ilk was just a prelude to gin and tonics at the country club. And, as I said, it never made much sense. I identified with Ram Dass when I heard him say, "I was Jewish on my parents' side."

Scott Adams, in the persona of Dilbert, sums up many of our attitudes about organized religion: "The creator of the universe works in mysterious ways. But he uses a base ten counting system and likes round numbers. … Informed decision-making comes from a long tradition of guessing and then blaming others for inadequate results. … Nothing defines humans better than their willingness to do irrational things in the pursuit of phenomenally unlikely payoffs. This is the principle behind lotteries, dating, and religion."

But we can approach the subject of spirituality, as opposed to organized religion, in a less sarcastic way. I use the word *numinous*, from the Greek *noumenon*, which refers to "an unknowable reality underlying all things." *Numinous* describes or relates to the power, presence, or realization of a divinity, "having a strong religious or spiritual quality; indicating or suggesting the presence of a divinity."[247] In 1923, Lutheran theologian Rudolf Otto wrote of the numinous as a "non-rational, non-sensory experience or feeling whose primary and immediate object is outside the self."[248]

In this chapter, you will continue the REWIREMENT process by understanding how spirituality and maintaining a spiritual practice are supportive of conscious aging and living your purpose in a creative life. Psychiatrist and transpersonal psychology pioneer Stanislav Grof stated, "We need a vast expansion of what we think the psyche is. … We need to recognize the importance of spirituality in naturalistic science. … We need to incorporate spirituality as the critical dimension in the psyche."[249] This is the inward journey of self-discovery and personal transformation in which our hero, Odysseus, ultimately returns home to Ithaca, to where he began, but is transformed.

The first time I saw a dead body, a cadaver, was in 1974, when I was taking a course on human anatomy at Berkeley. Most of us in my laboratory group had never seen a dead body before, and we were nervous – at least I was. Such is the nature of our avoidance and denial of anything having to do with aging, suffering, or death. It was just too remote, but soon I was going to face it – that dead body under the rubber sheet in the adjoining room. Several weeks before, Patty Hearst was famously abducted a few blocks from my apartment. Jokes had already formed, nervous jokes, you know the kind, trying to get us to calm our minds before facing what up to then had been an unspeakable horror. And to make matters worse, I was about to participate in the dissection of this thing. So anyhow, as we were waiting, one joke that was circulating around the room was this: "What's a Hearst burger? Lift the bun, and the Patty's gone." OK, maybe not so funny. But it did help me get through the novel experience of that morning. So, what's the point of all this? The point is that once the sheet was removed, and I saw what was underneath, I realized quite immediately this was not even a man. Whatever had made this package of flesh, this cadaver, a human had long gone. After that, although respected, the body was just a subject for dissection and learning. Further to my point, I realized this something, this life force, was the soul that had left.

My uncle Lloyd, an attorney most of his life, told me on his hospice deathbed that after this, there is nothing – like turning off a light switch, "when the music's over, turn out the lights."[250] I seriously doubt he really believed that. I believe this was how he was processing the moment, coming to terms with his impending ego-dissolution and loss of everything he had, knew, and held dear. But even if he did believe this, deep in his heart and soul, it doesn't matter. Each of us must make sense of our lives and an afterlife, if we believe in such things, and what that means to us.

About ten years ago, my brother Chip, known to most as Jim, died alone and suddenly, presumably within seconds, from an uncommon genetic disorder, idiopathic hypertrophic cardiomyopathy, a type of heart attack made "famous" by the sudden deaths of otherwise healthy athletes. There really are no signs or symptoms of the disorder; my brother was in excellent health at age fifty-eight, had no knowledge of any heart problems, and was not taking any medication. You may have heard of athletes who have just suddenly dropped dead; that is often hypertrophic cardiomyopathy. I read a medical journal article that said, "Typically the first symptom is death." I do not think the researcher was trying to be funny. This is a rare genetic disorder that appears to have fallen to my brother but not to me, my sister, or any of our children as far as we know. But his death brought home to me, in a very intimate way, how precious our lives are – and how precarious. Elisabeth Kübler-Ross, a Swiss American psychiatrist and influential writer on the subject of death and dying, wrote in 1969, "It's only when we truly know and understand that we have a limited time on earth – and that we have no way of knowing when our time is up – that we will begin to live each day to the fullest, as if it was the only one we had."[251]

Matthew Fox, author and Episcopal priest, gave a lecture at a recent Sage-ing International conference I attended on spiritual eldering and conscious aging in Chaska, Minnesota. Expulsed from the Catholic Church for revealing certain inconvenient inconsistencies, Fox wanted to reinvent the Western traditions of Christianity with a movement toward genuine spirituality removed from rigid dogma and superstition. When I briefly spoke with him after his talk, I knew I was directly in the presence of a great human, an articulate man of honest spirituality, knowledge, and humility. He said our "fear of death is the ultimate neurosis" and a product of our society's "patriarchal version of death." He called to us to wake up – to resurrect – in this lifetime so we "don't have to worry about the next."

Creation spirituality, not to be confused with anti-evolution fundamentalist "creationism," is an ancient philosophy. Matthew Fox has defined and described the principles of creation spirituality, as well as "The Four Vias," its four paths. He wrote, "Honoring all of creation as Original Blessing, Creation Spirituality integrates the wisdom of Eastern and Western spirituality and global indigenous cultures, with the emerging scientific understanding of the universe, and the passion of creativity. It is both a tradition and a movement, celebrated by mystics and agents of social change from every age and culture. It is also the tradition of the historical Jesus himself since it is the wisdom tradition of Israel."[252]

There are many psychological states that across time, cultures, and religions are appropriately called "spiritual" or "mystical." They are often very dramatic, not subtle. In his book, *DMT the Spirit Molecule: A Doctor's Revolutionary Research into the Biology of Near-Death and Mystical Experiences*, Rick Strassman has written, "All spiritual disciplines describe quite psychedelic accounts of the transformative experiences, whose attainment motivate their practice. Blinding white light, encounters with demonic and angelic entities, ecstatic emotions, timelessness, heavenly sounds, feelings of having died and being reborn, contacting a powerful and loving presence underlying all of reality – these experiences cut across all denominations. They also are characteristic of a fully psychedelic DMT experience."[253]

There is an entertaining and illuminating discussion, available on YouTube, on the nature of mystical experience and spirituality during an interview, more of an interplay, between Ram Dass and Matthew Fox.[254] The discussion took place at the first State of the World conference held in San Francisco in September 1995 and should be watched. Some of the main points of discussion included their individual views on psychedelics, spirituality, and mystical experiences that arise from different perspectives as well as the intimate link among well-being, creativity, spirituality, and depression. Fox and Ram Dass discussed the importance of ritual to humans and maintaining, reviving, or reinventing some of our earlier traditions surrounding ritual, still used in some cultures, but lost in our modern consumer culture of TV advertising and its generated feelings of personal inadequacy. No rituals, for example, effectively mark our passage from one life stage to the next. They discussed conscious aging, rites of passage and the importance of the conscious aging movement to producing a more socially just and environmentally sound society.

In the interview, Fox said, "We are all born mystics with a natural connection to the whole." But we have lost a sense of the sacred. It is through ritual where humans "connect with the cosmic," have real encounters, and is the basis for community sharing and fellowship. The emergence of the "rave scene" and popularization of MDMA, or ecstasy, at the time of the interview (1995) was seen as a way in which younger people, in the absence of any meaningful or sacred ritual and fellowship, were creating, through trance dance and community worship, transformational models for deeper spiritual and human connection.

Fox and Ram Dass spoke of how the Grateful Dead and its huge devoted following, although not specifically identified with the later rave scene, was a similar phenomenon. Ram Dass said he viewed the group "as close to a living spiritual process that had the minimum amount of oppressive structures. It was clearly ritualized, and the band didn't consider themselves other than a catalyst for a process that very definitely needed the audience for the totality of it to happen. And I feel that was a 25-year living religious experience." Fox agreed that "it really was a ritual for a lot of people who identified with it" and that the band represented something bigger. "They were not just doing rock; they were doing ritual. They blurred the boundaries between art and spirituality." This was indeed a sort of "healing of the masses, a task of religious prophets." Fox continued, "So in many ways, I think that the band was doing a religious task in addition to a musical task." Anyone, including myself, who ever went to a Grateful Dead concert, certainly while Jerry Garcia was still alive, can probably understand what Ram Dass and Fox were talking about because we experienced it.

In an interview with Robert Forte for the book, *Entheogens and the Future of Religion*, Jack Kornfield, psychologist and founder of Spirit Rock Meditation Center, discussed psychedelic experiences and spiritual practice:

> "I took LSD and other psychedelic's at Dartmouth though I was studying Eastern thought even before then, but they came hand-in-hand as they did for many people. It is true for the majority of American Buddhist teachers that they had experience with psychedelics either right after they started their spiritual practices or prior to it. … Many people who took LSD, mushrooms, or whatever it was, along with a little spiritual reading of the *Tibetan Book of the Dead* or some Zen texts, had the gates of wisdom open to a certain extent. They began to see that their limited consciousness is only one plane and one level and that there were a thousand new things to discover about the mind. There are many new realms, new perspectives on birth and death; on the nature of mind and consciousness as the field of creation, rather than the mechanical result of having a body, the biological result; and on the myth of separation and the truth of the oneness of things. Great kinds of wisdom opened up, and for some people, their hearts, too. … Even though there were some transformations from these experiences, they tended to fade for a lot of people, at least aspects of them. … And so, people undertook various kinds of spiritual disciplines. They did *kundalini yoga* and *bastrika* breathing, or they did serious *hatha yoga* … light and concentration exercises, visualizations, or Buddhist practices as a way to get back to those profound and compelling states that had come through psychedelics."[255]

On a cool, vibrant November morning in 2017, I had the great fortune to be in Dharamsala in the Himalayan foothills of Himachal Pradesh in India. That morning, I had a discussion with Venerable Khandro, a Buddhist nun from Australia, as we walked together down the hill from a meditation center into town. I asked her about self-actualization vis-à-vis Buddhist concepts, and she was familiar with Maslow's hierarchy.

It is clear that self-actualization does not specifically acknowledge the impermanence of body and mind as espoused by Buddhism nor does it equal enlightenment, a transcendence of the physical. Actualization can happen in multiple past lives, the present, or future lives. It may be viewed as a step on a spiritual path – not an end, not enlightenment, which is the ultimate aspiration through many lives. Enlightenment comes with recognition of and resignation to impermanence as well as unity with all things. Thich Nhat Hanh wrote, "We are here to awaken from our illusion of separateness."

While self-actualization may be achieved within a single lifetime, a higher level within the "hierarchy of needs," recognized by Abraham Maslow later in life, is self-transcendence, when a person is ultimately motivated by values that transcend the impermanence of personal self or ego and thus enters a connection with Spirit, not unlike enlightenment as defined in the spiritual philosophy of Buddhism. Sri Chinmoy has written, "There is only one dream that will always be perfect in your lifetime, and that is the dream of self-transcendence."[256] "Self-transcendence gives us joy in boundless measure. When we transcend ourselves, we do not compete with others. We do not compete with the rest of the world, but at every moment we compete with ourselves. We compete only with our previous achievements. And each time we surpass our previous achievements, we get joy."[257] Self-transcendence is a higher service to others, above one's self-interests, a sort of higher-level self-actualization, realization, and acceptance. Maslow noted that "transcendence refers to the very highest and most inclusive or holistic levels of human consciousness, behaving and relating, as ends rather than means, to oneself, to significant others, to human beings in general, to other species, to nature, and to the cosmos."[258]

In *Man's Search for Meaning* (1946), which may have profoundly influenced Maslow's later reconsideration of self-actualization, Viktor Frankl wrote, "The real aim of human existence cannot be found in what is called self-actualization. Human existence is essentially self-transcendence rather than self-actualization. Self-actualization is not a possible aim at all; for the simple reason that the more a [person] would strive for it, the more [they] would miss it. For only to the extent to which [people] commit [themselves] to the fulfilment of [their] life's meaning, to this extent [they] also actualize [themselves.] In other words, self-actualization cannot be attained if it is made an end in itself, but only as a side-effect of self-transcendence."[259]

I went through a brief period of allowing and actually paying strangers to draw on me, and I think I have given up that obsession. But I am especially happy to have a little tattoo on my left arm, a simple wave inspired by the wisdom of Thich Nhat Hanh, who said, "Enlightenment, for a wave in the ocean, is the moment the wave realizes it is water. When we realize we are not separate but a part of the huge ocean of everything, we become enlightened."

There is a sort of constant chatter in my mind, what the Buddhists call the "monkey mind," a term meaning "unsettled, restless, capricious, whimsical, fanciful, inconstant, confused, indecisive, uncontrollable."[260] We are constantly telling ourselves stories from the past and placing ourselves into the future in our mind. None of that has anything to do with being in the present, being mindful, except for being aware of this continual self-talk. That's the point of meditation – to let that internal, incessant self-talk subside and bring you into the present. To just slow down.

To say you can't take it with you is not entirely true. You just can't take anything physical with you. All the rest? You got that. You own it. Karma. Whatever you want to call whatever it is we're doing here. You can fix it now; you can fix it later. Doesn't matter – unless it does. But whatever "it" is, it will – and must – be fixed. Perhaps in some unexpected way. In Hawaiian, *kuleana pono* means to get your life in order, or your space in order; make it *pono*, make it good and spiritual.

Spiritual practice comes in many forms. My personal favorite is a form of mindfulness, the labyrinth, which can be done by walking a full labyrinth or by using a small desktop finger labyrinth. A labyrinth is a walking meditation, a metaphor of personal journey, and a tool for transformation. Unlike a maze, there is a single pathway spiraling to the center and then taken back out the same way. You return to where you began. The three phases or steps of a labyrinth walk are Release (walking in), Receive (at the center), and Return (walking back out). In her engaging and informative TEDx talk, "A Journey to Self-Discovery: Lessons of the Labyrinth," Kristin Keyes described what a labyrinth is and how it helps "quiet the mind, guide healing, deepen self-knowledge, and empower creativity."[261]

Chartres Cathedral labyrinth

Over several days at a retreat in New Harmony, Indiana, I was trained to facilitate labyrinth walks as a spiritual practice through Veriditas by Rev. Lauren Artress, a psychotherapist and Episcopal priest based at Grace Cathedral in San Francisco. The word *veriditas* originated with the twelfth-century German abbess and saint, Hildegard von Bingen, and is a blending of two Latin words for "green" and "truth." Her intent was to describe the divine healing power of nature as transferred from plants to humans. The mission of Veriditas is to inspire "personal and planetary change and renewal through the labyrinth experience … by training and supporting labyrinth facilitators around the world and offering meaningful events that promote further understanding of the labyrinth as a tool for personal and community transformation." Veriditas's vision "is that the labyrinth experience guides us in developing the higher level of human awareness we need to thrive in the 21st century."[262]

In *Walking a Sacred Path*,[263] Artress recounts how she had a precise replica of the eleven-circuit Medieval labyrinth on the floor of Chartres Cathedral in France built at Grace Cathedral. She defined the labyrinth as "a spiritual tool that has many applications in various settings. It reduces stress, quiets the mind, and opens the heart. It is a walking meditation, a path of prayer, and a blue-print where psyche meets Spirit. … To walk a sacred path is to discover our inner sacred space: that core of feeling that is waiting to have life breathed back into it through symbols, archetypal forms like the labyrinth, rituals, stories, and myths. … It quiets the mind and opens the soul."

The labyrinth is an effective meditation practice that can be used to rediscover a spiritual center, your purpose or path, and to ponder a question or concern. Walking the labyrinth serves to promote our mindfulness in daily life and to be transformative. Vietnamese Buddhist monk and peace activist Thich Nhat Hanh has written, "Mindfulness shows us what is happening in our bodies, our emotions, our minds, and in the world. Through mindfulness, we avoid harming ourselves and others." According to Sylvia Boorstein, psychotherapist and founding teacher of Spirit Rock Meditation Center in Marin County, California, "Mindfulness is the aware, balanced acceptance of the present experience. It isn't more complicated than that. It is opening to or receiving the present moment, pleasant or unpleasant, just as it is, without either clinging to it or rejecting it."

The labyrinth walking meditation represents an archetype, a mystical ritual found in most of the world's religious and secular traditions for thousands of years. It is a metaphor, not magic. A labyrinth is an arrangement of stones placed in a spiral by humans. The magic comes from you, from within. That's where the magic happens. An approach to visualizing the transformative power of walking the labyrinth is based on the threefold path of:

1. *Release* – walking in, likened to purgation, letting go of the details of your life
2. *Receive* – being at the center, likened to illumination, receiving what is there for you to receive
3. *Return* – walking back out the same way you came in, likened to union, empowering you to take back into your life and the world what you discovered at the center

Today, there are thousands of labyrinths linked in a global movement. The World-Wide Labyrinth Locator[264] website is jointly maintained by Veriditas and The Labyrinth Society to provide an easy, accessible and searchable database of labyrinths around the world. Try it; there is bound to be one near you.

Nancy Eubel, a quantum healing hypnosis practitioner and former executive director of A.R.E.,[265] prepared an exercise as part of a workshop based on her book, *Mindwalking: Rewriting Your Past to Create Your Future.*[266] The following is an excerpt from one of the exercises in that workshop, included here with her permission:

> "Labyrinths are a type of mandala found in many cultures. A mandala is a concentric diagram that represents wholeness. It has spiritual and ritual significance and is sometimes called a cosmic diagram. Its geometric art represents wholeness and sacred space and reminds us of our relation to the infinite – the quantum dimensions that extend beyond and within our bodies and minds. Walking the path of the labyrinth can focus the mind, slow the breathing, and induce a peaceful state. Some see it as a journey to an individual's center and then back out into the world. Each person experiences this spiritual journey

in her/his own way. That experience may be profound, or more subtle.

"When you walk a labyrinth, you turn 180 degrees each time you enter a different circuit. While shifting your direction you also shift your awareness from right brain to left brain, or vice versa, balancing the two hemispheres of the brain and also balancing the chakras (points of contact between the Spirit and the physical body, which might be likened to electrical outlets lined up along the spine).

"The labyrinth is a very powerful tool, which can provide you with the insights you need in order to recognize and transform limiting thoughts. You can do this by

- Selecting a question and focusing on it as you begin
- Entering the labyrinth and following it to the center
- Asking your question in a meditative way at the center
- Walking out and exiting the labyrinth, then pausing for a moment to allow the answer to come to you, and expressing thanks
- Anticipating and being watchful for additional guidance that comes in the hours and days after your walk.

"The benefits that can be gained are not limited to walking the labyrinth with your feet; they can also be reaped from walking a portable version with your finger. You do this by selecting your question and then using your right or left index finger (depending upon whether you are right or left-handed) to make the circuit of the labyrinth. A finger labyrinth has been included for your use.

"Exercise: Follow the steps as outlined and 'walk' the labyrinth asking this question: 'What must I do to maintain the connection with Higher Consciousness?' In the future you can use this labyrinth for your own questions any time you choose."

FINGER LABYRINTH

In his book, *The Divine Human*, John Robinson wrote of the modern wizards, elders who "are pioneers of a new and mystical consciousness that is constantly looking through the walls of denial and intellectualization. Sacred consciousness blossoms when we intentionally experience and integrate this awakened state into our lives. … We join together in a radical and profound shift in human awareness." There are great opportunities for awakenings and transformation through our aging. Robinson poses several questions, including: "What if we discover in this awakening that we are already divine? What if this realization transforms our very nature and purpose in the world?"[267]

I would like to conclude this chapter with a quote from astrophysicist Hubert Reeves, who wrote, "Man is the most insane species. He worships an invisible God and destroys a visible Nature, unaware that this Nature he's destroying is this God he's worshiping."

This chapter has reviewed how spirituality, mindfulness, and maintaining a spiritual practice are beneficial to conscious aging and living your purpose in a creative life. The next chapter will discuss how reengaging with community service and environmental and social justice activism, to the extent you feel compelled, responsible, and able, are important elements of conscious aging.

Chapter 13:

Not Fade Away

"The more one forgets himself –
by giving himself to a cause to serve or another person to love – the more human he is and the more he actualizes himself."
– Viktor Frankl, *Man's Search for Meaning*

"You are sacred, you are good, you belong, you have purpose ... and every time you raise your hand, you help other people know they are not alone."
– Lyla June Johnston[268]

"The most common way people give up their power is by thinking they don't have any."
– Alice Walker

Step 10: Take Back Your Power

Martin Seligman, psychologist and advocate of positive psychology, has written about the conditions for happiness, well-being, and a meaningful life. He has said, "You use your highest strengths and talents to belong to and serve something you believe is larger than the self."[269] In this chapter, you conclude the REWIREMENT process by understanding that facing the pain you feel for the world, empowering yourself to engage in community service as well as environmental and social justice activism, might just make you happier if not save you.

New worlds are always being born, but something is happening now – big time. As we become suspended between two worlds, one dying the other becoming, trying to find or build a bridge, we can always evolve, if not just adapt, by creating or recreating ourselves at any age. You are not becoming fossilized, locked into inflexible patterns of thought and action – unless you allow yourself to be a fossil. You can recover the awareness of your sacredness, your purpose – unless you choose to ignore that. You can embrace your pain and take on a steadfast commitment to change. One day when asked, "What did you do once you knew?" how will you respond? You can choose to channel your strengths, talents, and creative energies for the better and ultimately end your life well. This is important; just stop for a moment and think about that.

As Terry Tempest Williams has said, "we are eroding and evolving at once" both individually and as a society. It is apparent that our democracy, science, ecosystems, climate, decency, compassion, and trust are eroding. As she has asked, "How do we find the strength to not look away from all that is breaking our hearts? What if our undoing leads us to our becoming?" – eroding and evolving at once. Recognize the inevitable reality of all that is now dying. She reminds us also that "our denial is our collusion."[270]

"How do we be fully present to our world," said Joanna Macy, "at a time when the suffering and the prospects for conscious life forms are so grim. The living systems of earth are coming apart under the onslaught of the industrial growth society scrambling for the last dollars. There never has been guarantee for human life."[271]

In Chapter 2, I discussed how for over forty years, I worked in seventeen countries on a variety of environmental projects. But efforts at sustainable biodiversity conservation seemed only temporary, hindered by corruption, inertia, and lack of political will. I felt powerless and disillusioned. I became jaded and cynical. I yearned for something with more tangible results and for a sense of community, something nearly impossible when continually changing gears from country to country, project to project. And with this insecurity, this lack of being grounded, I became very depressed.

If you are a recovering news junkie like me, watching TV news can become an obsession. The hostile, confused, ignorant, and maddening state of the world can, in turn, become reflected in my own inner workings, my "monkey mind" gone wild in a state of delusion and illusion. One day I found myself on the couch (literally and figuratively) watching television news – and getting more and more angry – frustrated with political events. I could not hold back my tears as emotion swelled up in me. Innocent children were being forced away from their parents, who naively thought America might give them a chance for a better life – or just a life – instead of the injustice of cold, heartless cages. We know how that went.

But then it was soon after when I first heard Joanna Macy speaking about uncertainty and a world with no guarantees; it was transformative. Maybe I had heard it before; it seemed familiar. Was it how she said it? Was it because her eyes looked remarkably like my mother's, their shape and color? Or perhaps it was the timing – if heard under happier circumstances, I may have nodded in affirmation and just moved on, business as usual. Here is some of what she said, and how she said it, that touched me so much:

"I know that we're not sure how this story will end. I want so much to feel sure. I want to be able to tell people, 'Don't worry. It's going to be okay.' And you know what? I realize that would not be doing anyone a favor. First of all, we can't know. But secondly, if somehow, we could be given a pill to be convinced, 'Don't worry, it's going to turn out okay,' would that elicit from us our greatest creativity and courage? No. It's that knife edge of uncertainty where we come alive to our truest power. So we do ourselves the favor, we honor ourselves to live with sufficient realism and dignity to know, we're right with that knife edge of uncertainty. And we don't know how it's going to come out; there're no guarantees. Then we realize, 'But wait. There're no guarantees anyway.' … There never has been guarantee for human life. And it's in that uncertainty … that is the nature of life. All the wise ones tell us that. That's where we come alive."[272]

In this way, Joanna Macy urges us to take heart despite the intensity and pain of the current catastrophe inflicted on our biosphere. Our actions have led to a frightening and destabilizing loss of biodiversity, pollution, and climate change, or more specifically climate chaos, the unpredictability of temperature, precipitation, and storms. The following weekend, I went to the National Mall in Washington to join a protest demonstration, the first of many. It felt good. I had not marched in those streets since the Vietnam War. I felt somehow that I had come back.

In these times of crisis, wrote Ron Pevny, "the world teeters on a knife edge between cultural and ecological collapse and cultural transformation. Our world cannot afford to have millions of its citizens (many highly educated and skilled) believing that they are incapable of making a difference in their elder years. The work needs conscious elders who shine as beacons of hope in the darkness of fear, elders championing and modelling life sustaining values and using their wisdom and compassion to heal a wounded planet."[273]

If, like me, you are a boomer (or a proximity), then you may very well have been engaged with environmental and social justice activism when you were younger. This is our time once again; a time to rediscover something most of us "of a certain age" put on hold when we took up the responsibilities of career advancement, economic survival, and having families – becoming a "responsible adult" with kids and a mortgage. We were the generation against the war, championing civil rights and the women's movement, launching the environmental movement. I remember the first Earth Day in April 1970 and making a papier-mâché globe with the continents completely covered with pictures of people to stress overpopulation. But I think the world's population has nearly doubled since then. Some of us also experienced psychedelics and experimented with counterculture movements. Unfortunately, when psychedelics were banned, all the other movements began to be seen by society at large as linked to illegal activity and general "weirdness." These movements were – and still are – put into question and became less valued or important because of this link with what the media, with all their drama, would perpetually portray as elements of a disruptive and subversive counterculture.

One coaching approach to alignment that supports deep transformation is "calling out the power." My coaching mentor, Sharon Brown, once told me, "To call out the power in others requires that we visit our own edges and step into our own power." Community service, giving back, and rekindling a passion for environmental protection and social justice are important elements of conscious aging. You will know you can direct your understanding of ageism and conscious aging, transformation, and passion for change toward service to others and the planet in ways that best resonate with your values, strengths, interests, and abilities. Change in ourselves is fundamental before we can expect to effect change in others or the planet. And collective change, when organized and directed, is powerful. Writer and management consultant Margaret Wheatley wrote that "all change, even very large and powerful change, begins when a few people start talking with one another about something they care about."[274]

I participate in the Elder Action Network (EAN), formerly known as the Conscious Elders Network. EAN is "an educational, non-profit organization fostering a budding movement of vital elders, dedicated to growing in consciousness while actively addressing the demanding challenges facing our country. We work inter-generationally for social and economic justice, environmental stewardship, and sound governance. We bring our multiple talents and resources, offering these in service to the goal of preserving and protecting life for all generations to come."[275] I have engaged in EAN's social justice group, Elder Activists for Social Justice (EASJ), and the climate group, Elders Climate Action (ECA), in addition to the Conscious Living, Aging, and Dying (CLAD) group. More information about joining these groups and their activities can be found on the EAN website.

EAN regularly offers a live, online webinar course, "The Empowered Elder," which I have cofacilitated. The course addresses some fundamental questions, such as "How do we live in ways that will ensure our grandchildren's future?" and "What's my role as an elder in ensuring a healthy future for all?" The course draws from a body of work for transformation, the Work That Reconnects, first developed in 1978 from the teachings and experiential tools of Joanna Macy and others.[276] The 2014 book by Joanna Macy and Molly Brown, *Coming Back to Life*, is an updated comprehensive guide to the Work That Reconnects, which "explores how to evoke creative, compassionate and transformational responses to the ecological crises of our time. Drawing from deep ecology, systems theory, and spiritual traditions, the Work That Reconnects builds motivation, creativity, courage, and solidarity for the transition to a sustainable human culture."[277]

Foundations of the Work That Reconnects are based on "deep ecology, systems thinking, and the resurgence of nondualistic spirituality,"[278] which underlie several of the work's core assumptions. From the Work That Reconnects Network website, quoted here with permission, these assumptions include:

1. "*Our Earth is alive.* It is not a supply house and sewer for the Industrial Growth Society. As most indigenous traditions teach, the Earth is our larger body.
2. "*Our experience of moral pain for our world springs from our interconnectedness with all beings, including humans of all cultures, from which also arise our powers to act on their behalf.* When we deny or repress our pain for the world, or view it as a private pathology, our power to take part in the healing of our world is diminished. Our capacity to respond to our own and others' suffering – that is, the feedback loops that weave us into life – can be unblocked.
3. "*Unblocking occurs when our pain for the world is not only intellectually validated, but also experienced and expressed.* Cognitive information about the social and ecological crises we face is generally insufficient to mobilize us. Only when we allow ourselves to experience our feelings of pain for our world, can we free ourselves from our fears of the pain – including the fear of getting permanently mired in despair or shattered by grief. Only then can we discover the fluid, dynamic character of feelings. Only

then can they reveal on a visceral level our mutual belonging in the web of life and free us to act on our moral authority.

4. "*When we reconnect with life, by willingly enduring our pain for it, the mind retrieves its natural clarity.* We experience not only our interconnectedness in the Earth community and the human community, but also mental eagerness to match this experience with new paradigm thinking. Significant learnings occur as the individual re-orients to wider reaches of identity and self-interest.
5. "*The experience of reconnection with the Earth community arouses desire to act on its behalf, as well as on behalf of humankind.* As we experience our essential desire for the welfare of all beings, Earth's self-healing powers take hold within us. For these powers to function, they must be trusted and acted on. The steps we take can be modest ones, but they should involve some risk to our mental and social comfort, lest we remain caught in old, 'safe' limits. Courage is a great teacher and bringer of joy."[279]

In their article, "Choosing the Story We Want for Our World," Molly Brown and Joanna Macy identify "three stories commonly held in the industrialized world today: Business as Usual, the Great Unraveling, and the Great Turning. All three are boiled-down simplifications of global realities. Nevertheless, taken together, they can offer a useful perspective on the values and beliefs prevalent in the world today." Their book, *Coming Back to Life*, and this article, found on the Work That Reconnects website, go into more detail. But briefly and incompletely, these three stories of our times are summarized here.

- *Business as Usual* is "the story of the Industrial Growth Society, and the European-based colonial empires from which it emerged. It is the dominant enforcing mechanism of a predatory capitalist, imperialist economic system (in other words, the corporate financial military industrial complex) that perpetuates patriarchy and white supremacy for the profit and power of a few. Many people caught up in the Industrial Growth Society assume this story to be the only reality. The defining premise, which we hear from politicians, corporations, corporate-controlled media, and the military, is that there is little need to change the way we in the industrialized world live."

- *The Great Unraveling* is "the story told by scientists, journalists, and activists who have not been bought off or intimidated. Drawing attention to the disasters caused by Business as Usual, their accounts give evidence of the on-going derangement and collapse of biological, ecological, economic, and social systems. … Now the climate itself is unraveling world-wide and the sixth great extinction of species is underway."
- *The Great Turning* "involves the emergence of new and creative human responses, as well as a reawakening of sustainable indigenous traditions, that propel the transition from the Industrial Growth Society to a Life Sustaining Society. Attitudes shift from exploitation to respect, from extraction to regeneration, from competition to cooperation. More and more of us come to see how we are interwoven together as peoples, and that solidarity with one another is a way through these crises." [280]

EAN's "The Empowered Elder" course, designed by a team of EAN elders led by educator and eco-activist Constance Washburn,[281] covers seven main topics, one per week:

1. *Being an Elder* is an introduction to EAN and to the values, roles, and tasks of elderhood. The topic covers what it means to be an elder and ways to transition from being an un-empowered "senior" to an empowered elder.
2. *Growing in Consciousness* is an introduction to mindfulness and the "Story of Oneness" and covers how mindfulness and consciousness growth support our lives and interconnection with the larger living systems of Earth.
3. *Opening to the Crises Facing Our World* is a hard look at the environmental, socioeconomic, and spiritual crises and divisions

present in the world today and how facing these crises and feeling our pain for the world empowers us to take action.

4. *The Great Turning: The Sustainability Revolution* is an introduction to the new sustainable models of environmental, social, and economic systems. The topic covers how to shift from seeing only the problems that we hear so much about in the media to seeing the many solutions and movements around the world for more sustainable and harmonious ways to live with each other and Earth's living systems. The topic then considers how we can be part of the Great Turning and draws from Macy's *Active Hope: How to Face the Mess We're in Without Going Crazy*[282], David Korten's *The Great Turning*,[283] and Paul Hawken's *Blessed Unrest*,[284] among other resources.
5. *Sacred Activism* is an exploration and connection to what is "sacred" and important to us and how to take action from love not hate, from unity not division. The topic focuses on finding our calling, what we are being asked to do now in the role of elder. Resources include Andrew Harvey's *The Hope: A Guide to Spiritual Activism.*[285]
6. *Taking Action Together for the Earth* focuses on planning for how to engage as elders, such as how to form Elder Circles, Climate Action Chapters, or other community action groups. The emphasis is on shifting from "not knowing what I can do" to making a commitment to take action with others on behalf of all life on the planet. Resources include Thomas Berry's *The Great Work: Our Way into the Future.*[286]
7. *Elder Circles, Projects Creation, and Celebration* involves learning about elder circles, actions, groups, and individual projects created from plans made by workshop participants, reflecting on what has been learned, and establishing next steps.

There is a new intergenerational movement of spiritual activism established by theologian Matthew Fox with Skylar Wilson and Jennifer

Berit Listug, codirectors of "Wild Awakenings," an adult rites of passage organization that "offers wilderness immersion experiences for exploring our inner nature and the transformation of consciousness." [287] They have formed the "Order of the Sacred Earth" and have written a book by the same name.[288] The order asserts that "the planet doesn't need another church or religion. What it needs is a new Order, a sacred community and movement, a movement of communities welcoming all the peoples" regardless of "belief systems (or non-belief systems), genders, races, classes, abilities, and nations." The order is a sacred activism movement that is based on both Eastern and Western spiritual and wisdom traditions, science, and indigenous knowledge. As stated by its founders, the Order of the Sacred Earth is "not a new religion or a new church" but a "radically inclusive Order of mystic activists, uniting our energy and intention in one sacred vow: 'I promise to be the best lover and defender of the Earth that I can be.'"[289] I am proud to have taken that vow and will try my best to always uphold it.

Ask yourself, "What is my vision of the future?" Imagine this future, the way you would really like it to be. If you're not certain what that is, just go with your imagination because you can change it whenever you want. Dream big. Shakti Gawain, in her book, *The Path of Transformation: How Healing Ourselves Can Change the World*, has given us a way to do this. Close your eyes and "imagine your relationship with yourself as fulfilling as possible on all levels – spiritual, mental, emotional, and physical. Imagine everything in your life reflecting the balance and harmony within your own being – your relationships, your work, your finances, your living situation, your creative pursuits. Allow them all to be wonderfully successful and satisfying. Now expand your focus to imagine the future of the world around you – your community, your country, humanity, the natural environment, our planet. Allow them all to reflect the integration and wholeness you have found within yourself. Imagine the new world emerging and developing in a healthy, balanced, expansive way. Really let your imagination soar. Envision the world as you would love it to be, a paradise on Earth."[290]

Reb Zalman reminded us that "elderhood is a time of unparalleled inner growth having evolutionary significance in this era of worldwide cultural transformation. It is a call from the future, a journey for the health and survival of our ailing planet Earth. … Young and middle-aged people certainly can awaken their intuition and help preserve the earth from eco-destruction. But because the evolutionary plan calls for developing latent brain potential in the afternoon and evening of life, elders have a special responsibility to act as leaders in healing of the planet and ensuring our continued survival."[291]

"Out of 5.8 billion people in the world," said the Dalai Lama, "the majority of them are certainly not believers in Buddhism. We can't argue with them, tell them they should be believers. No! Impossible! And, realistically speaking, if the majority of humanity remain nonbelievers, it doesn't matter. No problem! The problem is that the majority have lost, or ignore, the deeper human values – compassion, a sense of responsibility. That is our big concern."[292]

Vietnam veteran Richard Pimentel, in a video on YouTube, talks about leadership and taking on responsibility as we age, in his case during his imminent retirement. He says that responsibility is made up of two words: response and ability. "Given my ability, what then will be my response? … What abilities do you have and, more importantly, what is your response?" He urges us to not strive for personal acceptance from others but rather to pay attention and encourage people who need the wisdom of our years. Pimentel said, "Leaders do not get people to believe in them. Leaders find ways to get people to believe in themselves."[293]

Everything we do and say matters. Pimentel reminds us that we do have a responsibility – to respond according to our ability. As Barack Obama told the Howard University graduating class of 2017, "You have to go through life with more than just passion for change; you need to have a strategy. … Not just awareness, but action."[294] You might be wrong, but so what? You'll learn from that as you develop and refine your plan. Just pick your movie and finish it. There is much to do. And remember this: "When a change wants to happen," said Joanna Macy, "it looks for people to act through. How do we know when a change wants to happen? We feel the want inside us. There is a desire, a tugging at us to be involved." Is she talking about you?

Now ask yourself, "Given my character strengths, abilities, core values, rediscovered purpose, and vision of the future, what most draws me to service?" Reflect on that and then pose a few more questions to yourself: "When push comes to shove, do I really care about the state of the world and what future generations may endure – politically, socially, environmentally? If I have them, do I care at all what sort of world my grandchildren are inheriting? What am I denying, not facing?" Be honest. Is it an uneasy discomfort of uncertainty, the pain of apathy, the need to somehow have a guarantee of a positive outcome – an assurance that all will turn out just fine before I will act? Do I really need that guarantee before I will start anything? Am I following through on what I say I want to see as change in myself, if not in this world?

"Is this the darkness of the tomb," asked Valerie Kaur, "or the darkness of the womb?".[295] Would you be willing to be a midwife, a *doula*, to the birthing of a new society? You will need to act. First, take personal responsibility and then "respond according to your ability." Caroline Myss has said, "We are the engines of climate change. It is not happening around us; it is happening through us and because of us."

But how to act? Appendix 1 provides you with some additional resources – books and organizations to help you with continual learning, growth, and becoming engaged with others in the social and environmental movements of the Great Turning. I heard this some time ago but have no idea who said it: "Find what breaks your heart the most and make that your passion."[296] If you are concerned about climate disruption, for example, and want to do something, the best thing you can do is first educate yourself about the problem, the issues, and become involved in a local organization such as 350.org, which is found on the list in Appendix 1. You can then decide how to take personal action – your response according to your ability.

"Leave safety behind," implored Gray Panther founder Maggie Kuhn, "Put your body on the line. Stand before the people you fear and speak your mind – even if your voice shakes. When you least expect it, someone may actually listen to what you have to say. Well-aimed slingshots can topple giants." And United States Representative John Lewis said, "If you're gonna get yourself into trouble, make it Good Trouble, Necessary Trouble." I appreciate that!

And in conclusion, "When we lose touch with the rhythms of nature," wrote Angeles Arrien, "we become unbalanced. To be fully present within our nature, we must be in balance with the land around us. We benefit by taking time from our daily routines of work, relationships, and other commitments to return to nature. It provides a way to renew ourselves."[297] Stand up, go outside, breathe the air, and know you are alive. How wonderful if this could be your daily practice.

In this chapter, we have explored some ways to rekindle your passion for community service and become engaged in activism for environmental and social justice – for the two are inseparable – in the face of uncertainty. Joanna Macy reminds us, "it's that knife edge of uncertainty where we come alive to our truest power." And Caroline Myss asserts that "we have to live what we claim to believe"[298] – that is the aim, the struggle, an almost daily battle to remain clear-headed and proactive despite the bombardment of lies, the myths of ageism that creep in to confuse and divert us from this aim. Otherwise – figuratively and literally – it's back to the couch.

You have now completed all ten steps of the REWIREMENT process. Not an end, just a beginning. And remember this: "The breeze at dawn has secrets to tell you," Rumi told us, "Don't go back to sleep! You must ask for what you really want. Don't go back to sleep! People are going back and forth across the doorsill where the two worlds touch. The door is round and open. Don't go back to sleep!"[299]

In Part 3, we turn to potential obstacles that may block your way along the journey of conscious aging. This is followed by a concluding summary of the REWIREMENT process. The final chapter will identify a way forward to reinforce your efforts to re-fire your purpose and, in this way, stop worrying so much about "retirement" and other insecurities – and about the lack of any guarantees – as you age.

PART 3

RETURN to the Game Rewired

Chapter 14:
Friend of the Devil

"Men are so quick to blame the gods:
they say that we devise their misery.
But they themselves – in their depravity –
design grief greater than the griefs that fate assigns."
– Homer, *The Odyssey*

Pitfalls and Logjams

In this chapter, you will become more aware of your own potential pitfalls, annoying logjams along the path of conscious aging, identifying the mostly self-imposed obstacles and mental blocks that can hold you back. These can be overcome by being vigilant on your wizard's journey, your *Odyssey* into and through the labyrinth of conscious aging.

I begin with an observation about myself. I need to be vigilant, to be careful how I use my time because everything I say and do matters. If I say I want to make a difference, resist policies that go against my values, then I should not just talk about it but rather actually do something. But there are mind traps, pitfalls, and logjams. Thich Nhat Hanh has reminded us that "in modern society most of us don't want to be in touch with ourselves; we want to be in touch with other things like religion, sports, politics, a book – we want to forget ourselves. Anytime we have leisure, we want to invite something else to enter us, opening ourselves to the television and telling the television to come and colonize us."[300]

I am so very uncomfortable and ashamed to admit I have an addiction. It's now very much under control, but nothing has simultaneously calmed me more and made me angrier than television. And I tend to go to the news, which makes me even more irritable. I justify this by telling myself, "I must be informed." But the incessant happy inane jingles about macaroni and cheese creep in. Or "I want it all. I want it now" – more BS from Grub Hub; don't need it, don't want it. Or the moronic Pom Worry Monster who is somehow supposed to be entertaining in some way and get us to buy something we don't need or want to drink. And when all else fails, "just call Len the plumber;" that's comforting.

Television has been my diversion, but I rarely pay full attention to what is dancing around and making noise on the screen. I am often doing something else. Multitasking? But, on its own, it gives me the illusion of doing something. I accomplish nothing when I watch TV, this enabler of my procrastination and missed opportunities and regrets. At some point, it begins to irritate me. It allows me to disconnect from the world, from nature, from others and from myself. Someone should start a twelve-step Television Anonymous program to wean people from the thing. But day by day, it has a weaker grip on me. Now, I feel you condescending and raising your eyebrow because you "don't watch TV." Good for you. I mean that sincerely.

I grew up with TV. We were the first generation to do so. It was my babysitter, my comforter, my escape – a sort of kindly co-parent. I still got outside a lot, perhaps much more than the current generation. But it created a fantasy world, full of fictional lifestyles, all better than this reality that faced me. Leave It to Beaver. I say no more. For a few brief hours, the tube enabled me to escape, for example, the pain of facing a couple of relentless bullies for an entire year in eighth-grade, a couple of Del Ray "greasers" – John Johnson and Robert Holloway (names unchanged to protect no one) – and then come home from school, my mother passed out on the kitchen floor from a day of drinking to self-medicate.[301] So what would be my response? Go into what we called the "TV room" – more of a numbing state of mind than a physical room – shut the door, sit in the comfy chair, potato chips, and a Mountain Dew, watch one of the four moronic pre-cable channels available and be transported someplace else; to not think. Twelve-year-olds don't have access to alcohol and opioids. All about pain avoidance and comfort, the TV room required no thought, just passive acceptance. Then there was an agony of breaking free of that room and getting to the next agony of homework, busy work, so I could face the next day of school without getting yelled at. Eighth grade was without question the absolute worst year of my life, and I was very pleased many years later when I discovered the city finally razed Thomas Jefferson Middle School.

TV became my escape into a sort of temporary oblivion – not unlike when someone with a weight problem runs for cake as soon as he feels threatened or sad and can't break free from the cycle of loss and gain, loss and then gain again. It's the underlying issue, the root cause, the psychic pain, that must eventually be addressed. I get it. And we all have our own horror stories. Actually, I think I got off pretty easy compared to many.

But consider this. I am unlikely to be writing about you in the following context if you have come this far – but consider this anyhow. Is your ultimate goal really to retire one day to a sandy, seaside condo in Miami Beach, a life of coconut palm luxury and ease, maybe a boat? Isn't that what we've all been told we should want? Let's forget about the fact that sea level rise will probably do away with that folly. But that's not going to affect you anyhow – right? After all, you'll probably be dead before any of that nonsense starts to reduce your property values. And let me apologize to everyone living a very nice life in Miami Beach – I am sorry for singling you out – quite unfair.

Televangelist Rev. Ike once said, "The best thing you can do for the poor people is not be one of them." Mail in money (cash preferred) and he would mail you back a prayer scarf that would do what, I never quite figured out. This is horrible exploitation and highly cynical. But I do think the best thing you can do for your children and grandchildren is not be a miserable, disempowered, cranky "elderly senior citizen." That is not what you want them to see. I do not want anyone's pity especially if it has to do with me engaging with the natural life process of aging. Be a mentor. Be a role model, an inspiration. Be who you wish you had as a role model. Write a book, start a business, participate in a demonstration, do a little dance, anything – just get off the couch; don't just soak in the pity and don't keep angrily identifying obvious problems.

But even if you really cared about "our future generations," surely your own grandchildren and their children, you might still think, 'that sucks for them, but that's their problem.' You know what goes around comes around. You'll be back somehow dealing with all this again – in some form – but with amnesia. So, in anticipation of these unhappy events, you might just want to start doing something for a brighter future if not just your own. And, as I expect you genuinely do want to do something, there are things you can do that will have an impact. Linking up with a couple of the communities and organizations listed in Appendix 1 is a good start. And there are many more not listed but equally worthy of your time and energy.

A pitfall, a logjam, is always within you – rarely are you called on to fight an external demon. For example, do you feel apathetic, on the couch, just not really caring? Or do you nobly decry the apathy of others in the face of what we see in a world that needs our attention, if only for our own self-interest? Or is it really pain you feel and an inability to face your pain? Pain for what?

Joanna Macy spoke about our apathy; I quote her here due to my inability to express this pain any more eloquently. "So it's good to look at what this apathy is, to understand it with respect and compassion. *Apatheia* is a Greek word that means, literally, non-suffering. Given its etymology, apathy is the inability or refusal to experience pain. What is the pain we feel – and desperately try not to feel – in this planet-time? It is of another order altogether than what the ancient Greeks could have known; it pertains not just to privations of wealth, health, reputation, or loved ones, but to losses so vast we can hardly comprehend them. It is pain for the world."[302]

There is pain from loss of biodiversity; destroyed ecosystems; rampant pollution of air, soil, and water; climate change; a fragile biosphere that may someday be incapable of sustaining our own life. But there is also pain for ourselves, our regrets, our physical diminishments, loneliness, self-doubt, internal and external ageism, and all it entails. Your "apathy" toward the world, fellow humans and yourself is the pain you cannot face. But that is only what you tell yourself. You can step up. You can improve your life situation – take back your power. You can, through your action and wisdom, have an impact on reversing what our species is doing to our home. After all, the word ecology comes from the Greek word *oikos*, meaning home – the study of our home.

John Robinson's excellent and illuminating book on the *Odyssey* as a parable of male aging,[303] *What Aging Men Want*, was presented in Chapter 2. Parallels are drawn between Odysseus and his epic journeys, the *Iliad* and the *Odyssey*, and ourselves (men or women) as we leave an "adult war" to consciously age with new transformational challenges. There is so much in Robinson's book to ponder for the parallels are astonishing. But I can only provide here (with an intention to get you to read his book) a summary of his list of what we really want. While these were identified in the context of aging men, the topics themselves are relevant to each of us. All require some explanation, but I leave it to you to find that meaning.

We all, I think, want:

- "to leave the war,
- to come home to love,
- to help,
- to share our lives with others,
- forgiveness,
- to matter,
- to stay involved,
- passion filled and meaningful work,
- to have fun,
- to be seen as unique individuals,
- to keep learning,

- to find meaning,
- physical connection and experiences,
- to stay as independent as is reasonable,
- prepare for death,
- awaken a spiritual comprehension of life,
- and finally, we want 'our culture to wake up from the incessant drumbeat of fear, competition and war.'"[304]

Think about these topics. Then ask yourself, "What do I want?" Come to face and understand your current and potential obstacles and mental blocks and learn how to overcome them – become inspired. Identify your triggers, that which sets you off or keeps you the way you are, protects you even. You are now at a stage in your life where you can let go of the adult way of striving for success, moving away from the *Iliad*. For the most part, that war is over. You are now coming home, on your *Odyssey*. And it took Odysseus ten years to get home to Ithaca and Penelope, overcoming many obstacles along the way while lost at sea. This letting go or coming home, or whatever metaphor you choose, is just the beginning – the beginning of being of service. But depression, a giving in to our myths, can prevent us from cracking out of ourselves and being of service to others.

"I know depression is a suffering – I know it all too well," wrote Caroline Myss in an article on the 2014 suicide of Robin Williams. "When clinical depression merges with a spiritual crisis, that's when the psyche loses its capacity to breath, to remain connected to the life force in any vital way. A crisis of the spirit – of the soul – shatters one's connection to purpose and meaning, to feeling hope itself. ... Indeed, as I have witnessed with many people who battle mental and emotional sufferings, some of their pain is rooted in their astute powers of observation and not just from their personal lives." For, as Jiddu Krishnamurti has said, "It is no measure of health to be well adjusted to a profoundly sick society." Myss continued, "All pain is not personal. A spiritual crisis can look like depression. It has many of the same inner sufferings, but the differences are very profound. Unfortunately, we cannot ask a suicide victim any of the essential questions that would help one discern whether he is suffering from clinical depression or experiencing a spiritual crisis." She then offered a prayer for those coping with the pain of depression.[305]

You have survived. Are you not better for having gone through all the difficulties, the challenges, failures, sweat, frustration, confusion, defeats, loves, and successes? And what have you given? What are you leaving behind? "There is an important principle in Judaism, a source of hope," wrote Rabbi Jonathan Sacks, "one of the structuring principles of the Torah. It is the principle that God creates the cure before the disease. Bad things may happen, but God has already given us the remedy if we know where to look. So, when we give, it is not just our contribution but we who are raised up. We survive by what we are given; we achieve dignity by what we give."[306]

I acknowledge that what happens to many people when finally faced with this long-awaited freedom of "retirement," once the initial euphoria fades, is a pervasive fear of losing an identity and those things that are most valuable. This may include being a respected and productive member of society, having an impact, shaping children to become happy adults, or being an empowered member of a goal-oriented team. At some point, a self-defeating, but quite understandable, sense of loss – loss of meaning and purpose – corresponds to a feeling of retirement from life as we know it, a hopefully painless diminishment toward an ultimate inevitability.

I find that some of the biggest mistakes of our so-called baby boomer generation include thoughts of changing while keeping on doing the same things, the same dysfunctional activities that kept some of us in an unhappy, unfulfilled, unawake state – a naive desire to gain all but lose nothing. It is convenient to think there is "all the time in the world" to do stuff; we'll get to this or that eventually – a sort of "benign" procrastination or becoming "comfortably numb" to the pain of ourselves and the world.

We know ageism creeps around from both outside and within; we must be vigilant. Most of us have internalized the materialistic myths of our consumer, youth, and achievement-oriented society – and have made them our dysfunctional own. Do you really – I mean really – now view yourself as useless, innocuous, invisible, not respected, "over the hill?" Do you know someone who feels they must now "retire" from life, become invisible with shame, with no value to society, a winding down toward the inevitability of death? Really? But it is our evolutionary ability and resolve to adapt and flourish under changing circumstances that will save us from those unhappy stories. Who would you be if you could dispel those myths once and for all?

We see those with no purpose at retirement statistically do not live very long; some turn to opioids and alcohol, some take their own lives from despair and perceived hopelessness. The biggest problem can be dealing with health issues, and those will certainly complicate our mental state at some point. Ask yourself, "What are the top five things that frustrate me on an average day?" Would this not be doing something you really do not want to do? What are the circumstances, work or chores, the people who frustrate you the most? What can you do about that? Do you have some assumptions such as, "The best has come and gone, but somewhere along the way I missed it?" Will you be relegated to a rocking chair or worse, greeting the arrival of those "A Place for Mom" people?

And it's not really all about conscious aging and its platitudes, despite my enthusiasm and devotion to the concept; it's about conscious living, continually, ongoing, at any age, and this awareness should have started long before now. But maybe you didn't plan, didn't focus on the inner work. Or maybe you did, you tried your best, but life happened and your "best laid plans" fell apart. But you still can choose your path forward, change course, start again, in any step. Rumi wrote some wisdom about this that translates as, "Come, come, whoever you are. Wanderer, worshiper, lover of leaving. It doesn't matter. Ours is not a caravan of despair. Come, even if you have broken your vows a thousand times. Come, yet again, come, come." I like that. We always have possibilities, the opportunity to choose, to try again. We'll get there eventually, one way or another – in our own terms.

In the next and final chapter, we will consider a way forward that can reinforce your efforts to rewire and re-fire and, in this way, stop worrying so much about "retirement" and other insecurities, participate as a force for global change – and accept the lack of any guarantees – as you age.

Chapter 15:

Eyes of the World

"We shall not cease from exploration
And the end of all our exploring
Will be to arrive where we started
And know the place for the first time.
Through the unknown, remembered gate
When the last of earth left to discover
Is that which was the beginning."
- **T.S. Eliot, *Little Gidding, Four Quartets***

"A society grows great when old people plant trees
under whose shade they will never sit."
— Anonymous "Greek Proverb"

You Can Make the Difference You Want to See

You are Odysseus on your own challenging journey home to Ithaca, having left the war behind. But being lost at sea as we are, there remain many perils – and delights. You are an elder, or an "elder-in-training," with the capability and responsibility to mentor the young and with the potential for great continual learning and insight. You are a wizard, learning to create your reality by how you label what happens, until you begin to stop labeling and see, with new eyes, the world as a spectrum, as polarities, rather than as black-and-white dualities. You are already whole, someone who is transforming and thereby an instigator of transformation, turning the base metal of your relationships and this world into gold. You are a co-conspirator, happy to be in your age cohort, in this new age of meaning, finding the wizard within as you reclaim what has always been yours – your purpose – what already exists within you.

You understand how society's myths about ageism, the patriarchy, and money are disempowering and interrelated and can be released through self-exploration, attitude, and taking action. You can now reinvent and transform the last third of your life with creativity, meaningful work, and financial sustainability. You are able at any time to direct this understanding, mental freedom, and passion for change toward service to others and environmental activism.

By following the ten REWIREMENT steps in the previous chapters, you learned about ways to confront ageism, embrace conscious aging, discover your values, character strengths, vision, and goals; live your purpose; find work in line with your values and abilities; improve your mind-set about money; expand your consciousness; engage in a spiritual or mindful practice; and consider applying your abilities to catalyze change in the world. The following summarizes these ten steps.

Step 1: Recognize Your Ageism

"There's this youth culture that is really, really powerful and really, really strong," said singer-songwriter and political activist Annie Lennox on turning sixty in 2014, "but what it does is it really discards people once they reach a certain age. … I actually think that people are so powerful and interesting – women, especially – when they reach my age. We've got so much to say, but popular culture is so reductive that we just talk about whether we've got wrinkles, or whether we've put on weight or lost weight, or whether we've changed our hair style. I just find that so shallow."

You understand how society's myths about ageism, and how you have internalized these myths, impede your ability to thrive as you age. You know you do not have to settle for discrimination from ageism, and you can confront these myths. You have learned ways to act to avoid succumbing to its debilitating influences, impacts that may affect your ability to find purpose and new work and manage your finances – myths and discrimination that keep you from being secure and happy as you age.

Step 2: Embrace Conscious Aging

This book is all about aging – and doing so consciously. It focuses largely on your conscious aging challenges and opportunities. This is the inward journey of awareness, self-discovery, and personal transformation in which our hero, Odysseus, leaves the war, becomes lost at sea, and returns home to Ithaca, to where he began, but is transformed through challenges along the way.

This is about being an "elder," an "older," and even a "mentern," both mentor and continual learner. This, of course, is not a single step but one composed of many steps. The IONS example represents a conscious aging program that can be examined and studied in much more detail to explore "self-compassion, forgiveness, life review, transformative practices, death makes life possible, surrender or letting go, and creating a new vision of aging." You have reflected on your attitudes about aging. In the context of your current situation, you have begun to apply what you have learned to improve your well-being.

Your aim is to be secure, fulfilled, and happy as you age. What is important is that you embrace the reality of aging, fully coming into your potential, being able to express your gifts in ways that bring you happiness and serve others. You have the potential to improve conditions for others and for the planet. Through being more aware, more conscious, you can awaken to approaches that can transform society. Ron Pevny wrote, "The gifts and wisdom of conscious elders are critical for restoring our world with balance, seasoned experience, wholeness, and an understanding of interrelationship. These elements are necessary for the cultural transformation that can assure a future for our descendants and our planet's ecosystems."

Step 3: Wake Up to Your Values and Strengths

You have discovered some of your core values, character strengths, and distinctive personality traits. You have identified what makes you unique. By identifying your needs, values, strengths, and personal gifts in the context of aging and retirement, you can live your years to the fullest and improve your general well-being. Your strengths and personal abilities can now inform your decisions and enhance a trajectory toward rediscovering your purpose as you consciously age.

Step 4: Identify Your Vision and Goals

You have explored ways to establish your personal vision that is most aligned with your core values and character strengths. This has helped to inform your conscious aging process. Identifying your vision was accomplished through following the guidelines set forth in this step. You understand the importance of identifying where to focus your attention, areas you have highlighted for improvement. In line with your vision, you have then identified your main goals and are committed to taking action to achieve those goals.

Step 5: Re-fire Your Purpose

A translation from the writings of Patañjali, compiler of the *Yoga Sutra* from the second century BCE, says, "When you are inspired by some great purpose, some extraordinary project, all your thoughts break their bonds: Your mind transcends limitations, your consciousness expands in every direction, and you find yourself in a new, great, and wonderful world. Dormant forces, faculties, and talents become alive, and you discover yourself to be a greater person by far than you ever dreamed yourself to be." In this way, your life changes in a "new, great and wonderful world." You know how to rediscover and reimagine your purpose, your "reason to be." You know that your purpose is not something you create but rather something you uncover and that there are helpful ways to do this and find meaning to your life.

However, the continual barrage of consumerism, advertising that tells you how much you lack, is all about "aborting the artist" within you, killing your creativity, pulling you away from your purpose. Without creativity and following your purpose, without this meaning, you are likely fall into a depression. But this "dark night of the soul" is a signal, a powerful spiritual message, to you that you have lost your way. You are no longer on the right track, and it is time to get back – to take back your power, to create, to live with purpose – and get on with life.

Step 6: Envision Your Work

As you age consciously, you can gain clarity and envision more meaningful work. This "work" may be a new occupation that is more in alignment with your values, character strengths, vision, and goals and that strengthens your purpose and financial goals. When you expand your view from one based on limiting beliefs, you can begin to explore and embody a much wider range of alternative viewpoints. You have the resources to envision and make the change you want to see in your work and to begin securing your financial future – this only requires you settle on a plan and then act.

Step 7: Manifest Your Prosperity

You have identified ways to achieve financial security and prosperity while recognizing the many myths we hold about money. You understand how our materialistic society's consumer myths have been internalized– and how this is holding you back from financial security. You know that you can overcome a mind-set of money shame, scarcity, and fear.

The real reason for this pain, this insecurity over your money, is not poor financial planning or investments gone wrong or any other excuse you can think of; it's all about your mind-set. We have seen how myths of ageism and multiple feelings of inadequacy brought about by our culture and its continual onslaught of "you're not good enough without this" advertising, have made you miserable. It's not your fault. But it is your fault if you have knowledge and see a way forward but you take no action.

It is your responsibility, and yours alone, to change your ways, get off the couch, and shape your life in alignment with your values and dreams.

Step 8: Expand Your Consciousness

Rabbi Zalman Schachter-Shalomi said, "Why should anybody live longer than the time of begetting and raising their children? If we do live longer, then nature must have a task. There must be a purpose. The purpose is to hothouse consciousness, generation by generation, so that the older generation can transmit something to the younger." Expanding consciousness is all about transformation, and there are many tools and methods for that. You learned about ways to expand your consciousness through a variety of experiential means and integrate your experiences to effect sustained transformation. All the REWIREMENT steps up to this point may be considered as a foundation, a prerequisite, to this step. You can combine consciousness expansion with a lifetime of learning and practical application of knowledge, now tempered by wisdom.

What our society urgently needs now is a cadre of entheogenic elders, psychedelic sages, wise mentors, activists who have rebooted and reinvented themselves – modern elders who have rewired their consciousness, have experienced to some degree the ego dissolution and reconstruction of mystical experience. We need them to be spiritual activists – spiritual warriors – to effectively impart their wisdom and knowledge to others, the youngers, to help heal our societal dysfunctions and our planetary environmental crisis. For many, this sounds funny. I get that. It may appear like old people unwisely "defying age" or running around at Burning Man ("Oh, isn't Granny cute") and other baggage connected with the word "psychedelic". For many of us, it was impossible to not have the experience and be changed in some way in consciousness and how we forever view ourselves and the world.

Step 9: kNow the Numinous

This step focused on your spirituality. You understand how spirituality, in whatever form you choose, and maintaining a spiritual practice, can be of tremendous benefit to conscious aging and living your purpose in a creative life. You learned about the potential of the labyrinth to inspire change and renewal and to serve as a guide to help you develop greater self-awareness and understanding. Lauren Artress, "chief promoter" of the labyrinth as a spiritual practice, has said, "Religion is for those scared to death of hell. Spirituality is for those who've been there."

Authentic spirituality is service. Full stop. Service to your community, service to the planet – but also service to yourself with the realization, responsibility, and application that everything you do or say has meaning and consequences, positive or negative. Going to church or temple regularly, meditating faithfully, going vegan, wearing special hats or robes to identify you – none of that, in and of itself, makes you a spiritually centered person. All those spiritual practices, whether they be meditation, mindfulness, yoga, diet, or something else, are a means to this end – service.

Step 10: Take Back Your Power

"Adults keep saying we owe it to the young people, to give them hope. But I don't want your hope," said sixteen-year-old Greta Thunberg at the World Economic Forum conference in Davos, Switzerland, in January 2019. "I don't want you to be hopeful. I want you to panic. I want you to feel the fear I feel every day. I want you to act. I want you to act as you would in a crisis. I want you to act as if the house is on fire, because it is." And to fix this problem, we must also fix ourselves.

How can you become empowered to engage in community service and the interconnection of environmental and social justice activism? I can't answer that for you. But you have explored some ways to rekindle your passion for service and become engaged in conscious activism[307] that supports environmental and social justice – for the two are inseparable – in the face of uncertainty. Conscious aging calls up your courage to challenge the past and embody a better future by being a positive force for change. Reconnect with nature and with your community, your family, yourself.

Viktor Frankl wrote, "Being human always points, and is directed, to something, or someone, other than oneself – be it meaning to fulfill or another human being to encounter. The more one forgets himself – by giving himself to a cause to serve or another person to love – the more human he is and the more he actualizes himself."[308] Now can be your time to reconnect more meaningfully with others and the diversity of life around you. It can be a time of service, using your experience and wisdom to make the changes you want to see.

Now, the question to ask yourself is do you want to take a deeper dive here, totally immersing yourself into the pain and exhilaration of change or are you content with merely dipping a toe into the chaos. In that safe place, you will be comfortable, aloof, but fooling yourself into a conceit that you are doing something to make a difference, a difference that requires very little from you. However, if, on the other hand, you really, sincerely, deeply want to make a difference in yourself, your community, or our planet, then that is your choice, but much will be required according to your ability. Immersing yourself into this pain, accepting it, and rising above all despite it, can bring great exhilaration. This is the exhilaration – a wonder and an awe even – that comes with being alive, being a fully conscious human. And when you are fully conscious, you do not exist for yourself alone – not just your oh so very special ego – but rather for all your other selves, those in your home and community, those on the other side of town whom you have never met, and those on the other side of the planet speaking some incomprehensible language but whose life and survival are also bound to yours. Ethnicity, class, language, religion, gender, and culture are illusions that serve to divide us; deep down you know we are all the same, from and of the same source.

I have a notepad on my desk with a quote on it, "That which I no longer need now leaves my life. Everything around me serves a purpose." I have no idea who said that, and it doesn't matter. What is important is that you ask yourself, as you move into your later years, "What is most important now?" Bessie Stanley of Lincoln, Kansas, wrote a winning essay in 1905 for a newspaper contest on "What Constitutes Success?" The quote is often incorrectly ascribed to Ralph Waldo Emerson, who never said, "He has achieved success . . . who has left the world better than he found it, whether by an improved poppy, a perfect poem, or a rescued soul; who has never lacked appreciation of earth's beauty or failed to express it; who has always looked for the best in others and given the best he had; whose life was an inspiration" But also, success comes to he "who has lived well, laughed often, and loved much."[309]

You are facing a transformation, a transition from the prospect of becoming disempowered, resigned to a downward spiral, to becoming empowered and living a creative, conscious life. There is no need to fall back onto old, comfortably numb ways of dealing with your time, with people, and with your future. You understand this process and how to avoid falling back. Transform your mind-set from one that views a seemingly inevitable prospect of decline, becoming a disempowered "senior citizen," to a person who is empowered, conscious, and creative. You are an "elder," bringing a high level of awareness and intentionality to every facet of your life as you continue to grow, learn, and age.

Appendix 1 provides you with some additional resources – books and organizations to help you with continual learning and growth. But changing our behaviors and habits requires practice and doing a thing repeatedly. Choose and adjust your practices to change the results you are getting. There are not too many self-study, self-help programs that have a lasting effect – a cumulative effect over long periods of time perhaps – but few people are able to maintain a program that requires radical shifts in thought and practice to produce a sustainable change for the better – for example, achieving an ideal weight and overall health, overcoming procrastination, initiating an exercise program, meditation, or mindfulness practice. This is no different. They all require changing your mind.

It is my hope you will direct your understanding about conscious aging, mental freedom, and passion for change toward service to others and the planet in the way that best resonates with you – your character strengths, values, and abilities. You can chart a new course to reinvent and transform yourself, your community, and the planet, and live the last third of your life with creativity, purpose, action, meaningful work, financial freedom, and fun. You can identify and unleash your wisdom and gifts, your passion for life, living an examined life.

With a mind-set of healthier attitudes toward money, meaning, and what it means to be "older," you can take action on behalf of yourself, your community, and the health of our planet. I hope you will follow up with these steps, some in greater detail. My sincere wish for you is that you do act and that your actions will be based on clear goals for where you want to be with a plan on how to get there.

And now for some Dead: "Lately it occurs to me. What a long strange trip it's been."[310] But you know this trip, this "sunshine daydream," is far from being over. Get back into the game, and – most importantly – remind yourself to just "Be Here Now," really, mindful and present, listening, learning, and serving. And remember this:

- *Wake Up*! to society's myths of ageism and unrealistic expectations that keep you insecure.
- *Cheer Up*! as you transform from disempowered "senior citizen" to confident older or "elder," repurposing a lifetime of skills and experience.
- *Push Back*! on a mind-set of despair, invisibility, and irrelevance to a clarity that comes from rewiring attitude and consciousness.
- *Let Go*! of blockages to your creativity and opportunities for purpose, work, prosperity, and service to positive change.

Finally, the most impactful and loving act you can do as a legacy for your children and grandchildren is to be that wizard. Be a role model for conscious aging and active engagement. Show them how good the later years can be – by your good example. Show them their later years are not something to be regarded with dread and shame. They do not have to buy into the lies and pain you have overcome. Rather, this is a time of great anticipation, personal growth, and hope – a time when all comes into alignment, when the base metal turns to gold. You are exactly where you need to be, right here, not there, right now, not earlier, not later. In that way, you have no idea how much of an impact you will make on those you love, those you have never met, and all future generations. Somehow, I just know it's going to be much more than you think.

"Still round the corner there may wait
A new road or a secret gate
And though I oft have passed them by
A day will come at last when I
Shall take the hidden paths that run
West of the Moon, East of the Sun."
– J.R.R. Tolkien, ***The Lord of the Rings***

Endnotes

Dedication

1 Fox, Matthew (2012). *Hildegard of Bingen: A Saint for Our Times*. Namaste Publishing, Vancouver, Canada.

Introduction

2 C.R.E.A.M. " (Cash Rules Everything Around Me) is a song by the Wu-Tang Clan from their 1993 album, Enter the Wu-Tang (36 Chambers).
3 From presentation by Matthew Fox given at Sage-ing International Conference, Chaska, Minnesota, 28 October 2018.
4 David Orr, writer, environmental activist and professor of environmental studies and politics at Oberlin College, quoted from his talk, "*Is There a Future for our Democracy? Why Everything Depends on the Answer*," at the 30th annual Bioneers Conference, 18 October 2019, San Rafael, California.
5 Hart, Ingrid (2013). *My Year in California: A Journey Toward Midlife Renewal*. My Year in California, Costa Mesa, California.
6 Bratter, Bernice and Helen Dennis (2008). *Project Renewment: The First Retirement Model for Career Women*. Scribner, New York.
7 Dr. Norm Shealy, Keynote at Monroe Institute 2016 Professional Seminar: "*The Biochemistry and Physics of Health and Longevity," YouTube, Published on May 18, 2016*: https://www.youtube.com/watch?v=zOxGDspeeFQ&fbclid=IwAR0k1kVsz8PwYTncWAV80VmZDlJIIkG14ntHJuxAZpl5ZvtwMToqIlE-Pfc

Chapter 1

8 Morpheus to Neo in the Warner Bros. movie "The Matrix" (1999): "*I know exactly what you mean. Let me tell you why you're here. You're here because you know something. What you know, you can't explain. But you feel it. You've felt it your entire life. That there's something wrong with the world. You don't know what it is, but it's there – like a splinter in your mind – driving you mad. It is this feeling that has brought you to me. Do you know what I'm talking about?*"
9 David Gilmour & Roger Waters, "Comfortably Numb," Pink Floyd, Columbia, 1979
10 This quotation has been attributed to Albert Einstein, but there is no

evidence that he ever said it.

11 Definition of ennui from Oxford Living Dictionaries

12 Excerpts and Jerry Garcia quote from: Richardson, Peter (2014). *No Simple Highway: A Cultural History of the Grateful Dead.* St. Martin's Press, New York.

13 The Greatest Generation refers to those who grew up during the Great Depression and fought World War II, or whose labor helped win it. The title was coined by former NBC Nightly News anchor and author Tom Brokaw in his book, "The Greatest Generation," which profiled people who came of age during World War II, especially those in the United States.

14 Mather, Mark, Linda A. Jacobsen and Kelvin M. Pollard (2015). *Aging in the United States.* Population Bulletin 70, no. 2. Population Reference Bureau, Washington, D.C.

15 Benson, William F. (ca. 2011). *CDC Promotes Public Health Approach to Address Depression among Older Adults.* CDC Healthy Aging Program, US Center for Disease Control.

16 Kessler, R.C. et al. (2005). *Prevalence, severity, and comorbidity of 12-month DSM-IV disorders in the National Comorbidity Survey Replication (NCS-R).* Archives of General Psychiatry 62(6):617-627.

17 *Anthony Bourdain, Renegade Chef Who Reported from the World's Tables, Is Dead at 61* by Kim Severson, Matthew Haag and Julia Moskin, *New York Times*, June 8, 2018

18 Fottrell, Quentin (2014). *Boomers face a greater risk of depression and suicide.* MarketWatch, 17 August 2014.

19 U.S. Surgeon General (1999). Older adults and mental health. In: Mental Health: A Report of the Surgeon General. Available at www.surgeongeneral.gov/library/mentalhealth/chapter5/sec1.html

20 NIMH (2007). National Institute of Mental Health. *Depression booklet.* Available at www.nimh.nih.gov/health/publications/depression/index.shtml

21 "Dark Night of the Soul" (*La noche oscura del alma*) is a poem written by 16th century Spanish mystic and poet Juan de Yepes y Álvarez (St. John of the Cross).

22 Actually, I am a firm believer in some version of option 3, but I try to keep that to myself – but no longer it would seem!

23 Ashton Applewhite, "*Let's end ageism,*" TED Talk, April 2017: https://www.youtube.com/watch?v=WfjzkO6_DEI

Chapter 2

24 *The Meaning of Life, Part 7 – Death*, by Monty Python from the 1983 film *The Meaning of Life*: https://www.youtube.com/watch?v=YoBTsMJ4jNk

25 Hollis, James (1994). *Under Saturn's Shadow: The Wounding and Healing of Men.* Inner City Books, Toronto, Canada.

26 Lourdes Viado's interview with James Hollis: The Secrets Men Carry. 21 April 2017: https://lourdesviado.com/40-the-secrets-men-carry-with-james-hollis-phd/

27 Robinson, John (2013). *What Aging Men Want: The Odyssey as a Parable of Male Aging*. Psyche Books, John Hunt Publishing, Ltd., Alresford, Hants, UK

28 Excerpt from p. 22 in Robinson, John (2013). *What Aging Men Want: The Odyssey as a Parable of Male Aging*. Psyche Books, John Hunt Publishing, Ltd., Alresford, Hants, UK

29 Excerpt from p. 64 in Robinson, John (2013). *What Aging Men Want: The Odyssey as a Parable of Male Aging*. Psyche Books, John Hunt Publishing, Ltd., Alresford, Hants, UK

30 Quote from Israel "Iz" Kamakawiwoʻole, singer-songwriter, musician and Hawaiian sovereignty activist

31 A few years later, I discovered a book, "*Everyday Enlightenment: How to be a Spiritual Warrior at the Kitchen Sink*" by the Buddhist nun, Venerable Yeshe Chodron. (Harper Collins Publishers PTY Ltd., 2006).

32 Werner Erhard quote from: *Epistemological and Contextual Contributions of est to General Systems Theory*. Presented by Werner Erhard and Victor Gioscia to the symposium on Evolving Trends in General Systems Theory and the Future of the Family at the Sixth World Congress of Social Psychiatry, Opatija, Yugoslavia, 5 October 1976.

33 Maslow, Abraham (1954). *Motivation and Personality*. 1st edition: 1954, Harper & Brothers, New York.

34 Quote from Kyle Cease in a short video, *It's the End of Control*: https://upliftconnect.com/end-of-control/

35 Excerpted from: *The Supreme Siddhi of Mahamudra*. Translated by Sean Price, Adam Kane and Gerardo Abboud, from *Notes on Mahamudra* by Pema Karpo, page 46.

36 Lyrics from Grateful Dead, *Uncle John's Band*, written by Jerome J. Garcia, Robert C. Hunter © Universal Music Publishing Group, Warner/Chappell Music, Inc.

37 Schlitz, Marilyn Mandala, Cassandra Vieten and Tina Amorok (2007). *Living Deeply: The Art and Science of Transformation in Everyday Life*. New Harbinger Publications and Noetic Books, Oakland, California.

38 Excerpt from p. 61 in Robinson, John (2013). *What Aging Men Want: The Odyssey as a Parable of Male Aging*. Psyche Books, John Hunt Publishing, Ltd., Alresford, Hants, UK

39 From *The Dictionary of Obscure Sorrows*. https://en.wikipedia.org/wiki/The_Dictionary_of_Obscure_Sorrows

40 Tobe, Edward H. (2013). *Mitochondrial dysfunction, oxidative stress, and major depressive disorder*. Neuropsychiatric Disease and Treatment 9: 567–573.

41 Excerpt from p. 58 in Robinson, John (2013). *What Aging Men Want: The Odyssey as a Parable of Male Aging*. Psyche Books, John Hunt Publishing, Ltd., Alresford, Hants, UK

42 Excerpt from p. 73 in Robinson, John (2013). *What Aging Men Want: The Odyssey as a Parable of Male Aging*. Psyche Books, John Hunt Publishing, Ltd., Alresford, Hants, UK

43 Excerpt from p. 45-46 in Robinson, John (2013). *What Aging Men Want: The Odyssey as a Parable of Male Aging*. Psyche Books, John Hunt Publishing, Ltd., Alresford, Hants, UK

Chapter 3

44 From: *Carl Jung's 'Stages of Life'* by Tim Ruggiero, philosophical society.com

45 Based on a sermon given by Rev. Toni Fish, "*They Ain't Anything 'Til I Call 'Em*," at Unity of Fairfax, Oakton, Virginia, on 26 August 2018. Rev. Fish is minister at Unity of Frederick, Maryland.

46 When in Berkeley, these hotdogs are an experience not to be missed (I get nothing for this endorsement, thank you): http://www.topdoghotdogs.com/index.html

47 Emily Levine, a true wizard, on "*How I Made Friends with Reality*". TED 2018: https://www.ted.com/talks/emily_levine_how_i_made_friends_with_reality?language=en

48 Chopra, Deepak (1995). *The Way of the Wizard: Twenty Spiritual Lessons for Creating the Life You Want*. Harmony Books, New York.

49 From Deepak Chopra, *The Way of the Wizard* (p. 10): "Being a seer, the wizard has no gender, and it is only the clumsiness of English that turns Merlin into a 'he' (as our language does with *God, prophet, seer*, and many other words that are far beyond male and female). *Wizardess* is a clumsy word, so please know that *wizard* applies to women as well as men. If anything, the return of the magical has been greeted more quickly by women in our society than by anyone else."

50 Adapted from a sermon given by Rev. Toni Fish, "*They Ain't Anything 'Til I Call 'Em*," at Unity of Fairfax, Oakton, Virginia, on 26 August 2018. Rev. Fish is minister at Unity of Frederick, Maryland.

51 From Foreword by David W. Orr, in Stone, Michael K. and Zenobia Barlow (Eds.). (2005). *Ecological Literacy: Educating Our Children for a Sustainable World.* The Bioneers Series. Sierra Club Books, San Francisco.

52 Roosevelt, Eleanor (1939). *This is My Story.* Garden City Publishing, 3rd edition. Eleanor Roosevelt also famously said, upon learning that a rose had been named for her that she "... was very flattered. But I was not pleased to read the description in the catalogue: 'No good in a bed, but fine up against a wall.'"

53 "Think Different. Here's to the crazy ones." Apple TV commercial:

https://www.youtube.com/watch?v=P9jY3mPy7cs
54 Institute of Noetic Sciences (IONS) https://noetic.org/experience/conscious-aging/
55 Coaching for Transformation (CFT) and Leadership That Works are accredited by the International Coach Federation (ICF): http://www.leadershipthatworks.com/Public/Home/
56 Veriditas is a 501c3 nonprofit incorporated in California in 1995: https://www.veriditas.org/

Chapter 4

57 This quote is attributed to Marcus Tillius Cicero, 106-43 BC, "Roman statesman, writer, lawyer and orator, murdered by Antonius"
58 Jong, Erica (2006). *Fear of Fifty: A Midlife Memoir.* TarcherPerigee (Penguin, Random House), New York.
59 Wikipedia on Ageism: https://en.wikipedia.org/wiki/Ageism
60 Amazon Echo – Saturday Night Live: https://www.youtube.com/watch?v=YvT_gqs5ETk
61 Stopping the Elderly Suicide Epidemic video: https://www.youtube.com/watch?v–NH6LondGsvw
62 From a *Journal of the American Medical Association* psychiatry study, Medical City / LifeLines
63 *Many Seniors Don't Accept Stereotypes About Aging.* By Marlene Cimons, *The Washington Post,* 17 April 2018.
64 From Bill Thomas' Changing Aging website: "TED Talks and a New Spin on Aging" by Phyllis Goldberg: https://changingaging.org/elderhood/ted-talks-and-a-new-spin-on-aging/
65 Freedman, Marc (2018). *How to Live Forever: The Enduring Power of Connecting the Generations.* PublicAffairs, Perseus Books, New York.
66 *The Truth About HR Hiring Practices* by David Stewart, *Ageist,* January 2019.
67 Applewhite, Ashton (2018). *This Chair Rocks: A Manifesto Against Aging.* Networked Books.
68 Rauch, Jonathan (2018). *The Happiness Curve: Why Life Gets Better after 50.* Thomas Dunne Books, St. Martin's Press, New York City.
69 Applewhite, Ashton (2018). *This Chair Rocks: A Manifesto Against Aging.* Networked Books.
70 Maggie Kuhn (1905-1995), American activist and founder of the Gray Panthers movement: https://en.wikipedia.org/wiki/Maggie_Kuhn
71 The Radical Age Movement: Confronting Ageism https://radicalagemovement.org/
72 *Conscious Aging,* 2018, Eckhart Tolle Teachings, Inc.: https://youtu.be/6WFKQmYbt0Y

73 *Biophysicist discovers new life after death*: Joyce Hawkes at TEDx Bellevue: https://youtu.be/MyaBeHeRK6M
74 Ashton Applewhite, "*Let's end ageism*," TED Talk, April 2017: https://www.youtube.com/watch?v=WfjzkO6_DEI
75 Pharr, Suzanne (1988). *Homophobia A Weapon of Sexism*. Little Rock Arkansas: The Women's Project.
76 Neumark, David, Ian Burn and Patrick Button (2015, revised 2017). *Is It Harder for Older Workers to Find Jobs? New and Improved Evidence from a Field Experiment.* NBER Working Paper Series, Working Paper 21669, National Bureau of Economic Research, Cambridge, Massachusetts (revised November 2017). http://www.nber.org/papers/w21669
77 For example, *How the Patriarchy Harms Men and Boys*, by Terri Coles. Huffington Post, Living, 10 November 2017: https://www.huffingtonpost.ca/2017/11/10/patriarchy-men-boys_a_23273251/
78 Hollis, James (1994). *Under Saturn's Shadow: The Wounding and Healing of Men*. Inner City Books, Toronto, Canada.
79 Lourdes Viado's interview with James Hollis: *The Secrets Men Carry*. 21 April 2017: https://lourdesviado.com/40-the-secrets-men-carry-with-james-hollis-phd/
80 bell hooks (2004). *The Will to Change: Men, Masculinity and Love.* Washington Square Press, New York.
81 Bettina Aptheker on Feminism and Ageism. A public lecture at Pacific Institute. San Francisco, 8 May 2008, quoted in: https://www.livingwellah.com/blog/category/feminism-and-ageism/
82 Doris Bersing, PhD blog: Feminism and Ageism: *Aging Women: From Crone to Mentor*: https://www.livingwellah.com/blog/category/feminism-and-ageism/
83 Institute of Noetic Sciences (IONS) Conscious Aging program and workshops: https://noeticprograms.org/in-person-workshops/conscious-aging/_
84 From: *Conscious Aging: Cultivate Wisdom, Connect with Others, Celebrate Life – Group Process Guidelines for Facilitators* by Kathleen Erickson-Freeman, Institute of Noetic Sciences (IONS), 2012.
85 Thanas, Katherine (2018). *The Truth of This Life: Zen Teachings on Loving the World as It Is.* (page 59) edited by Natalie Goldberg and Bill Anelli, Shambhala Publications, Boston, Massachusetts.
86 Lyla June Johnston, *Nihimá Nahasdzáán: Healing Women and Nature Through a Diné (Navajo) Lens.*
Bioneers Conference, San Rafael, California, 21 October 2018, beginning at 5:30 on video: https://www.youtube.com/watch?v=YZQiihDC__E
87 Schachter-Shalomi, Zalman and Ronald S. Miller (1995, updated 2014). *From Age-Ing to Sage-Ing: A Revolutionary Approach to Growing Older.*

Time Warner Books.

Chapter 5

88 From: "*Deepening the Sage Within*" course description, Sage-ing International, Indianapolis. https://www.sage-ing.org/

89 Singer, Michael A. (2007). *The Untethered Soul: The Journey Beyond Yourself.* New Harbinger Publications/ Noetic Books, Oakland, California.

90 Pevny, Ron (2014). *Conscious Living, Conscious Aging: Embrace & Savor Your Next Chapter*. Atria, New York, & Beyond Words, Hillsboro, Oregon.

91 Moody, Harry R. (2002). "*Conscious Aging: A Strategy for Positive Development in Later Life*" In: Judah Ronch and Joseph Goldfield (eds.) *Mental Wellness in Aging: Strength-based Approaches*. Human Services Press

92 From an article by Robert C. Atchley, "*Conscious Aging: Nurturing a New Vision of Longevity*," derived from his book: Atchley, Robert C. (2000). *Social Forces in Aging*. 9th edition, Wadsworth, Belmont, California.

93 Sage-ing International: https://www.sage-ing.org/

94 From YouTube channel "We Plants Are Happy Plants." *The Peculiar Humor of Terence McKenna* (*Part 4*). 21 October 2019: https://www.youtube.com/watch?v=Fsax_JFUQyg

95 Freedman, Marc (2018). *How to Live Forever: The Enduring Power of Connecting the Generations*. PublicAffairs, Perseus Books, New York.

96 Conley, Chip (2018). *Wisdom @ Work*. Currency, New York.

97 Institute of Noetic Sciences (IONS) https://noetic.org/

98 About IONS: https://noetic.org/about/

99 Institute of Noetic Sciences (IONS) Conscious Aging program and workshops: https://noetic.org/experience/conscious-aging/

100 Schlitz, Marilyn Mandala, Tina Amorok and Marc Micozzi (2004). *Consciousness and Healing: Integral Approaches to Mind-Body Medicine*. Churchill Livingstone, Elsevier, London. AND Schlitz, Marilyn Mandala, Cassandra Vieten, and Tina Amorok (2007). *Living Deeply: The Art and Science of Transformation in Everyday Life*. Noetic Books, Institute of Noetic Sciences, New Harbinger Publications, Oakland, California.

101 From: Erickson-Freeman, Kathleen (2012). *Conscious Aging: Cultivate Wisdom, Connect with Others, Celebrate Life – Group Process Guidelines for Facilitators.* Institute of Noetic Sciences (IONS), Petaluma, California.

102 Joan Halifax on "compassion and the true meaning of empathy," TEDWomen, December 2010: http://www.youtube.com/watch?v=dQijrruP9c4

103 For more information about the SCS self-compassion test or its variants, you can visit Kristin Neff's website: https://self-compassion.org/

104 Luskin, Frederic (2002), *Forgive for Good: A Proven Prescription for Health and Happiness.* Harper Collins, New York.

105 Lyla June Johnston, 2017, YouTube video, HumansandNature.

org, published on Mar 22, 2017: https://www.youtube.com/watch?v=Dn-BWEBt7nk0

106 *Neuroscience Reveals: Gratitude Literally Rewires Your Brain to be Happier*, by Daily Health Post Editorial, 21 July 2019. https://dailyhealthpost.com/gratitude-rewires-brain-happier/?utm_source=link&utm_medium=fb&utm_campaign=sq&utm_content=dhp&fbclid=IwAR1Jaqb8PoCWfKtVmcG8YprLSbpisoYATjfM1mR1byrtV8lVtg5C-lPcXvU

107 *In Praise of Gratitude*, Harvard Mental Health Letter, Harvard Health Publishing, Harvard Medical School: https://www.health.harvard.edu/mind-and-mood/in-praise-of-gratitude

108 Phifer, Nan Merrick (2010). *Memoirs of the Soul: A Writing Guide*. Ingot Press.2016).

109 Newhouse, Margaret L. (2016). *Legacies of the Heart: Living a Life that Matters*. EBook Bakery Books.

110 Freed, Rachael (2013). *Your Legacy Matters: Harvesting the Love and Lessons of Your Life*. Minerva Press, Minneapolis, Minnesota.

111 Video: *An Introductory Presentation on Life Review in Advancing Age* by Dr. Tom Meuser, Director, Gerontology, University of Missouri, St. Louis, 2009: https://www.youtube.com/watch?v=F5TZUTHDfKU&fbclid=IwAR1u-t95iK5JiBISUXWN_C9fYBF7q2EkJEMwGqMoenkx1Bi48MKmh0ORN4Cg

112 Pevny, Ron (2014). *Conscious Living, Conscious Aging: Embrace & Savor Your Next Chapter*. Atria, New York, & Beyond Words, Hillsboro, Oregon.

113 Thich Nhat Hanh (2010). *You Are Here: Discovering the Magic of the Present Moment*. Shambhala, Boulder, Colorado.

114 Schlitz, Marilyn Mandala, Cassandra Vieten and Tina Amorok (2007). *Living Deeply: The Art and Science of Transformation in Everyday Life*. New Harbinger Publications and Noetic Books, Oakland, California.

115 Definitions of transformation and alignment from: Lasley, Martha, Virginia Kellogg, Richard Michaels and Sharon Brown (2015). *Coaching for Transformation: Pathways to Ignite Personal & Social Change*. 2nd ed., Discover Press.

116 "Sometimes in order to reconstruct yourself afresh, the complete destruction of who you have been is required." From: Schlitz, Marilyn Mandala, Cassandra Vieten and Tina Amorok (2007). *Living Deeply: The Art and Science of Transformation in Everyday Life*. New Harbinger Publications and Noetic Books, Oakland, California (p. 38).

117 "*Noetic* is" from "a Greek word that refers to knowledge that is subjective – the things you know through your own direct experience. Thus, noetic experiences are those in which there's a deeply subjective and internal experience of knowing." From: *Living Deeply: The Art and Science of Transformation in Everyday Life* (p. 40).

118 Non-ordinary states of consciousness, as doorways to transformation, can be "achieved through meditation, shamanic healing arts, trance, past-life regression, hypnosis, art, dance, music, deep play, sex, being in nature, ritual and ceremony, prayer, the sacred use of plants ... as well as many other means. These states can also arise spontaneously." From: *Living Deeply: The Art and Science of Transformation in Everyday Life* (p. 48).
119 *9 Ways to Rewire Your Brain for Creativity*, by Deep Patel, contributor to "Entrepreneur", 7 November 2018. https://www.entrepreneur.com/article/322792
120 Video and transcript of his commencement address is found in the article, *Steve Jobs: 'Death is very likely the single best invention of life.'* The Guardian: https://www.theguardian.com/technology/2011/oct/06/steve-jobs-pancreas-cancer
121 Eckert Tolle on *Acceptance and Surrender*: https://www.youtube.com/watch?v=aAoiuoFXW0o
122 Pinkson, Tom (2013). *Fruitful Aging: Finding the Gold in the Golden Years*. Wakan (p. 126).
123 Excerpted from IONS' 2012 conscious aging telecourse, Lesson 8: "*Creating a New Vision of Aging*" by Dr. Tom Pinkson, and as presented in *Conscious Aging: Cultivate Wisdom, Connect with Others, Celebrate Life – Group Process Guidelines for Facilitators* by Kathleen Erickson-Freeman, Institute of Noetic Sciences, 2012 (pp. 91-92).
124 Emma Knight class assignment as seen on https://www.pinterest.com/pin/175710822933938581/?lp=true

Chapter 6

125 Maslow, Abraham (1954). Motivation and Personality. 1st edition: 1954, Harper & Brothers, New York.
126 Image from Wikimedia Commons, the free media repository. *A pyramid chart with examples of the categories*. Date: 10 April 2019. Author: Chiquo.
127 Image from Wikimedia Commons, the free media repository. *Dynamic hierarchy of needs of Abraham Maslow* referring to Krech, D., Crutchfield, R. S., Ballachey, E. L. (1962), Individual in society, Tokyo etc. 1962, S. 77; Date: 16 October 2016; Author: Philipp Guttmann.
128 For a good list of core values commonly used by leadership institutes and programs, see: https://jamesclear.com/core-values
129 Adapted from Lasley, Martha, Virginia Kellogg, Richard Michaels and Sharon Brown (2015). *Coaching for Transformation: Pathways to Ignite Personal & Social Change*. 2nd edition, Discover Press, p. 94.
130 *Yale's Most Popular Class Ever: Happiness* by David Shimer. New York Times, Jan. 26, 2018: https://www.nytimes.com/2018/01/26/nyregion/at-yale-

class-on-happiness-draws-huge-crowd-laurie-santos.html
131 Log into University of Pennsylvania's Authentic Happiness website: https://www.authentichappiness.sas.upenn.edu/user/login?destination=node/423
132 Log into Univ. Penn. PERMA™ well-being survey: https://www.authentichappiness.sas.upenn.edu/user/login?destination=node/628
133 VIA Institute of Character website: Character Strengths Survey: http://www.viacharacter.org/www/Character-Strengths-Survey and Video: http://www.viacharacter.org/www/Character-Strengths-Survey
134 To access the Jung Typology personality test: http://www.humanmetrics.com/cgi-win/jtypes2.asp#questionnaire

Chapter 7

135 Audre Lorde quote from "*The Cancer Journals, Special Edition*," Aunt Lute Books, San Francisco, CA, 1997, p. 13.
136 Marianne Williamson, from "*A Return to Love: Reflections on the Principles of a Course in Miracles*" (1992, HarperCollins)
137 Adapted from *Exploring Your Vision, in Seven Steps*, Chapter 2 In: Lasley, Martha (2004). *Courageous Visions: How to Unleash Passionate Energy in Your Life and Your Organization.* Discover Press.
138 *Create a Personal Vision Statement That Can Guide Your Life* by Susan M. Heathfield, 7 January 2019: https://www.thebalancecareers.com/create-your-personal-vision-statement-1919208
139 Adapted from: Mitchell, Arthur H., Khairul Alam & Abdul Bari (2004). *Assessment of the Forest Department's Institutional Organization and Capacity to Manage the Protected Area System of Bangladesh*, Government of Bangladesh, Ministry of Environment and Forestry, USAID/Bangladesh, Dhaka.
140 From *Alice's Adventures in Wonderland* by Lewis Carroll, 1865
141 Lasley, Martha, Virginia Kellogg, Richard Michaels and Sharon Brown (2015). *Coaching for Transformation: Pathways to Ignite Personal & Social Change.* 2nd edition, Discover Press, p. 212.
142 SMART definitions from Lasley, Martha, Virginia Kellogg, Richard Michaels and Sharon Brown (2015). *Coaching for Transformation: Pathways to Ignite Personal & Social Change.* 2nd edition, Discover Press, pp. 189-190.
143 Categories and questions adapted from Lasley, Martha, Virginia Kellogg, Richard Michaels and Sharon Brown (2015). *Coaching for Transformation: Pathways to Ignite Personal & Social Change.* 2nd edition, Discover Press. AND the Chopra Center Life Coaching Discovery Session questionnaire.

Chapter 8

144 Quote by Leo Rosten from "*The Myths by Which We Live*," The Rotarian (Evanston, Illinois) volume 107, no. 3, September 1965, p. 55.
145 Nawalkha, Ajit (2018). *Live Big: The Entrepreneur's Guide to Passion,*

Practicality and Purpose. BenBella Books, Dallas, Texas.
146 Pevny, Ron (2014). *Conscious Living Conscious Aging: Embrace & Savor Your Next Chapter*. Atria Paperback, New York, and Beyond Words, Hillsboro, Oregon.
147 Dan Buettner and Blue Zones: https://www.bluezones.com/dan-buettner/; Dan Buettner TED Talk:
148 *3 Lessons in Having Purpose from Those Who Live to 100* by Melissa Eisler, Chopra Center's Mind-Body Medical Group
149 "*Caroline Myss' Advice for Getting to the Heart of Who You Really Are*," an interview with Oprah Winfrey, www.oprah.com, January 2013.
150 Myss, Caroline (2009). *Defy Gravity: Healing Beyond the Bounds of Reason*. Hay House
151 Frankl, Viktor (1946, Vienna, Austria & 1959 United States). *Man's Search for Meaning*. Verlag für Jugend und Volk (Austria) & Beacon Press (English)
152 Myss, Caroline - *op. cit.*
153 Newhouse, Margaret, with Judy Goggin (2004). *Life Planning for the 3rd Age: A Design and Resource Guide*. Civic Venture, San Francisco, California.
154 Envisioning your purpose questions adapted from: Lasley, Martha, Virginia Kellogg, Richard Michaels and Sharon Brown (2015). *Coaching for Transformation: Pathways to Ignite Personal & Social Change*. 2nd edition, Discover Press, p. 137.
155 Leider, Richard J. (2015). *The Power of Purpose: Find Meaning, Live Longer, Better*. 3rd edition. Berrett-Koehler, Oakland, California.
156 Leider, Richard J. (2015). *A Guide to Unlocking the Power of Purpose*. Richard Leider - Inventure - The Purpose Company, Edina, Minnesota. The seven reflections on purpose are used here with permission from the author.

Chapter 9

157 Adapted from: Lasley, Martha, Virginia Kellogg, Richard Michaels and Sharon Brown (2015). *Coaching for Transformation: Pathways to Ignite Personal and Social Change*. 2nd edition, Discover Press.
158 From: *The Dictionary of Obscure Sorrows*. https://en.wikipedia.org/wiki/The_Dictionary_of_Obscure_Sorrows
159 Lasley, Martha, Virginia Kellogg, Richard Michaels and Sharon Brown (2015). *Coaching for Transformation: Pathways to Ignite Personal & Social Change*. 2nd edition, Discover Press, p. 123.
160 *How Your Thoughts Create Your Reality: Discover the Potential of Your Mind* by Pam Grout, 11 April 2016:
161 Connie Schultz - TEDx Talk, Cleveland, 21 October 2016: https://www.youtube.com/watch?v=97d2P7U1Ukk
162 Mather, Mark, Linda A. Jacobsen and Kelvin M. Pollard (2015). *Aging*

in the United States. Population Bulletin 70, no. 2. Population Reference Bureau, Washington, D.C.

163 *The Baby Boomer Numbers Game: This massive generation could change our notions about retirement*. by Dave Bernard, *US News and World Report*, March 23, 2012.

164 *The Baby Boomer Number Game: This massive generation could change our notions about retirement.*
by Dave Bernard, *US News and World Report*, March 23, 2012

165 *Age 65 Retirement: The German Precedent*. Social Security History, US Social Security Administration: https://www.ssa.gov/history/age65.html

166 *The Baby Boomer Number Game: This massive generation could change our notions about retirement.*
by Dave Bernard, *US News and World Report*, March 23, 2012

167 *Number of older Americans in the workforce is on the rise*. by Bruce Drake, 7 January 2014, Facttank: News in the Numbers, Pew Research Center, Washington, D.C.

168 "Instead of feeling secure, many retirees feel betrayed" A "Washington Post" review by Cynthia Estlund, New York University, of the book by Katherine S. Newman (2018). *Downhill from Here: Retirement Insecurity in the Age of Inequality*. Metropolitan. "The Washington Post," 3 February 2019.

169 "*Retirees thought GE would take care of them forever. It didn't.*" by Natasha Rausch, Bloomberg, 19 December 2018.

170 Fottrell, Quentin (2014). *Boomers face a greater risk of depression and suicide*. MarketWatch, 17 August 2014.

171 Peter Greeman quoted in Newhouse, Margaret, with Judy Goggin (2004). *Life Planning for the 3rd Age: A Design and Resource Guide*. Civic Venture, San Francisco, California.

172 Excerpt from *Stages of Life*, an article by Carl Jung (ca. 1944) in *The Portable Jung*, ed. by Joseph Campbell, 1976

173 Fottrell, Quentin (2014). *Boomers face a greater risk of depression and suicide*. MarketWatch, 17 August 2014.

174 Nelson, John E. and Richard N. Bolles (2010). *What Color Is Your Parachute? For Retirement: Planning a Prosperous, Healthy, and Happy Future*. Crown Publishing, Ten Speed Press, Berkeley, California.

175 White, Elizabeth (2016). *55, Underemployed, and Faking Normal: Your Guide to a Better Life*. Simon & Schuster, New York.

176 Elizabeth White, *An honest look at the personal finance crisis*. TEDx VCU, Richmond, Virginia, February 2017, https://www.ted.com/talks/elizabeth_white_an_honest_look_at_the_personal_finance_crisis?language=en

177 *What is the 'Gig' Economy?* by Bill Wilson, business reporter, BBC News, 10 February 2017: https://www.bbc.com/news/business-38930048

178 The South Park Underwear Gnomes Profit Plan: https://vimeo.com/79954057
179 "The author of this proverb is unknown. It is commonly misattributed to Plato due to Benjamin Jowett's popular idiomatic 1871 translation of Plato's *Republic*, where in Book II, 369c, his translation reads: 'The true creator is necessity, who is the mother of our invention.' - Wikipedia
180 "*The Advantages Older Adults Bring to First-Time Entrepreneurship*" by Derek Lidow, *Forbes*, 5 March 2019: https://www.forbes.com/sites/dereklidow/2019/03/05/the-advantages-older-adults-bring-to-first-time-entrepreneurship/#677eac0544e7
181 Discussed in Hannon, Kerry E. (2019). *Never Too Old to Get Rich: The Entrepreneur's Guide to Starting a Business Mid-Life*. Next Avenue. John Wiley & Sons, Inc., Hoboken, New Jersey (pp 4-5).
182 Conley, Chip (2018). *Wisdom @ Work*. Currency, New York.
183 For more information on the Modern Elder Academy (MEA): https://www.chipconley.com/modern-elder-academy
184 Leider, Richard and David Shapiro (2015). *Work Reimagined: Uncover Your Calling*. Berrett-Koehler, Oakland CA.
185 Episode 155 - Microdosing LSD with Dr. James Fadiman, YouTube, vinicio510, Published Aug 31, 2017: (22:07) https://www.youtube.com/watch?v=77VgLYG7eTo&fbclid=IwAR1fKhpHMLbpGQvEZVLIqxjgAAgKyMl6ZFB6if3hvNI6skjPVRXOTRz9Ir4

Chapter 10

186 Nemeth, Maria (1997). *The Energy of Money: A Spiritual Guide to Financial and Personal Fulfillment*. Ballentine Wellspring, Random House Publishing Group, New York.
187 "*Let's get honest about our money problems*," Tammy Lally, TEDx Orlando, June 2017: https://www.youtube.com/watch?v=jlhtTKPkg5M
188 Lally, Tammy (2018). *Money Detox: Your Invitation to Liberation*. Little Lindsey Press, New York.
189 *The Baby Boomer Number Game: This massive generation could change our notions about retirement.*
by Dave Bernard, *US News and World Report*, March 23, 2012
190 Sean Williams, The Motley Fool, December 20, 2018, "*Social Security: Why claiming early could be all the rage next decade*"
191 Law of Attraction website: http://www.thelawofattraction.com/
192 Law of Abundance, Brian Tracy (for example): https://www.briantracy.com/blog/financial-success/the-law-of-abundance/
193 Levin, Nancy (2016). *Worthy: Boost Your Self-Worth to Grow Your Net-Worth*. Hay House, Inc., Carlsbad, California.
194 Price, Deborah L. (2003). *Money Magic: Unleashing Your True Potential*

for Prosperity and Fulfillment. New World Library, Novato, California.
195 Campbell, Joseph (1949). *The Hero with a Thousand Faces*. Bollingen Foundation, Pantheon Books.
196 Nemeth, Maria (1997). *The Energy of Money: A Spiritual Guide to Financial and Personal Fulfillment*. Ballentine Wellspring, Random House Publishing Group, New York.
197 Twist, Lynn (2003). *The Soul of Money: Transforming Your Relationship with Money and Life*. W.W. Norton & Company, New York.
198 Lynn Twist and the Soul of Money Institute, information and courses, website: https://soulofmoney.org/
199 Orman, Suze (2012). *The 9 Steps to Financial Freedom: Practical and Spiritual Steps So You Can Stop Worrying*. Three Rivers Press, Random House, New York (first published 1997).
200 Prior, Pam (2018). *Your First CFO: The Accounting Cure for Small Business Owners*. Morgan James Publishing, New York.
201 Pam Prior financial advisor website: https://pamprior.com/
202 Cameron, Julia (1992). *The Artist's Way: A Spiritual Path to Higher Creativity*. Jeremy P. Tarcher/Putnam, New York.

Chapter 11

203 Schachter-Shalomi, Zalman and Ronald S. Miller (1995, updated 2014). *From Age-Ing to Sage-Ing: A Revolutionary Approach to Growing Older*. Time Warner Books.
204 Rabbi Zalman Schachter: Spiritual Eldering (excerpt) -- A Thinking Allowed DVD w/ Jeffrey Mishlove, Thinking Allowed TV, Published 31 August 2010: https://www.youtube.com/watch?v=9QHekfSByMY
205 Medical definition of psychotechnology – the application of psychological methods and results to the solution of practical problems and an application of technology for psychological purposes such as personal growth or behavior change.
206 Schachter-Shalomi, Zalman and Ronald S. Miller (1995, updated 2014). *From Age-Ing to Sage-Ing: A Revolutionary Approach to Growing Older*. Time Warner Books.
207 Atlantic City Pop Festival, 1-3 August 1969: https://en.wikipedia.org/wiki/Atlantic_City_Pop_Festival
208 *The Great Lost Rock Festival of 1969*, by Jeff Tamarkin: https://bestclassicbands.com/atlantic-city-pop-festival-1969-8-4-15/
209 Bourzat, Françoise with Kristina Hunter, Foreword by Ralph Metzner (2019). *Consciousness Medicine: Indigenous Wisdom, Entheogens, and Expanded States of Consciousness for Healing and Growth*. North Atlantic Books, Berkeley, California.
210 *Plant Intelligence and the Importance of Imagination In Science*, a pre-

sentation by Dr. Monica Gagliano, a presentation given at the 2018 Bioneers Conference, San Rafael, California, October 2018: https://bioneers.org/monica-gagliano-plant-intelligence-and-the-importance-of-imagination-in-science/

211 *Plant Intelligence and Human Consciousness: Into the Mystery*, a panel discussion with Michael Pollan, Monica Gagliano and J.P. Harpignies at the 2018 Bioneers Conference, San Rafael, California, October 2018: https://bioneers.org/plant-intelligence-and-human-consciousness-into-the-mystery-bioneers-conference-panel/

212 Weil, Andrew and W. Rosen (1993). *From Chocolate to Morphine: Everything You Need to Know About Mind-Altering Drugs*. Houghton Mifflin, New York.

213 Godlaski, Theodore M (2011). *The God within*. Substance Use and Misuse 46(10): 1217–1222.

214 Walsh, Chales & Charles S. Grob, eds. (2005). *Higher Wisdom: Eminent Elders Explore the Continuing Impact of Psychedelics*. State University of New York Press, Albany, New York.

215 Excerpted from: Chögyam Trungpa Rinpoche (2010). "Facing Yourself," in *Smile at Fear: Awakening the True Heart of Bravery* by, page 4, Edited by Carolyn Rose Gimian. Shambhala Publications, Boulder, Colorado

216 Chödrön, Pema (2017). *When Things Fall Apart: Heart Advice for Difficult Times*. Thorsons Classics, London.

217 Myss, Caroline (2009). *Defy Gravity: Healing Beyond the Bounds of Reason*. Hay House.

218 Grof, Stanislav and Christina Grof (2010). *Holotropic Breathwork: A New Approach to Self-Exploration and Therapy*. (SUNY Series in Transpersonal and Humanistic Psychology). Excelsior Editions, State University of New York Press, Albany, New York. – and - Grof, Stanislav (2012). *Healing Our Deepest Wounds: The Holotropic Paradigm Shift*. Stream of Experience Productions.

219 Stanislav Grof quoted directly from a webinar, Psychology of the Future: Exploring the Leading Edge of Psychology, Healing & Self-Discovery. 22 February 2019, The Shift Network: https://theshiftnetwork.com/PsychologyOfTheFuture

220 Pollan, Michael (2018). *How to Change Your Mind: What the New Science of Psychedelics Teaches Us About Consciousness, Dying, Addiction, Depression, and Transcendence*. Penguin Press.

221 *Bill Wilson's Experience with LSD*: https://aaagnostica.org/2015/05/10/bill-wilsons-experience-with-lsd/

222 *Psilocybin: A Journey Beyond the Fear of Death?* By Richard Schiffman. Scientific American, December 2016.: https://www.scientificamerican.com/article/psilocybin-a-journey-beyond-the-fear-of-death/

223 *Hallucinogens Have Doctors Tuning in Again*. By John Tierney, The New

York Times, 11 April 2010.
224 *Going Out on a High: The Doctor Advocating LSD for the Dying*. By Eugene S. Robinson, The Daily Dose, 2 December 2018.
225 Multidisciplinary Association of Psychedelic Studies (MAPS): https://maps.org/
226 *Psilocybin for the masses Oregon considering legalizing mushrooms: Oregon state legislature is considering a bill that would decriminalize psychedelic mushrooms*. by Lilly Dancyger, 5 December 2018 (This article originally appeared in *Rolling Stone*): https://www.salon.com/2018/12/05/psilocybin-for-the-masses-oregon-considering-legalizing-mushrooms_partner/#.XC-um7YLhIM.twitter
227 *Medicine for the Modern World: Go beyond eco-tourism with a transformative travel immersion to the Amazon Rainforest*. Pachamama Alliance: https://landing.pachamama.org/medicine-for-the-modern-world
228 Pachamama Alliance online course, *Awakening the Dreamer*: https://www.pachamama.org/engage/awakening-the-dreamer
229 Fadiman, James (2011). *The Psychedelic Explorer's Guide: Safe, Therapeutic and Sacred Journeys*. Park Street Press, Rochester, Vermont.
230 Interview with Dr. James Fadiman, *The Psychedelic Explorer's Guide – Risks, Micro-Dosing, Ibogaine and More*. By Tim Ferriss, 21 March 2015: https://tim.blog/2015/03/21/james-fadiman/
231 Disclaimer: *Do not use any legal or illegal drugs or substances without consulting a medical professional or other trained professional. The information provided here is for informational purposes only*.
232 The Third Wave website: https://thethirdwave.co/
233 Anderson, Thomas, Rotem Petranker, Adam Christopher, Daniel Rosenbaum, Cory Weissman, Le-Anh Dinh-Williams, Katrina Hui, and Emma Hapke (2019). *Psychedelic microdosing benefits and challenges: an empirical codebook. Harm Reduction Journal*, Volume 16, Article 43 (published: 10 July 2019). https://harmreductionjournal.biomedcentral.com/articles/10.1186/s12954-019-0308-4
234 Waldman, Ayelet (2017). *A Really Good Day: How Microdosing Made a Make a Difference in My Mood, My Marriage and My Life*, Alfred A. Knopf, New York.
235 Disclaimer: *Do not use any legal or illegal drugs or substances without consulting a medical professional or other trained professional. The information provided here is for informational purposes only.*
236 *What is psychospiritual coaching*? https://evergreen-therapy.com/psychospiritual-coaching/
237 Jung C. G. (1963). *Memories, Dreams, Reflections*. Pantheon, New York.
238 Lasley, Martha, Virginia Kellogg, Richard Michaels and Sharon Brown (2015). *Coaching for Transformation: Pathways to Ignite Personal & Social Change.*

2nd ed., Discover Press (p. 73).
239 Caroline Myss, "*Shadow: On Truth, Betrayal, and Trump*" (SoulFeed Podcast), YouTube: https://www.youtube.com/watch?v=qpARDWvxPS0
240 Zweig, Connie (2017). *Meeting the Shadow of Spirituality: The Hidden Power of Darkness on the Path*. iUniverse, Bloomington, Indiana. – and - Zweig, Connie, and Steve Wolf (1997). *Romancing the Shadow: A Guide to Soul Work for a Vital, Authentic Life*. Ballantine Wellspring, New York.
241 *Psychedelic Integration 101: The What, Why, When & How of Integrating Psychedelic Journeys*. By Sherree Malcolm Godasi: www.PsychedelicIntegrationCoach.com
242 From: *Psychedelic Integration Coaching Sessions* guidelines: https://psychedelicintegration-oc.com/?olaS=meet-up-psychedelic-psycho-spiritual-integration-oc
243 Deborah Servetnick, psychedelic integration coach, Pikesville, Maryland, deborah@psychedelicoach.com
244 II Corinthians 4.1:18
245 St. Francis of Assisi quoted in "*Love Poems from God: Twelve Sacred Voices from the East and West*," edited by Daniel Ladinsky (Penguin Group, New York, 2002).

Chapter 12

246 Jung, Carl (1934). *The Meaning of Psychology for Modern Man.*
247 *Numinous* definition from Oxford English Dictionary.
248 Otto, Rudolf (1923). *The Idea of the Holy: An Inquiry into the Non-Rational Factor in the Idea of the Divine*. Oxford University Press (published in 1917 in German as *Das Heilige*).
249 Stanislav Grof quoted directly from a webinar, *Psychology of the Future: Exploring the Leading Edge of Psychology, Healing & Self-Discovery*. 22 February 2019, The Shift Network: https://theshiftnetwork.com/PsychologyOfTheFuture
250 Lyric from the song, *When the Music's Over*, by the Doors from the 1967 album *Strange Days* by Elektra Records.
251 Kübler-Ross, Elisabeth (1969). *On Death and Dying*. Scribner; Classic edition (July 2, 1997)
252 For more information on Matthew Fox and Creation Spirituality: http://www.matthewfox.org/what-is-creation-spirituality/
253 N,N-dimethyltryptamine, DMT, is a short-acting and very powerful psychedelic naturally occurring in plants and animals, including humans. It is the psychoactive substance, for example, in *ayahuasca*, the Amazonian plant medicine.
254 Ram Dass interview with Matthew Fox. *Part 1*: https://www.youtube.com/watch?v=ukCwYDWiIoM; *Part 2*: https://www.youtube.com/watch?v=5vMf1xmnDUQ

255 Forte, Robert, ed. (2012). *Entheogens and the Future of Religion*. Park Street Press, Rochester, Vermont (originally published in 1997 by the Council on Spiritual Practices)

256 Sri Chinmoy (1991). *Twenty-seven thousand aspiration-plants.* Part 163, Agni Press.

257 Sri Chinmoy (2004). *The oneness of the Eastern heart and the Western mind.* Part 3, Agni Press.

258 Abraham Maslow, "*The Farther Reaches of Human Nature,*" New York, 1971, p. 269.

259 Frankl, Viktor (1946 Austria & 1959 United States). *Man's Search for Meaning*. Verlag für Jugend und Volk (Vienna, Austria) & Beacon Press (Boston, Massachusetts).

260 Definition of "mind monkey" or monkey mind from Wikipedia

261 Kristin Keyes, *A Journey to Self-Discovery: Lessons of the Labyrinth*, TEDx Coeur d'Alene, 21 November 2017. https://www.youtube.com/watch?v=vNN8ZMHC9r0

262 Veriditas Labyrinth website: https://www.veriditas.org/

263 Artress, Lauren (2006). *Walking a Sacred Path: Rediscovering the Labyrinth as a Spiritual Practice*. Riverhead Books, New York.

264 Veriditas & The Labyrinth Society World-Wide Labyrinth Locator: https://labyrinthlocator.com/

265 A.R.E. = Association for Research and Enlightenment, Virginia Beach, Virginia

266 The course drew from the book: Eubel, Nancy (2010). *Mindwalking: Rewriting Your Past to Create Your Future*. A.R.E. Press, Virginia Beach, Virginia.

267 Robinson, John C. (2016). *The Divine Human: The Final Transformation of Sacred Aging*. O-Books, John Hunt Publishing, Ltd., Alresford, Hants, UK.

Chapter 13

268 Lyla June Johnston, *Nihimá Nahasdzáán: Healing Women and Nature Through a Diné (Navajo) Lens*. Bioneers Conference, San Rafael, California, 21 October 2018, beginning at 05:30 on video: https://www.youtube.com/watch?v=YZQiihDC__E

269 Quoted in: *There's More to Life Than Being Happy: Meaning comes from the pursuit of more complex things than happiness*. by Emily Esfahani Smith, The Atlantic, 9 January 2013.

270 Terry Tempest Williams, writer, educator, conservationist, and activist, quoted from her talk, "*Erosion: Our Undoing is our Becoming,*" at the 30th annual Bioneers Conference, 18 October 2019, San Rafael, California.

271 Joanna Macy and The Great Turning (Trailer) FMTV- Food Matters, published 16 March 2017: https://www.youtube.com/watch?v=BUkoXMff1Vw

272 *Joanna Macy on Uncertainty*, free484, published 30 January 2014: https://www.youtube.com/watch?v=KcH4Byo7snU
273 Pevny, Ron (2014). *Conscious Living, Conscious Aging: Embrace & Savor Your Next Chapter*. Atria, New York, & Beyond Words, Hillsboro, Oregon.
274 Wheatley, Margaret J. (2009). *Turning to One Another: Simple Conversations to Restore Hope to the Future*. Berrett-Koehler Publishers, Oakland, California.
275 Elders Action Network (EAN) website for more information: https://www.eldersaction.net/
276 To learn more about the Work That Reconnects visit: www.workthatreconnects.org
277 Macy, Joanna and Molly Brown (2014). *Coming Back to Life*. New Society Publishers, British Columbia, Canada.
278 Work That Reconnects Network website: https://workthatreconnects.org/
279 Core Assumptions of the Work That Reconnects: https://workthatreconnects.org/foundations-of-the-work/
280 *Choosing the Story We Want for Our World* by Molly Brown and Joanna Macy may be found on the Work That Reconnects website: https://workthatreconnects.org/choosing-the-story-we-want-for-our-world/#more-6894
281 Constance Washburn website for more information: https://www.constancewashburn.com/
282 Macy, Joanna and Chris Johnstone (2012). *Active Hope: How to Face the Mess We're in Without Going Crazy*. New World Library, Novato, California.
283 Korten, David C. 2006). *The Great Turning: From Empire to Earth Community*. People-Centered Development Forum, Kumarian Press (Bloomfield CT) and Barrett-Koehler Publishers (San Francisco CA).
284 Hawken, Paul (2008). *Blessed Unrest: How the Largest Social Movement in History Is Restoring Grace, Justice, and Beauty to the World*. Penguin Books, New York.
285 Harvey, Andrew (2009). *The Hope: A Guide to Spiritual Activism*. Hay House, Carlsbad, California.
286 Berry, Thomas (1999). *The Great Work: Our Way into the Future*. Bell Tower, New York.
287 Wild Awakenings website for more information: http://wildawakenings.com/
288 Fox, Matthew, Skylar Wilson and Jennifer Berit Listug (2018). *Order of the Sacred Earth: An Intergenerational Vision of Love and Action*. Monkfish Book Publishing Company, Rhinebeck, New York.
289 Order of the Sacred Earth website for more information: https://www.orderofthesacredearth.org/

290 Gawain Shakti (2000). *The Path of Transformation: How Healing Ourselves Can Change the World.* 2nd edition. Nataraj Publishing, a division of New World Library, Novato, California.
291 Schachter-Shalomi, Zalman and Ronald S. Miller (1995, updated 2014). *From Age-Ing to Sage-Ing: A Revolutionary Approach to Growing Older.* Time Warner Books.
292 The Dalai Lama, quoted in *Time*, December 1997
293 Richard Pimentel, "*How to Live the Life You Never Imagined,*" Goalcast, video published on 26 April 2018: https://www.youtube.com/watch?v=-teUd1GB8kgU
294 Quote from Pres. Barack Obama, commencement address, Howard University, Washington, D.C., 10 Feb. 2017
295 Valerie Kaur, civil rights attorney, activist, and founder of the Revolutionary Love Project, quoted from her talk, "*Breathe! Push! The Labor of Revolutionary Love,*" at the 30th annual Bioneers Conference, 19 October 2019, San Rafael, California.
296 *Resolutions: Find What Breaks Your Heart.* Blog posted by serenaellens, January 18, 2017: https://thestorycafeblog.wordpress.com/2017/01/18/resolutions-find-what-breaks-your-heart/
297 Arrien, Angeles (2007). *The Second Half of Life: Opening the Eight Gates of Wisdom.* Sounds True, Boulder Colorado (first published 2005).
298 Caroline Myss on the Spiritual crisis (part 3/3), YouTube, Lilou Mace, Published on Jul 2, 2010: https://www.youtube.com/watch?v=1tQwkJ80N5U
299 From page 16 in *The Essential Rumi.* Translated by Coleman Barks. 2004. Harper, San Francisco.

Chapter 14

300 From: *Being Peace* by Thich Nhat Hanh
301 I don't mean to besmirch my mother's memory. She was a good woman with an illness. She had her own demons and did the best she could to survive as a widow with three young children during the madness and hypocrisy of the '50s and '60s. I have forgiven her. She showed me unconditional love, and for that I will always be grateful.
302 Macy, Joanna and Molly Brown (2014). *Coming Back to Life.* New Society Publishers, British Columbia, Canada.
303 Robinson, John (2013). *What Aging Men Want: The Odyssey as a Parable of Male Aging.* Psyche Books, John Hunt Publishing, Ltd., Alresford, Hants, UK
304 Robinson, John (2013). *What Aging Men Want: The Odyssey as a Parable of Male Aging.* Psyche Books, John Hunt Publishing, Ltd., Alresford, Hants, UK (pp. 142-144).
305 Excerpt from "In Memory of Robin Williams: Prayers for Depression"

by Caroline Myss, Aug 13, 2014, Hay House, Heal Your Life: https://www.healyourlife.com/in-memory-of-robin-williams. In addition, Myss offers these prayers for all those who are coping with depression: "*My prayer on this day is that I receive the graces of hope and fortitude during this time in my life. Help me to make it through those moments when I feel like giving up. Hover over me, God, with guidance through my thoughts and through my dreams.*" And another, "*Guide me through this darkness, Lord. Hover over me especially when I cannot seem to hold on for another moment. Flood me with the graces of hope and fortitude. Send your angels to watch over me as I sleep through the night. Remind me during the day that from this small dark cocoon, I will emerge a butterfly.*"

306 "*The Gratitude of Labour (Terumah, Covenant & Conversation 5775 on Ethics)*" by Rabbi Jonathan Sacks, *The Times of Israel*, 18 February 2015: http://blogs.timesofisrael.com/the-gratitude-of-labour-terumah-covenant-conversation-5775-on-ethics/

307 The Earthways Foundation briefly defines conscious activism as "*engagement in the world that expresses and reveals our most profound understanding of the nature of reality.*" See also: O'Dea, James (2014). *The Conscious Activist: Where Activism Meets Mysticism.* Watkins Publishing, London, England, UK.

308 Frankl, Viktor E. (1946). *Man's Search for Meaning.*

309 Quoted by many, including Angeles Arrien in *The Second Half of Life*, as being from Ralph Waldo Emerson, but an article about the correct author and her winning essay, published in the *Emporia Gazette*, Emporia, Kansas, 11 December 1905 may be found here: https://quoteinvestigator.com/2012/06/26/define-success/ (Even the quote I use here is not precisely what she wrote!)

310 Lyrics from "*Truckin'*, written by Jerry Garcia, Phil Lesh, Robert C. Hunter, Bob Weir, © Universal Music Publishing Group. "*What a Long Strange Trip It's Been: The Best of the Grateful Dead,*" released by Warner Bros. on 18 August 1977, was the Grateful Dead's second compilation album.

Appendix 1

Additional Resources

Books: Discover and Learn!

This is just the tip of the iceberg. The following is neither a bibliography of works cited (see Endnotes) nor an attempt at giving you a list of all the best offerings out there. This is but a sampling of books relevant to each main topic. Topics often overlap, but these should be obvious. All these resources are, in my opinion, excellent, appropriate, and useful.

Ageism and the Patriarchy

Applewhite, Ashton (2018 & 2019). *This Chair Rocks: A Manifesto Against Aging*. Melville House, Brooklyn, New York.

Gillick, Muriel R. (2007). *The Denial of Aging: Perpetual Youth, Eternal Life, and Other Dangerous Fantasies*. Harvard University Press, Cambridge, Massachusetts.

Gullette, Margaret Morganroth (2013). *Agewise: Fighting the New Ageism in America*. University of Chicago Press.

Hollis, James (1994). *Under Saturn's Shadow: The Wounding and Healing of Men*. Inner City Books, Toronto, Canada.

hooks, bell (2004). *The Will to Change: Men, Masculinity and Love*. Washington Square Press, New York.

Jensen, Robert (2017). *The End of Patriarchy: Radical Feminism for Men*. Spinifex Press, North Geelong, Victoria, Australia.

MacDonald, Barbara (2001). *Look Me in the Eye: Old Women, Aging, and Ageism*. Spinsters Ink, Tallahassee, Florida.

Nambangi, LaBelle with foreword by Imbolo Mbue (2018). *Women Who Soar: Stories of Challenging the Status Quo and Breaking the Global Patriarchy*. Wise Ink, Minneapolis, Minnesota.

Nelson Todd D. (ed.) (2004). *Ageism: Stereotyping and Prejudice against Older Persons*. A Bradford Book. MIT Press, Cambridge, Massachusetts.

Conscious Aging

Arrien, Angeles (2005). *The Second Half of Life: Opening the Eight Gates of Wisdom*. Sounds True

Fischer, Norman (2008). *Sailing Home: Using the Wisdom of Homer's Odyssey to Navigate Life's Perils and Pitfalls.* North Atlantic Books, Berkeley, California.

Freed, Rachael (2013). *Your Legacy Matters: Harvesting the Love and Lessons of Your Life.* Minerva Press, Minneapolis, Minnesota.

Freedman, Marc (2018). *How to Live Forever: The Enduring Power of Connecting the Generations.* PublicAffairs, Perseus Books, New York.

Gawande, Atul (2014). *Being Mortal: Medicine and What Matters in the End.* Picador, New York.

Halifax, Joan (2009). *Being with Dying: Cultivating Compassion and Fearlessness in the Presence of Death.* Shambhala, Oakland, California.

Hollis, James (2018). *Living an Examined Life: Wisdom for the Second Half of the Journey: A 21-Step Plan for Addressing the Unfinished Business of Your Life.* Sounds True, Boulder, Colorado.

Luskin, Frederic (2002). *Forgive for Good: A Proven Prescription for Health and Happiness.* Harper Collins, New York.

Martin, William (2010). *The Sage's Tao Te Ching: Ancient Advice for the Second Half of Life.* The Experiment, Tenth Anniversary Edition.

Newhouse, Margaret L. (2016). *Legacies of the Heart: Living a Life that Matters.* EBook Bakery Books.

Ostaseski, Frank (2017). *The Five Invitations: Discovering What Death Can Teach Us About Living Fully.* Flatiron Books, New York.

Pevny, Ron (2014). *Conscious Living, Conscious Aging: Embrace & Savor Your Next Chapter.* Atria, New York, & Beyond Words, Hillsboro, Oregon.

Phifer, Nan Merrick (2001). *Memoirs of the Soul: A Writing Guide.* Ingot Press.

Pipher Mary (2019). *Women Rowing North: Navigating Life's Currents and Flourishing as We Age.* Bloomsbury Publishing, London.

Pinkson, Tom (2013). *Fruitful Aging: Finding the Gold in the Golden Years.* Wakan.

Ram Dass (2000). *Still Here: Embracing Aging, Changing, and Dying.* Riverhead Books.

Ram Dass and Mirabai Bush (2018). *Walking Each Other Home: Conversations on Loving and Dying.* Love Serve Remember Foundation. Sounds True, Boulder, Colorado.

Rauch, Jonathan (2018). *The Happiness Curve: Why Life Gets Better after 50.* Thomas Dunne Books, St. Martin's Press, New York City.

Robinson, John (2013). *What Aging Men Want: The Odyssey as a Parable of Male Aging.* Psyche Books, John Hunt Publishing, Ltd., Alresford, Hants, UK

Robinson, John (2012). *The Three Secrets of Aging: A Radical Guide.* O Books.

Schachter-Shalomi, Zalman and Ronald S. Miller (1995, updated 2014). *From Age-Ing to Sage-Ing: A Revolutionary Approach to Growing Older.* Time Warner Books.

Schlitz, Marilyn Mandala, Cassandra Vieten, and Tina Amorok (2007). *Living Deeply: The Art and Science of Transformation in Everyday Life.* Noetic Books, Institute of Noetic Sciences, New Harbinger Publications, Oakland, California.

Schlitz, Marilyn Mandala, Tina Amorok and Marc Micozzi (2004). *Consciousness and Healing: Integral Approaches to Mind-Body Medicine.* Churchill Livingstone, Elsevier, London.

Shealy, C. Norman (2014). *Living Bliss: Major Discoveries Along the Holistic Path* (Foreword by Caroline Myss). Hay House, Carlsbad, California.

Thomas, William H. (2004). *What Are Old People For? How Elders Will Save the World.* Van der Wyk & Burnham, Acton, Massachusetts.

Tornstam, Lars (2005). *Gerotranscendence: A Developmental Theory of Positive Aging.* Springer Publishing, New York.

Wyatt Karen M. (2012). *What Really Matters: Seven Lessons for Living from the Stories of the Dying.* Sunroom Studios.

Zweig, Connie (in press, 2020). *Reinventing Age from the Inside Out: How to Cross the Threshold from Role to Soul.*

Values, Strengths, Vision, and Goals

Deiner, Ed and Robert Biswas-Diener (2008). *Happiness: Unlocking the Mysteries of Psychological Wealth.* Wiley-Blackwell.

Eubel, Nancy (2010). *Mindwalking: Rewriting Your Past to Create Your Future.* A.R.E. Press, Virginia Beach, Virginia.

Lasley, Martha, Virginia Kellogg, Richard Michaels, and Sharon Brown (2015). *Coaching for Transformation: Pathways to Ignite Personal & Social Change.* 2nd edition, Discover Press.

Lasley, Martha (2004). *Courageous Visions: How to Unleash Passionate Energy in Your Life and Your Organization.* Discover Press.

Levin, Nancy (2014). *Jump ... And Your Life Will Appear: An Inch-by-Inch Guide to Making a Major Change.* Hay House Inc.

Maslow, Abraham (1954). *Motivation and Personality.* 1st edition: 1954, Harper & Brothers, New York.

Seligman, Martin (2011). *Flourish: A New Understanding of Happiness and Well-Being - and How to Achieve Them.* Free Press, New York.

Seligman, Martin (2002). *Authentic Happiness: Using the New Positive Psychology to Realize Your Potential for Lasting Fulfillment.* Free Press, New York.

Purpose

Agronin, Marc E. (2018). *The End of Old Age: Living a Longer, More Purposeful Life.* Da Capo Lifelong Books, Cambridge, Massachusetts.

Frankl, Viktor (1946, Vienna, Austria & 1959 United States). *Man's Search for Meaning.* Verlag für Jugend und Volk (Austria) & Beacon Press (English)

Leider, Richard J. (2015). *The Power of Purpose: Find Meaning, Live Longer, Better.* 3rd edition. Berrett-Koehler, Oakland, California.

Richard Leider and David Shapiro (2004). *Reclaiming Your Place at the Fire: Living the Second Half of Your Life on Purpose.* BerrettKoehler.

Newhouse, Margaret, with Judy Goggin (2004). *Life Planning for the 3rd Age: A Design and Resource Guide*. Civic Venture, San Francisco, California.

Work

Bratter, Bernice and Helen Dennis (2008). *Project Renewment: The First Retirement Model for Career Women*. Scribner, New York.

Conley, Chip (2018). *Wisdom @ Work*. Currency, New York.

Hannon, Kerry E. (2019). *Never Too Old to Get Rich: The Entrepreneur's Guide to Starting a Business Mid-Life*. Next Avenue. John Wiley & Sons, Inc., Hoboken, New Jersey.

Leider, Richard and David Shapiro (2015). *Work Reimagined: Uncover Your Calling*. Berrett-Koehler, Oakland CA.

Nelson, John E. and Richard N. Bolles (2010). *What Color Is Your Parachute? For Retirement: Planning a Prosperous, Healthy, and Happy Future*. Crown Publishing, Ten Speed Press, Berkeley, California.

White, Elizabeth (2016). *55, Underemployed, and Faking Normal: Your Guide to a Better Life*. Simon & Schuster, New York.

Prosperity

Lally, Tammy (2018). *Money Detox: Your Invitation to Liberation*. Little Lindsey Press, New York.

Levin, Nancy (2016). *Worthy: Boost Your Self-Worth to Grow Your Net-Worth*. Hay House, Inc., Carlsbad, California.

Nemeth, Maria (1997). *The Energy of Money: A Spiritual Guide to Financial and Personal Fulfillment*. Ballentine Wellspring, Random House Publishing Group, New York.

Orman, Suze (2012). *The 9 Steps to Financial Freedom: Practical and Spiritual Steps So You Can Stop Worrying*. Three Rivers Press, Random House, New York (first published 1997).

Price, Deborah L. (2003). *Money Magic: Unleashing Your True Potential for Prosperity and Fulfillment*. New World Library, Novato, California.

Prior, Pam (2018). *Your First CFO: The Accounting Cure for Small Business Owners*. Morgan James Publishing, New York.

Twist, Lynn (2003). *The Soul of Money: Transforming Your Relationship with Money and Life*. W.W. Norton & Company, New York.

Consciousness Expansion

Bourzat, Françoise with Kristina Hunter, Foreword by Ralph Metzner (2019). *Consciousness Medicine: Indigenous Wisdom, Entheogens, and Expanded States of Consciousness for Healing and Growth*. North Atlantic Books, Berkeley, California.

Dispenza, Joe (2012). *Breaking the Habit of Being Yourself: How to Lose Your Mind and Create a New One*. Hay House, Carlsbad, California.

Fadiman, James (2011). *The Psychedelic Explorer's Guide: Safe, Therapeutic and Sacred Journeys*. Park Street Press, Rochester, Vermont.

Forte, Robert, ed. (2012). *Entheogens and the Future of Religion*. Park Street Press, Rochester, Vermont (originally published in 1997 by the Council on Spiritual Practices)

Grof, Stanislav (2012). *Healing Our Deepest Wounds: The Holotropic Paradigm Shift*. Stream of Experience Productions.

Harris, Rachel (2017). *Listening to Ayahuasca: New Hope for Depression, Addiction, PTSD, and Anxiety*. New World Library, Novato, California.

McKenna, Terrence (1993). *Food of the Gods: The Search for the Original Tree of Knowledge A Radical History of Plants, Drugs, and Human Evolution*. Bantam, New York, NY.

Pollan, Michael (2018). *How to Change Your Mind: What the New Science of Psychedelics Teaches Us About Consciousness, Dying, Addiction, Depression, and Transcendence*. Penguin Press.

Richardson, Peter (2014). *No Simple Highway: A Cultural History of the Grateful Dead*. St. Martin's Press, New York.

Strassman, Rick (2000). *DMT: The Spirit Molecule: A Doctor's Revolutionary Research into the Biology of Near-Death and Mystical Experiences*. Park Street Press, Rochester, Vermont.

Waldman, Ayelet (2017). *A Really Good Day: How Microdosing Made a Difference in My Mood, My Marriage, and My Life*. Alfred A. Knopf, New York.

Walsh, Charles and Charles S. Grob, eds. (2005). *Higher Wisdom: Eminent Elders Explore the Continuing Impact of Psychedelics*. State University of New York Press, Albany, New York.

Spirituality

Artress, Lauren (2006). *Walking a Sacred Path: Rediscovering the Labyrinth as a Spiritual Practice*. Riverhead Books, New York.

Fox, Matthew (2012). *Hildegard of Bingen: A Saint for Our Times*. Namaste Publishing, Vancouver, Canada.

Fox, Matthew (2000). *Original Blessing*. Jeremy P. Tarcher / Putnam, New York

Fox, Matthew (2008 *The Hidden Spirituality of Men: Ten Metaphors to Awaken the Sacred Masculine*. New World Library, Novato, California.

Robinson, John C. (2016). *The Divine Human: The Final Transformation of Sacred Aging*. O-Books, John Hunt Publishing, Ltd., Alresford, Hants, UK.

Rohr, Richard (2011). *Falling Upward: A Spirituality for the Two Halves of Life*. Jossey-Bass.

Singer, Michael A. (2007). *The Untethered Soul: The Journey Beyond Yourself*. New Harbinger Publications/ Noetic Books, Oakland, California.

Zweig, Connie (2017). *Meeting the Shadow of Spirituality: The Hidden Power of Darkness on the Path*. iUniverse, Bloomington, Indiana.

Empowerment, Service, and Activism

Berry, Thomas (1999). *The Great Work: Our Way into the Future*. Bell Tower, New York.

Fox, Matthew, Skylar Wilson and Jennifer Berit Listug (2018). *Order of the Sacred Earth: An Intergenerational Vision of Love and Action.* Monkfish Book Publishing Company, Rhinebeck, New York.

Gawain Shakti (2000). *The Path of Transformation: How Healing Ourselves Can Change the World.* 2nd edition. Nataraj Publishing, a division of New World Library, Novato, California.

Harvey, Andrew (2009). *The Hope: A Guide to Spiritual Activism.* Hay House, Carlsbad, California.

Hawken, Paul, ed. (2017). *Drawdown: The Most Comprehensive Plan Ever Proposed to Reverse Global Warming.* Penguin Books, New York.

Hawken, Paul (2008). *Blessed Unrest: How the Largest Social Movement in History Is Restoring Grace, Justice, and Beauty to the World.* Penguin Books, New York.

Korten, David C. (2015). *Change the Story, Change the Future: A Living Economy for a Living Earth.* Berrett-Koehler Publishers, Oakland, California.

Korten, David C. (2006). *The Great Turning: From Empire to Earth Community.* People-Centered Development Forum, Kumarian Press (Bloomfield CT) and Barrett-Koehler Publishers (San Francisco CA).

Macy, Joanna and Molly Brown (2014). *Coming Back to Life.* New Society Publishers, British Columbia, Canada.

Macy, Joanna and Chris Johnstone (2012). *Active Hope: How to Face the Mess We're in Without Going Crazy.* New World Library, Novato, California.

O'Dea, James (2014). *The Conscious Activist: Where Activism Meets Mysticism.* Watkins Publishing, London, England, UK.

Plotkin, Bill (2008). *Nature and the Human Soul: Cultivating Wholeness and Community in a Fragmented World.* New World Library.

Robinson, John C. (2020). *Mystical Activism: Transforming A World in Crisis.* Changemakers Books, John Hunt Publishing, UK.

Organizations: Get Involved!

Following is a list of some organizations relevant to conscious ageing and related topics in this book. In no way is this list exhaustive.

350.org. "350.org is building a global grassroots movement to solve the climate crisis. Our online campaigns, grassroots organizing, and mass public actions are led from the bottom up by thousands of volunteer organizers in over 188 countries. …We're an international movement of ordinary people working to end the age of fossil fuels and build a world of community-led renewable energy for all." https://350.org/about/

Aging2.0. "Founded in 2012 by Stephen Johnston and Katy Fike, Aging2.0 strives to accelerate innovation to address the biggest challenges and opportunities in aging. Aging2.0's international, interdisciplinary and intergenerational community has grown to 40k+ innovators across 20+ countries. Our volunteer-run chapter network, which spans 75+ cities, has hosted more than 550 events around the world. Aging2.0 is run by a 'small-but-mighty' team out of San Francisco, California and Chapter Ambassadors in 75+ cities around the globe." https://www.aging2.com/

A Tribe Called Aging. "Heartfelt activists and thinkers are trying to understand and change our culture's outlook, policies and fears about aging and dying. We agree on the fundamental need to identify, expose and dismantle ageism, both societal and internalized. We believe that people can change their minds, their actions and their feelings—indeed, we believe life is change. We appreciate the beauty and power of impermanence." https://www.atribecalledaging.com/

Art of Dying Institute. The Art of Dying Institute is "designed to address the need for a cultural awakening around the themes of death, how we die and the consequences for how we live. … Our Vision: To awaken a deeper inquiry and more conscious engagement with death and dying. … Our Mission: The Art of Dying Institute, an initiative of the New York Open Center, offers a variety of innovative programs, addressing the need for cultural awakening around themes of death, how we die, and the consequences for how we live." https://www.opencenter.org/art-of-dying-institute/

Bioneers. "Bioneers is an innovative nonprofit organization that highlights breakthrough solutions for restoring people and planet. Founded in 1990 in Santa Fe, New Mexico by social entrepreneurs Kenny Ausubel and Nina Simons, we act as a fertile hub of social and scientific innovators with practical and visionary solutions for the world's most pressing environmental and social challenges. A celebration of the genius of nature and human ingenuity, Bioneers connects people with solutions and each other." https://bioneers.org/

Center for Conscious Eldering. "Conscious Eldering (also called Conscious Aging) is an understanding of aging which recognizes and incorporates all these facets of a fulfilling life while emphasizing the importance of continual growth of our inner life. Conscious Eldering holds that built into the human psyche is a call to the archetypal role of elder, a role that has long been characterized by continual growth toward wholeness of body, mind and spirit. We at The Center for Conscious Eldering passionately believe that true 'elders' are urgently needed in today's (and tomorrow's) world, contributing to their communities as they have throughout history." https://www.centerforconsciouseldering.com/

Creation Spirituality Communities. "Creation Spirituality is a way of living within the community of earth that deepens our reverence for life, participates in the creativity of the cosmos, and develops our passion for justice and human transformation. Creation Spirituality Communities is a network of individuals and communities who are attentive to the sacredness of creation through study and practice of Creation Spirituality." http://creationspirituality.info/

Elders Action Network (formerly, *Conscious Elders Network*). "EAN is an educational, non-profit organization fostering a budding movement of vital elders, dedicated to growing in consciousness while actively addressing the demanding challenges facing our country. We work inter-generationally for social and economic justice, environmental stewardship, and sound governance. We bring our multiple talents and resources, offering these in service to the goal of preserving and protecting life for all generations to come." https://www.eldersaction.net/

Elder Activists for Social Justice (EASJ). "As Elders, we feel a moral responsibility to address the many challenges facing our communities and to discover ways in which to offer our resources, wisdom, and generativity in service of the preservation and protection of life for future generations. The purpose of the EASJ Team is to educate and engage a movement of Elders with social justice issues so that together we can create a more just and thriving world for all. Our mission is to educate ourselves, share our growing understanding of these issues, and encourage collaborative, active engagement to address these issues as we build the EASJ Team."

https://www.eldersaction.net/easj_team

Elders Climate Action (ECA). "Elders Climate Action is building a non-partisan movement of elders committed to making our voices heard. We are determined to change our nation's policies while there is still time to avoid catastrophic changes in the earth's climate. Because of this concern and because we vote consistently, elders are in a unique position to influence national policy. We are committed to using our voices, our votes, and our collective power to push for policies that will reduce greenhouse gases to a level consistent with life thriving on our planet." https://www.eldersclimateaction.org/

Encore.org. "Encore.org is building a movement to make it easier for millions of people to pursue second acts for the greater good. … an innovation hub tapping the talent of people 50+. … Mission: To engage millions of boomers in 'encore careers' that provide continued income doing work that is personally fulfilling and helps address some of society's biggest challenges. … jobs that combine personal meaning, continued income and social impact – in the second half of life. … Our new five-year campaign, Generation to Generation, will mobilize 1 million people over 50 to help young people thrive, and unite all ages to create a better future." https://encore.org/

EveryAGE Counts. "EveryAGE Counts is an advocacy campaign aimed at tackling ageism against older Australians. The EveryAGE Counts campaign vision is 'a society where every person is valued, connected and respected regardless of age and health.' We recognise that change can take years to grow and embed in individual and collective attitudes, interpersonal relationships, community behaviours, professional practices and government policies, programs and laws." https://www.everyagecounts.org.au/about

Fetzer Institute. "Helping build the spiritual foundation for a loving world. At the Fetzer Institute, we believe in the possibility of a loving world: a world where we understand we are all part of one human family and know our lives have purpose. In the world we seek, everyone is committed to courageous compassion and bold love—powerful forces for good in the face of fear, anger, division, and despair." https://fetzer.org/

FrameWorks Institute - Reframing Aging Project. "Eight national aging-focused organizations have formed an unprecedented partnership to create a better public understanding of older adults' needs and contributions to society—and to use communications and outreach to drive a more informed conversation about aging and its implications for our communities. FrameWorks is the research partner for the Reframing Aging Project, an initiative of the Leaders of Aging Organizations (AARP, the American Federation for Aging Research, the American Geriatrics Society, the American Society on Aging, the Gerontological Society of America, Grantmakers in Aging, the National Council on Aging, and the National Hispanic Council on Aging.) Together they represent and have direct access to millions of older adults and thousands of individuals working in aging-related professions." http://frameworksinstitute.org/reframing-aging.html

Gaiafield Project: Subtle Activism for Global Transformation. "The Gaiafield Project develops 'subtle activism' practices, theories, and programs and works with like-minded groups to co-create local, national, and global networks of subtle activists to support a shift to a planetary culture of peace. Subtle activism involves harnessing the power of consciousness-based practices like meditation and prayer to support collective transformation, as in a globally synchronized meditation for peace. We believe that in our turbulent times there is a deep need for fostering greater coherence in the energetic fields that underlie communities at every scale."

http://gaiafield.net/what-is-subtle-activism/

Gray is Green. "Gray is Green is an online gathering of older adult Americans aspiring to create a green legacy for the future. As environmentally conscious elders, we respond to a generational call: to co-create a future of economic justice, ecological sustainability and social justice. We hold next generations of humans in mind and consider the future of ecosystems and other species. We are alert to the historic challenges facing our planet. And we are aware of the question arising from descendants' generations hence: What did you do, when you knew?" http://grayisgreen.org/

Gray Panthers. "The original Gray Panthers Project Fund dissolved in 2015 and was replaced by the National Council of Gray Panthers Networks. Gray Panthers mission is to work for social and economic justice and peace for all people." https://www.facebook.com/GrayPanthers

Humanity Healing. "Humanity Healing International is a humanitarian, nonpolitical, nondenominational spiritual organization promoting Spiritual Activism as a means to foster Healing for communities around the world that have little or no Hope. Our Mission is to seek out and identify specific projects worldwide and to implement definable and sustainable solutions. Our initiatives are not broad mandates to eradicate poverty, end famine, or stop violence in war-torn countries." http://humanityhealing.org/

Institute for Sacred Activism. "When the deepest and most grounded spiritual vision is married to a practical and pragmatic drive to transform all existing political, economic, and social institutions, a holy force – the power of wisdom and love in action – is born. This force I define as Sacred Activism. The economic, political, spiritual world crisis that we currently find ourselves in is a call to action. It is an opportunity for us to understand the realities around us and to rally together to do something different. We now have before us the possibility of using this current crisis to empower ourselves, and others, to actually get the planet to work."

https://andrewharvey.net/

Institute of Noetic Sciences (IONS). "At the Institute of Noetic Sciences (IONS), we are inspired by the power of science to explain phenomena not previously understood, harnessing the best of the rational mind to make advances that further our knowledge and enhance our human experience. The mission of the Institute of Noetic Sciences is to reveal the interconnected nature of reality through scientific exploration and personal discovery, creating a more compassionate, thriving, and sustainable world." https://noetic.org/

Interfaith Power and Light. "Interfaith Power & Light is mobilizing a religious response to global warming. The mission of Interfaith Power & Light is to be faithful stewards of Creation by responding to global warming through the promotion of energy conservation, energy efficiency, and renewable energy. This campaign intends to protect the earth's ecosystems, safeguard the health of all Creation, and ensure sufficient, sustainable energy for all. Since the year 2000, IPL has helped thousands of congregations address global warming by being better stewards of energy." https://www.interfaithpowerandlight.org/

Life Planning Network. "A community of professionals from diverse disciplines dedicated to helping people redesign and navigate the second half of life. Projects, Publications, Webinars, Groups, and Conferences that engage LPN's members in professional collaboration to create effective approaches, build better practices, guide older adults toward meaningful work, find solutions for the complex issues of later life, and plan fulfilling and purposeful lives." https://myredstring.com/lifeplanningnetwork/

McMaster Optimal Aging Portal. "Your source for healthy aging information that you can trust. Don't trust your health to Dr. Google. Instead, consult our evidence-based Blog Posts, Web Resource Ratings and Evidence Summaries for trustworthy information about healthy aging. Best way to navigate our content? Browse by pre-set health topics or Search your specific term or question. You are, of course, welcome to register to receive full access to our professional content."

https://www.mcmasteroptimalaging.org/

ManKind Project. "The ManKind Project is men's community for the 21st Century. MKP is a nonprofit training and education organization with three decades of proven success hosting life-changing experiential personal development programs for men. MKP supports a global network of free peer-facilitated men's groups and supports men in leading lives of integrity, authenticity, and service. We believe that emotionally mature, powerful, compassionate, and purpose-driven men will help heal some of our society's deepest wounds. We support the powerful brilliance of men and we are willing to look at, and take full responsibility for, the pain we are also capable of creating – and suffering. We care deeply about men, our families, communities, and the planet." https://mankindproject.org/

Multidisciplinary Association for Psychedelic Studies (MAPS). "Founded in 1986, the Multidisciplinary Association for Psychedelic Studies (MAPS) is a 501(c)(3) non-profit research and educational organization that develops medical, legal, and cultural contexts for people to benefit from the careful uses of psychedelics and marijuana. We envision a world where psychedelics and marijuana are safely and legally available for beneficial uses, and where research is governed by rigorous scientific evaluation of their risks and benefits." https://maps.org/

National Center for Creative Aging (NCCA). "Our Mission: To ensure that older people have the ability to amplify their creative potential by leading and serving a diverse network of organizations and individuals to advance the creative aging field. … professionals in many disciplines are keenly interested in the theory and practice of creative work by, and for, older people—whether fully active or frail. Those in creative fields are finding an extraordinary opportunity: to transform the experience of being old in America by giving meaning and purpose, not only to aging, but to the community at large." https://creativeaging.org/

Next Avenue. "News and Information for People Over 50. Next Avenue is public media's first and only national journalism service for America's booming older population. Our daily content delivers vital ideas, context and perspectives on issues that matter most as we age. Our mission is to meet the needs and unleash the potential of older Americans through the power of media." https://www.nextavenue.org/

Old School: Anti-Ageism Clearinghouse. "Old School is a clearinghouse of free and carefully vetted resources to educate people about ageism and help dismantle it. You'll find blogs, books, articles, videos, speakers, and other tools (workshops, handouts, curricula etc.) that are accessible to the general public. Our goal is to help catalyze a movement to make ageism (discrimination on the basis of age) as unacceptable as any other kind of prejudice." https://oldschool.info/

Order of the Sacred Earth. "In the midst of global fire, earthquake and flood - as species are going extinct every day and national and global economies totter – the planet doesn't need another church or religion. What it needs is a new Order – a sacred community and movement: A movement of communities welcoming all the peoples of Earth: our varied belief systems (or non-belief systems), genders, races, classes, abilities, and nations. A deeply spiritual movement, grounded in the Wisdom traditions of both East and West, in leading-edge science and indigenous tradition. A radically inclusive Order of mystic activists, uniting our energy and intention in one sacred vow: 'I promise to be the best lover and defender of the Earth that I can be.'" https://www.orderofthesacredearth.org/

Pachamama Alliance. "Pachamama Alliance is a global community that offers people the chance to learn, connect, engage, travel and cherish life for the purpose of creating a sustainable future that works for all. With roots deep in the Amazon rainforest, our programs integrate indigenous wisdom with modern knowledge to support personal, and collective, transformation that is the catalyst to bringing forth an environmentally sustainable, spiritually fulfilling, socially just human presence on this planet. Our unique contribution is to generate and engage people everywhere in transformational conversations and experiences consistent with this purpose. We weave together indigenous and modern worldviews such that human beings are in touch with their dignity and are ennobled by the magnificence, mystery, and opportunity of what is possible for humanity at this time." https://www.pachamama.org/

Sage-ing International. "Sage-ing International is dedicated to helping elders reclaim their role as leaders, sharing wisdom and spirit essential to creating a better world for current and future generations. Sage-ing International is committed to transforming the current paradigm of aging to "sage-ing" through learning, community building, and service. We share the Sage-ing® philosophy worldwide by providing workshops, conferences, webinars, and publications for the public and we train a network of Sage-ing® Leaders through the CSL certification program. We encourage and support elders in serving their families, communities, and others around the world. We provide opportunities for individuals on their sage-ing journeys to share and connect with others through interactive opportunities that include chapter programs and wisdom circles. We collaborate with the Conscious Aging Alliance member groups and others who share our vision." www.sage-ing.org

Stria News. "Stria is a media platform for the longevity market. We provide information, experiences and content that inspire cross-sector solutions for our aging society. Stria brings together the most important ideas, people and news from the longevity market. Our reporting and events deliver a foundation of understanding and insight for longevity professionals. And our client services help partners create powerful content and communication strategies that advance their position in the field. Stria is for and about the entire aging ecosystem. We unify the multiple lines of business, service and study that define our field—surfacing the issues and ideas that matter most." https://strianews.com/

The Radical Age Movement. "The Radical Age Movement is a national non-profit based in New York City that rejects long-standing misinterpretations of aging. Our goal is to end these misperceptions and skewed attitudes toward aging so that people of all ages, races, classes, genders, and sexualities can participate productively in areas of cultural, professional and community life." https://radicalagemovement.org/

The Revolutionary Love Project. "The Revolutionary Love Project envisions a world where love is a force for justice and wellspring for social change. … We produce stories, tools, curricula, conferences, films,

TV moments, and mass mobilizations that equip and inspire people to practice the ethic of love. … Our mission: to equip our movements and communities with tools to labor in love — love for others, our opponents, and ourselves. When we pour love in these three directions, then love becomes revolutionary." https://revolutionarylove.net/

The Shift Network. "We are a transformative education company that partners with the top teachers, experts, and healers on the planet, across many diverse fields, to offer powerful experiences that support your growth and transformation — and the evolution of the collective. We aim to empower you with the wisdom of the planet's brightest teachers, connect you with a global community, support you to give your greatest gifts and work together to create a better world. We aim to create a sustainable, peaceful, healthy and prosperous world. … We hold a vision where, not only are everyone's basic needs met while living in peace, but the very best in all of us is expressed and humanity's full creative potential is set free." https://theshiftnetwork.com/

Work That Reconnects. "To those of us growing up in the Industrial Growth Society, a breathtakingly new view of reality arises from deep ecology, systems thinking, and the resurgence of nondualistic spirituality. These three streams attest to our mutual belonging in the web of life, and to powers within us for the healing of our world. They are basic to the core assumptions of the Work That Reconnects. The central purpose of the Work That Reconnects is to bring us back into relationship with each other and with the self-healing powers in the web of life, motivating and empowering us to reclaim our lives, our communities, and our planet from corporate and colonial rule." https://workthatreconnects.org/

A few more organizations and websites of relevance to REWIREMENT topics:

Clear View Project: http://clearviewproject.org/

Erowid: https://www.erowid.org/

Fierce with Age http://fiercewithage.com/

Fruitful Aging and Recognition Rites for Elders https://drtompinkson.com/recognition-rites-for-a-new-vision-of-aging-honoring-elders/

Legacy of Wisdom Project https://www.legacyofwisdom.org/legacy-of-wisdom/en/home.html

Presencing Institute: https://www.presencing.org/

PsychedeLiA: Psychedelic Integration Los Angeles: https://www.psychedeliaintegration.org/

Sarvodaya Sharmadana Movement: https://www.sarvodaya.org/

Shalom Center: https://theshalomcenter.org/

Sixty and Me http://sixtyandme.com/

Spirituality and Practice: Elder Spiritual Project: http://www.spiritualityandpractice.com/

The Eden Alternative: http://www.edenalt.org/

The Global Consciousness Project: http://noosphere.princeton.edu/_

The Monroe Institute: https://www.monroeinstitute.org/

The Third Wave: https://thethirdwave.co/

Appendix 2

Conscious Aging Articles by Ron Pevny

Claiming Your Elderhood

by Ron Pevny [2]

Listen carefully and you will hear a rumbling, as the first of the baby-boom generation cross the threshold into our sixties. This rumbling will soon become a demographic earthquake. In an America that worships youth, the proportion of the population over sixty will reach unprecedented heights, and the resulting impact up on every aspect of American life will be profound. Each day, we need look no further than the media and the Internet to find predictions of the demographic sea change that is nearly upon us.

Listen even more carefully and you will detect another rumbling at a different frequency. This is the sound of a rapidly increasing number of seniors and baby-boomers questioning the mainstream contemporary models for aging. These are people having a sense—sometimes a vague yearning tinged with frustration and fear, sometimes a persistent deep feeling of inner calling -- that there are more possibilities for their senior years than are generally recognized and supported. They feel a call to elderhood, and sense that there is a difference between being old or senior, and being an elder. But, they often don't know what this would look like or how to get there. And, living in a society in which there is no designated role for elders, there is no prescription. The good news is that a general shape of elderhood in America is beginning to emerge.

Throughout much of recorded history, up until the Industrial Revolution, elders have had honored roles in society that were defined and supported. This remains true among the world's remaining indigenous peoples. Elders have been the nurturers of community, the spiritual leaders, the guardians of the traditions, the teachers, mentors and initiators of the young. They have been the storytellers who have helped their people

2 This article, used in the IONS Conscious Aging workshops, is copyrighted by the author, Ron Pevny, with permission granted to Art Mitchell to reprint it here.

see the enduring wisdom and deeper meanings of life that lie beneath superficial models of reality and persist through life's changes.

Elders have been the ones who, over long lives of experience and growth, have converted knowledge and experience into wisdom and whose revered role is to model this wisdom as they teach the younger generations about what it means to mature, discover one's calling and use one's gifts in service to the larger community.

So much has changed since then. The impending demographic shift is a result of societal advances that now make it possible for large numbers of people to live, often healthily, well into their seventies, eighties and even longer. Such life spans for huge numbers of people are unprecedented in human history. It is no longer just the rare few who live long lives.

At the same time, for the last century at least, modern culture has adopted the machine as the new metaphor for how human life is viewed. We are assembled and programmed during the years of youth. We efficiently produce material goods and new ideas and information during the years of adulthood, and our value is directly tied to what we contribute to the economy. We go to therapy if we are unable to continue to be efficient. In the senior years we slow or break down, no longer able to compete with those younger, and we are taken out of service or make that choice ourselves. In a world of ever-accelerating change, most of what older people have learned about work and technology – about contributing to the economy – is considered out-of-date and no longer useful.

In dismissing the elderly for these reasons, modern society also dismisses its prime potential source of deep wisdom and enduring values, informed by long experience, about how to live in balance and harmony with fellow human beings and with the earth. So, we shuffle off, at an increasingly earlier age, into retirement, often leading lonely, isolated existences or segregating ourselves into communities of others like us. We have made our contribution. It is time for us to get out of the way so younger, more energetic people can have the jobs. And society races on, worshipping youth, discounting the lessons of the past, and continually looking to what is new for its "vision" of what the good life looks like.

So, we live in an America that will soon be composed of record numbers of seniors facing the prospect of many years, even decades, of life. What are the contemporary models for aging that shape our visions for how we will live these years?

Many seniors and baby-boomers, especially those with financial security and good health, see our senior years as a time of well-deserved rest from responsibility and plentiful opportunities for recreation, travel, adventure and learning. As early a retirement as possible is the ideal for many, and moving to leisure-oriented communities of people like ourselves may well be part of this vision.

For those not so economically fortunate and healthy, the prospects for our senior years can appear much less appealing. They envision years of living alone, with our children or in elder care facilities, with few opportunities for contribution to the community and quite possibly the prospect of having to take low-paying service jobs to keep body and soul together.

Of course, this categorization is too simple. More and more seniors in both categories are volunteering in our communities. Many retirees are choosing to work part-time as consultants in their former professions or to pursue entirely different careers for reasons that may or may not include economic necessity. The models are not nearly as clear-cut as they were ten or twenty years ago. The cultural landscape is being redefined, and will be so even more profoundly as the baby-boomers, who have led so much cultural change since the 60s, reach sixty. The distinction between being elder and being old is becoming blurred. But what is this distinction?

We human beings seem to be genetically wired with a need for living passionate lives of purpose, meaning and service to the greater good, a good which is larger than the state of the economy. Throughout the last century, the mainstream visions of aging have largely seen the senior years as a time for withdrawing from contribution to the larger community, a time for winding down. At the same time, as life expectancy has dramatically increased, for many the years after retirement can be a significant portion of one's life. Can we find fulfillment and passion by "winding down" for twenty or thirty years? By devoting our lives to golf or other recreation? By "puttering" around the house? And what about the urgent need for elder wisdom in a complex and threatened world where true wisdom seems to be in short supply?

The emerging definition of what elderhood can be in today's world is very much linked to the crucial question of how, as a senior, to meet this need for purpose, meaning and service to the larger community. The challenge for those feeling these needs is to envision, create and claim elder roles for ourselves in a society greatly in need of elder wisdom but offering few such roles or models to its seniors. Meeting this challenge is not something that is easily done alone. And it requires conscious preparation at all levels—physical, psychological and spiritual.

This is where meaningful rites of passage, in critically short supply, can play such an important role. Throughout most of known human history, significant changes in life status have been marked by rites of passage or initiation into the next stage of life. The intent has been to provide extensive psychological and spiritual preparation for the transition, followed by a significant ceremony to mark the life passage, with the goal being to help the initiate to consciously and fully move into his/her next role. Through such powerful processes, people were assisted in letting go of attitudes, behaviors and self concepts that would not fit their new life roles.

Concurrently they were guided in identifying and strengthening the wisdom, the psychological resources and the spiritual connection necessary for claiming and effectively filling their new statuses.

Contrast this with today's world, where meaningful, empowering rites of passage are rare, and people are expected to move from one stage to another largely on their own, with little psychological and spiritual preparation. Teens graduate and are assumed and expected to be adults. Adults retire and are assumed and expected to be—what? Old? In decline? No longer able to significantly serve the community? Out of the way so the young can make the contributions? Drains on the budget?

This is a call for meaningful rites of passage for those feeling the call to elderhood. It is a call to the leaders of the many spiritual traditions in our country, as well as those others who, through various means have stepped into and owned the wisdom of their own eldering, to develop inspiring programs of preparation for elderhood, culminating in ceremonies of passage. It is also a call to seniors and soon-to-be-seniors who feel called to serve their communities as elders to request and seek out such support. A few programs already exist and are having a dramatic impact upon those who utilize them. As burgeoning numbers of people stand on or near the threshold to their senior years and feel a call to an elderhood of passion and engagement, the need for rites of passage for elders will greatly increase.

Whatever form they take, effective rites of passage into elderhood will not prescribe a particular form or role for emerging elders. The ways in which these elders will share their wisdom and skills with the larger community will be as unique as each individual and as diverse as the American population.

What we new elders will have in common, however, is a commitment to continual growth, deepening spiritual connection, passion, discovery of purpose and service. We will realize that our wholeness, our wisdom and gifts, and the well-being of the larger society and our planet itself, cannot be separated.

Current and soon-to-be seniors can play a critical role in shaping a positive future if we choose to not withdraw as we age, but rather to nurture ourselves and our communities by claiming our roles as conscious elders.

Ron Pevny *is Founding Director of the Center for Conscious Eldering. He is also a Certified Sage-ing® Leader, author of Conscious Living, Conscious Aging published by Beyond Words/Atria Books, and served as the host/interviewer for the Transforming Aging Summits presented by The Shift Network. Visit his Center for Conscious Eldering website at:*

www.centerforconsciouseldering.com

The Inner Work of Eldering

by Ron Pevny [3]

On one of the Choosing Conscious Elderhood retreats that I lead, a participant in her early 60's said something that had a powerful impact on all present. In reflecting on her intentions for her retreat, she spoke of two significant older people in her life. One, who was in relatively good physical health, was difficult to be around because of her seemingly constant anger, bitterness and negativity. She was old and miserable. People avoided her because she was a drain on their energy and joy. The other was a woman who, while not physically healthy, attracted people like a magnet. In her presence they felt joy, serenity, optimism, peace. People saw her as an elder whose radiance and wisdom lifted their spirits. Our retreat participant shared her intention, on this retreat and on her journey ahead, of growing into a radiant elder rather than a joyless old person; and her questions and concerns about how to accomplish this.

The aging process seems to bring out either the best or the worst in people— magnifying and emphasizing the flaws and shadow elements of some of us; amplifying the wisdom, radiance and compassion in others. The question carried by those of us committed to becoming peaceful, fulfilled elders is, "how can my aging bring out the best in me?" The inner work known by rubrics such as "conscious eldering," "conscious aging," "spiritual eldering" and "Sage-ing" holds important answers to this question.

The journey from late middle-age into fulfilled elderhood is facilitated by inner work that is focused and fueled by conscious intention. This journey can lead to the pinnacle of one's emotional and spiritual development. Undertaking this journey is in fact what our lives to that point have prepared us for. And as conscious elders, our service to our communities and to the community of all beings can be profound. Carl

---

3 This article, used in the IONS Conscious Aging workshops, is copyrighted by the author, Ron Pevny, with permission granted to Art Mitchell to reprint it here.

Jung succinctly expressed this potential: "A human being would certainly not grow to be seventy or eighty years old if this longevity had no meaning for the species. The afternoon of human life must also have a significance of its own…"

The word "conscious" is key in understanding the wide range of ways that the inner work of eldering may be done. It is also key to the distinction between being "old" and being an "elder." Conscious means aware. Aware of who we really are, of our authentic emotions, talents, aspirations, strengths and weaknesses. Aware of a growth process unfolding in our lives through all of our experiences, positive and painful. Aware of that within us which is conditioned by the myriad of disempowering messages that surround us, as well as that which is authentic, natural and life-supporting. Aware of those shadow elements in us—our dark sides—which can block our radiance and sabotage our potential.

Life Review

If the essence of conscious eldering is increasing awareness, then its core practice is Life Review. Wisdom does not come from having experiences. Wisdom comes from reflecting on one's life experiences. There are many ways of doing Life Review. Some entail structured exercises to focus on challenges, learning and growth during the stages of one's life, and they use pen, computer or art materials as tools. Oral history work with a knowledgeable friend or guide can be a powerful catalyst for remembering and finding the significance in life experiences. The grandmother of a colleague of mine creatively memorialized key events in the life of her family by creating a "family quilt" over a period of many years. Whichever method most resonates with us, what is critical is doing it. The awareness we gain is what makes virtually all the other inner work possible and effective. The elder wisdom we arrive at is a precious gift to the generations who will remember us as ancestors.

Healing the Past

Much of the inner work of eldering focuses on healing and letting go of old baggage. Actualizing our unique potential as elders requires that our energy be free and clear, that our psyches be capable of embracing the possibilities and opportunities of each present moment rather than stuck in the experiences of the past. We can't shine as radiant elders if our energy is continually sapped by old wounds, grudges, angers, hurts and feelings of victimhood. We can't move lightly and serenely through our days when we have not forgiven others and ourselves for the slights and hurts we have experienced and perpetrated through unconscious behavior. We cannot display our wholeness when unprocessed grief keeps open wounds that sap our energy.

When we review our lives, we become aware of the immense power of story. We become aware of the mythos we have constructed for our lives as the result of our experiences—the stories we tell ourselves (and oftentimes others) about our lives that shape who we become as the years pass. We see how disempowering these stories can be when they contain strong motifs of victimhood, inadequacy, unworthiness and regret. It is liberating to know that these stories can be changed, and doing so is perhaps the most powerful inner work we can do as we age. This process is often called "recontextualizing" or "reframing."

Recontextualizing

The essence of recontextualizing is viewing painful or difficult life experiences with the intention of finding what in those experiences has contributed—or has the potential to now contribute as we revisit it with conscious awareness—to our growth and learning. In the bigger picture of our lives, the job lost may have pushed us into a difficult search that led to a fuller expression of our gifts. The wounding inflicted on us by another may have taught us compassion or empathy for the suffering of others. The hurt we inflicted on another may have been a teacher for us about our shadow side—a critical awareness if we are to grow as human beings. A career decision we made that we regret may have been a crucial step toward our becoming who we are today, even if the mechanics of this are not obvious.

Recontextualizing of experiences that do not hold a strong emotional charge can be relatively easy. But, for emotionally charged experiences, if this practice is to truly impact our lives at the level of deep feeling and allow us to reshape the stories we live by, we must allow ourselves to feel deeply suppressed emotion, and do the inner work of grieving and forgiving. At its core recontextualizing is profoundly spiritual work. It requires a deep trust that the divine intelligence present in us has a purpose for our lives and is working through our experiences to achieve that purpose. We may not understand its workings, and they may not be what we would choose. But this wise inner guidance possesses the eagle's eye view of our lives that eludes the narrower view of our ego selves.

Deepening Spiritual Connection

Our ability to trust in a divine intelligence with a purpose for our lives depends greatly upon the strength of our connection to a Higher Power—to Spirit, Soul, God, the Great Mystery. The inner work of eldering is deeply spiritual work that requires us to find spiritual practices that nurture that connection. For the goal of all true spiritual practice is to help us experience ourselves and our lives in a wider context, framed in a truer story than the stories our ego selves tend to create about our lives. When we trust—with a trust grounded in the deep inner knowing that flows through spiritual connection—that our lives have prepared us to become elders with wisdom, talent and wholeness to give to our people, our unfolding stories become gifts to our communities.

Our deepening spiritual connection is intrinsically related to the shift from a life grounded in "doing" to one grounded in "being"—a shift that is a key dynamic in conscious eldering. When we make this shift, we move from living and acting with the primary goal of meeting the needs of our ego selves, to living and acting so that Spirit, however we may name it, shines through us as fully as possible.

Accepting Mortality

The world's spiritual traditions are aligned in teaching us that accepting our mortality is perhaps our biggest ally in helping us to truly embrace life and the wonder of each moment. Yet, we live amid pervasive denial of mortality. Illness and physical diminishment, realities for most of us as we age, have great power to transform denial into an acceptance that can give zest to each of our limited number of days.

Creating Legacy

We all leave a legacy – positive, negative or mixed – to the generations that follow us. Aging consciously implies becoming aware of the legacy we have created up to this point in our lives and being intentional about the legacy we want to create in our elderhood. As we review our lives and work to bring healing to the past, we help ourselves to acknowledge and build on the positives of this evolving legacy, and we free up the energy needed identify and move forward in building the legacy that is our gift to the future. Here again, a growing spiritual connection that allows us to see clearly our unique calling and gifts as an elder is key. This experience of calling (which is more powerful that a concept, an idea or a "should" alone) helps us become aware of the legacy we truly want to leave and of the path that will help us realize this goal. It opens our heart, strengthens our intention, focuses our action and taps our spiritual depths so that we bring our whole selves to the creation of legacy.

Letting Go

We cannot move fully from who we have been into the elder we can become without letting go of that which will not support us on this journey. We all have culturally instilled attitudes and beliefs about life and aging that are disempowering. Our inner work is to become conscious (aware) of these and let them go. We all have attachments to people, places, things, activities, ideologies, attitudes, old stories and self-identifications that may (or may not) have served us in the past but which will definitely not serve us in the future. Here again, our work is awareness and surrender. Life review is a valuable tool in becoming aware of what must be surrendered.

Rituals of letting go, whether conducted alone or with the support and witness of a group, can be powerful tools for transforming that awareness into willingness to let go of who we have been. Eldering rites of passage, such as those facilitated by the Center for Conscious Eldering, are powerful examples of rituals that help us to let go of outwork identifications. True, effective surrender requires cultivating deep trust that by letting go of what has come to feel familiar and safe, albeit constricting, we are supported by the wisdom and life force which is calling us into a new identity and positive new beginnings.

While the inner work of eldering is "work"—at times quite difficult work—it is also dynamic and enlivening. It can be the most important work we ever do. It may well be accompanied by tears of both sadness and joy as bound up energies are freed to reflect growing consciousness of who we are and what is possible. Its fruit can be the radiance, passion and service so needed by a world in need of conscious elders. I wish you well on your journey.

***Ron Pevny** is Founding Director of the Center for Conscious Eldering. He is also a Certified Sage-ing® Leader, author of Conscious Living, Conscious Aging published by Beyond Words/Atria Books, and served as the host/interviewer for the Transforming Aging Summits presented by The Shift Network. Visit his Center for Conscious Eldering website at:*

www.centerforconsciouseldering.com_

Acknowledgments

First, I must thank, of course, with deep love and gratitude, Monica, my long-suffering wife of thirty-eight years, for her understanding and support while, like Richard Dreyfus at the dinner table in *Close Encounters of the Third Kind*, I was making "mashed potato mountains" that made no sense to either of us.[4]

I especially want to thank all those who reviewed and provided comments to draft chapters. The book would have benefited tremendously had I heeded all your advice. I wish to thank the following people, by no means all, who have helped in various ways. Ron Pevny for his inspiration, permission to use his material in this book, and for introducing me to conscious aging during a six-day intensive workshop at Omega Institute. Nancy Levin for inspiring me to write this self-help book that reveals more about me than I would have liked – and in that way encouraged me to just "Jump!" Lauren Artress for inspiring me to learn about spiritual power of a labyrinth and for teaching me how to facilitate labyrinth walks. Sharon Brown, my coach, for enabling and empowering all things transformational. Lois Guarino, my other coach, for believing in me when I did not.

Many thanks also to Norm Shealy for being the embodiment of a wizard, a longevity guru, and for graciously writing the Foreword to this book. John Robinson for his inspirational life's work and books including permission to reference some of his material in Chapter 2. Reverend Toni Fish of Unity Frederick for her inspiring talk on beginners, journeymen, and wizards, and for permission to adapt that story in Chapter 3. Tom

4 Scene from *Close Encounters of the Third Kind*, Julia Phillips and Michael Phillips Productions, EMI Films, 1977: https://www.youtube.com/watch?v=yecJLI-GRuU

Pinkson for extensive quotes, Kerstin Sjoquist, and the Institute of Noetic Science (IONS) for permission to use some material in Chapter 5. Martha Lasley for excellent advice and allowing me to use her vision steps in Chapter 7 and some material from her book. Richard Leider for permitting me to use some of his "purposeful" material in Chapter 8. Jim Fadiman, who gave me sage advice on Chapter 11 and how to stay on topic, focusing on the reader (Sadly, I was not able to take up all his advice) – and for his encouragement: "*The reason you're a good coach is that you're not a psychologist and probably you get your clients more in touch with trees, and that is among the best therapies I know.*" Nancy Eubel for early rewiring inspiration and allowing me to include her finger labyrinth exercise in Chapter 12. Constance Washburn for consenting to my brief summaries of the Work That Reconnects and the Elder Action Network's "Empowered Elder" course material in Chapter 13.

I would also like to thank, in no special order, Katia Petersen, Jerome Kerner, Rick Moody, Bradley Grinnen, Chip Conley, Meg Newhouse, Sr. Maureen Spillane, Sr. Barbara Klodt, Ashton Applewhite, Elizabeth White, Anne Wennhold, Marc Blesoff, James Cox, Matthew Fox, Deborah Servetnick, Ingrid Hart, Nadya Zhilaev, Sherree Malcolm Godasi, Sandy Strauss, Suzanne St. George, Pam Prior, Corey Fuller, Angela Lauria, and Moriah Howell. Moriah, as editor, was able to cut through my obscurities and uncertainties and help me get all this done within strict time limits.

I also acknowledge the Morgan James Publishing Team: David Hancock, CEO & Founder; my author relations manager, Tiffany Gibson; Jim Howard; Bethany Marshall; and Nickcole Watkins.

I thank all those who are not included here, clients, family, and friends, with apologies for omission – for no other reasons than insufficient time or faulty memory. Writing this under duress to meet a publisher's deadline obliges me to be incomplete.

And finally, I thank, with a father's pride and love, my children, Katharine, Thomas, and Andrew, for being the amazing, awake humans they are and for understanding their father's sometimes uncomfortable self-revelations in this book.

Whoosh! Oops! There goes the deadline.
Thank you!
I have spoken.

Thank You!

Thanks for reading *Grateful, Not Dead* and following your REWIREMENT Steps!

My hope is you will use this guide to reflect on any self-limiting assumptions about age, opportunities, and the future to jumpstart your journey into the best years of your life with purpose and engagement.

This point in life isn't a dead end, but rather the beginning of a life changing and worthwhile journey. I hope this book has provided you with some peace of mind and encouragement as you plan or enter "retirement" – our so-called Third Act.

Now, you can read this and move on; read the next self-help book and move on, and the next. How about another "life-changing" workshop? Repeat as necessary. Move along. Nothing to see here. Or, you can stop and focus on what's right in front of you – with what you have up to now. You have the choice at any point to end any "paralysis by analysis," this "comfortably numb" hamster wheel, whenever you choose to do so. I know what I'm talking about. I have done it for myself. Up to you.

I can help show you how to make this transformation – and to make it sustainable. As a life coach, I help people to believe in themselves and create their empowered and purposeful future, focusing on specific goals and then achieving those goals or objectives within a set timeframe. I am here to help you get what you want. I listen, learn, and give you the opportunity to expand and clarify your awareness of who you are or are becoming as your most authentic self.

I would like to help you transform your life to one full of potential, opportunities, optimism, creativity, and power. We will explore your purpose and goals, identify blockages, then select actions to achieve your goals. I will work with you to identify what makes you feel alive and then turn your understandings and passion into actionable steps. You will come to maximize your creative potential through accessing your character strengths, experience, talents, vision, passions, and aspirations.

How do you get started?

You can visit my site (presumably no longer "under construction"), sign in, and receive useful *free worksheets* for self-assessment, vision, purpose, goal-setting, psycho-spiritual integration, time management, or other resources that may be available at the time – all are part of my integrated REWIREMENT Toolkit, to keep you on track during your transformation process.

You may schedule a free, confidential 30-40-minute *Transformation Appraisal and Strategy Session*, with no obligation. We will talk about whether working together is right for us. If you decide you want to move on to the next step, we will then schedule your first session, a discovery evaluation. At that time, you will receive a "Welcome to Transformation" package that includes some additional self-assessment and planning tools to make your first and all subsequent sessions more focused and productive.

Let's work together, in partnership, on achieving your goals and your personalized R-E-W-I-R-E-M-E-N-T.

We can begin anytime!

Art Mitchell

For a **free PDF version** of this book and for more information, go to:
https://mailchi.mp/e33d7da878c8/arthurhaynemitchell
or simply **E-mail** me: zaperonneau@gmail.com
Website (*under construction at time of writing*):
https://arthurhaynemitchell.com/

About the Author

"An autobiography is only to be trusted when it reveals something disgraceful. A man who gives a good account of himself is probably lying, since any life when viewed from the inside is simply a series of defeats."

- George Orwell

A so-called baby-boomer, Arthur Hayne Mitchell was born in 1951 in a snowstorm on the winter solstice in Washington, DC, and was raised across the Potomac in Alexandria, Virginia, until he escaped at age seventeen. Art began his career as a Peace Corps volunteer in Malaysia, where he was assistant chief game warden (wildlife officer) for the Malaysian state of Sabah in northeast Borneo. His first conservation planning project was preparing a national park management plan to protect the rainforest and indigenous Mentawai traditions on Siberut, a remote island west of Sumatra, Indonesia. This was one of the first strategies to incorporate indigenous people and traditional knowledge in park planning and management. As a conservation biologist for over forty years in seventeen countries, primarily in Southeast and South Asia but also East Africa and the Caribbean, he has led biodiversity conservation management projects on tropical rainforest, coastal, wetlands, and marine ecosystems as well as adaptation to climate disruption. He is a skilled facilitator and has established common visions for success at personal, project, and program scales, leading multidisciplinary and multicultural teams to realize their vision, achieve goals and objectives, and collaboratively deliver sustained results.

Art is also trained in transformation coaching, a supportive and goal-oriented partnership designed to empower clients to more fully live the life they want in line with their values and purpose. He is a certified professional coach (CPC) trained through Leadership That Works, accredited by the International Coaching Federation (ICF). His coaching focus is consciousness transformation and integration, specializing in "retirement," conscious aging, career transition, leadership, psycho-spiritual integration, creativity, goal setting, action planning, and engagement with community and global activism. He is also a trained Institute of Noetic Sciences (IONS) Conscious Aging workshop facilitator, Veriditas labyrinth facilitator, and an environmental advocate and activist.

Art has written and co-authored several books, including *Colonel Roosevelt and the White House Gang* and *An Acceptable Warrior*. He is working on a follow-up book, *Entheogenic Elders and Eco-Warriors for a Living Earth*, and a novel, *Passion of the Pauper*, which is based on true events surrounding the impacts of climate disruption in Bangladesh and five people who have been driven as a result to desperate poverty and life in the slums of Dhaka. Art has a BA from the University of California at Berkeley in zoology and M.Phil. and Ph.D. degrees from Yale University in biological anthropology (primatology) and forestry & environmental studies (conservation biology). He gratefully lives in the Sonoran Desert on the edge of western Tucson, Arizona, with his wife Monica.

CPSIA information can be obtained
at www.ICGtesting.com
Printed in the USA
JSHW011232071222
34492JS00001B/266

9 781642 796629